From the Series Editor

The number of women's colleges has shrunk from a peak of about 200 to about 70 over the past several decades. In spite of the prominence of institutions such as the "Seven Sisters" and Spelman, women's colleges confer one percent of all of the bachelor's degrees awarded in recent years. Why study women's colleges?

The power of case studies to illuminate sociological phenomena rarely rests on the typicality of the case. Instead, case studies frequently derive their analytic strength from their ability to consider the totality of a case. In *Contradictions in Women's Education*, Barbara Bank tackles pervasive tensions in women's education that are accentuated in a non-elite women's college. Over the past several decades, higher education for women has been portrayed as reinforcing traditional gender roles, a steppingstone to finding a husband and becoming a successful wife and mother. But women in higher education have also been exposed to an emancipatory ideology that emphasizes women's leadership potential and the strong social networks among educated women. Overlaid on top of this tension is a controversy regarding the purposes of an undergraduate education, and the extent to which it should prepare women for particular occupations or, instead, provide a broad exposure to the liberal arts that emphasizes independent thinking and intellectual creativity.

Bank explores how these twin tensions are manifested in the life of Central Women's College: in its culture, its sororities, and its communities. She shows how single-sex educational institutions can have powerful socializing effects on their students. This is a growing concern of educational policy, as there is continued evidence of the ways in which contemporary educational institutions at all levels of the system have shortchanged girls and women. Through her analyses, we learn both about the history of higher education for women in the United States and its future.

Aaron M. Pallas

Contradictions in Women's Education

Traditionalism, Careerism, and Community at a Single-Sex College

BARBARA J. BANK

WITH
HARRIET M. YELON

Teachers College
Columbia University
New York and London

Published by Teachers College Press, 1234 Amsterdam Avenue, New York, NY 10027

Library of Congress Cataloging-in-Publication Data

Bank, Barbara J.
    Contradictions in women's education : traditionalism, careerism, and community at a single-sex college / Barbara J. Bank with Harriet M. Yelon
        p. cm. — (Sociology of education series)
    Includes bibliographical references and index.
    ISBN 0-8077-4364-X (cloth : alk. paper) — ISBN 0-8077-4363-1 (pbk. : alk. paper)
    1. Women's colleges—United States—Case studies. 2. Women—Education (Higher)—United States—Case studies. I. Yelon, Harriet M. II. Title. III. Sociology of education series (New York, N.Y.)

LC1756.B36 2003
378'.0082'0973—dc21   2003041002

ISBN 0-8077-4363-1 (paper)
ISBN 0-8077-4364-X (cloth)

Printed on acid-free paper

Manufactured in the United States of America

10 09 08 07 06 05 04 03   8 7 6 5 4 3 2 1

To my sister Rosemarie
with whom I have spent many years
discussing and coping with
the contradictions of academic life.

Contents

Acknowledgments

During the 1990–1991 academic year, Harriet Yelon suggested that the two of us collaborate on some research. Neither of us suspected back then that our collaboration would be as extensive and long-lasting as it became. Harriet had been a graduate student at the University of Missouri, Columbia, and received her M.A. in Sociology in 1981. She began teaching at Central Women's College (CWC) in 1985, became a full-time faculty member at the college in 1987, and has always been a popular teacher and respected colleague. As such, she had an insider's ability to obtain the high levels of cooperation from CWC students, faculty, and staff that were so necessary for the successful completion of our study. Although the research on which this book is based would not and could not have been done without Harriet's instigation and efforts, she is not responsible for the book. As a result, readers will notice that I sometimes switch pronouns, writing about *our* research and *my* analyses, propositions, and conclusions. Harriet should be held blameless for the latter.

Not the least of Harriet's contributions to our research endeavor was her ability to obtain funds from CWC that we used to pay students who participated in Interviews I and III and the final survey and to hire Melinda Wrigley and Sarah Dudley who conducted Interview I. I am grateful to Melinda and Sarah and to the administration of CWC for this help and support.

My greatest debt of gratitude goes to the students who participated in our surveys and interviews. As we promised them, I have *not* used their real names in this book, although some of them had such interesting and important things to say that I am sorry not to be able to give them public credit.

Thanks also go to the faculty who participated in our survey and to those who talked to me informally about their experiences at CWC.

I was fortunate to be a Research Associate at the University of Missouri's Center for Research in Social Behavior during the years of our study of CWC. The staff and students employed by the Center helped with all of the data-management tasks. Special thanks go to Billye Adams who handled the budget for the last phase of the CWC study; to Kathy Craighead and Pat Shanks who transcribed Interviews I and III; to John Daniel, Jane Downing, Jim Earhart, Janie Eubanks, and Amy Wiard, who helped with the coding and data entry of the survey responses; and—again—to Janie Eubanks for her determined efforts to find all the students in our study who had left CWC, for conducting Interview II with them, for indexing the student newspapers, and for scheduling the students who participated in Interview III. More recently, Pat Shanks helped me to prepare the Appendices to this book, and I thank her very much for a job well done.

The writing of this book was greatly facilitated by a Research Leave and a Sabbatical Leave, granted by the University of Missouri, and I am grateful to the Graduate Research Council for supporting the former, and to the Department of Sociology and the College of Arts and Science for supporting both. I also had the privilege during my Research Leave of spending a month in residence at the Rockefeller Foundation's Bellagio Conference and Study Center on Lake Como in Italy. I thank not only the Rockefeller Foundation for creating a Center so conducive to scholarly work, but also those other residents who shared with me their views about women's colleges and higher education.

The intellectual debts this book owes to colleagues, both those I know personally and those I don't, are apparent from the many citations it contains. Special thanks are due to colleagues who supported various applications I made for financial support of this project and who gave me encouragement along the way. These include Kathleen Crittenden, Thomas L. Good, Cornelius Riordan, Alan Sadovnik, and Susan Semal.

It has been my good fortune to have Bruce J. Biddle as both a colleague and a spouse. He was the Director of the Center for Research in Social Behavior, which so greatly facilitated the study of CWC. He was instrumental in getting me to the Bellagio Center. His workaholic habits served as a constant prod to keep me focused on finishing this book, but he also served as my leisure-time companion when we put aside our respective manuscripts to enjoy international travel. He was always willing to listen while I tried to make sense of the CWC data and to develop the thematic structure of this book. And, he was willing to do more than his share of cooking and household management when he knew I really needed that. Could this book have been written without him? Probably, but it would have been much harder and less fun to do, and I would have felt far less supported.

Finally, I would like to thank Susan Liddicoat, acquisitions editor at TC Press, for her encouragement and many excellent suggestions. She has the rare ability of simultaneously making a manuscript better and allowing its author to speak with her own voice.

CHAPTER 1

Introduction

Higher education for women in the United States has been and continues to be characterized by tensions and contradictions. These contradictions both reflect and contribute to controversies in the larger society about the opportunities women should have and the kinds of lives they should lead. This linkage between education and the rest of social life means that the contradictions surrounding women's education are not the same as those experienced by men. Despite much talk about equal opportunity in higher education, and despite the fact that many women will experience more gender equity in college than in the workplace or the home, getting a college education continues to be a different process for women than for men. To say this is not to deny that women are encouraged to model their college careers on those of men and that most women do so. But, unlike the education of their male counterparts, women's higher education is enmeshed in a long tradition of gender-related contradictions and controversies.

CONTRADICTIONS SURROUNDING
WOMEN'S HIGHER EDUCATION

A central role in this long tradition has been played by women's colleges and the female seminaries and academies that preceded them. Although now existing as a small part of a wide range of options available to women seeking higher education, women's colleges were once their only option. The fact that women were excluded from the institutions of higher education that men attended was usually justified by claims having to do with the essential nature of men and women and with their appropriate roles in family and society. By the simple fact of their existence, institutions of higher education for women challenged some of these claims and placed themselves in the center of debates about what abilities women did and did not have and the social uses to which those abilities could best be put.

The exact content of these debates varied across place and time, and some of them, such as the one about whether women's intellectual development would undermine their reproductive capacity, now seem both outrageous and outdated. Nevertheless, it is the thesis of this book that these historic debates were part of a long tradition of arguments, contradictions, dilemmas, and tensions that continues to shape higher education for women in America today. Although this legacy is pervasive throughout the entire system of higher education, the focus of this book is on one women's college and on the ways in which three sets of contradictions surrounding women's higher education were evidenced in the official culture of the college, the student culture, and the experiences of individual students.

The first and most pervasive set of contradictions includes the dilemmas and tensions involving *gender traditionalism* that have characterized women's higher education since it began in the early decades of the 19th century. Controversy raged for more than a century about whether higher education was suitable or necessary for women and whether it would make them better wives and mothers. Women's colleges found themselves advocating a more emancipatory vision of what women could and should become while simultaneously defending themselves as contributors to the betterment of traditional family life. Their defense of traditionalism was a basis for a major assault on women's colleges in the 1970s when it was argued that they were anachronistic, irrelevant, and overly protective. To the contrary, recent defenders argue that women's colleges have been *more* emancipatory, hence less gender traditional, than coeducational institutions. The content of the contradictions has evolved, but concerns with how gender traditionalism and emancipation play themselves out in women's lives remain important issues in higher education.

Within this broader context, Greek-letter sororities have sometimes been cited as organizations that support and foster gender traditionalism. In the contemporary period, sororal traditionalism refers not so much to becoming good wives and mothers as it does to being sociable, concerned with one's appearance, and male-oriented. As with women's colleges, however, sororities are also extolled as emancipatory venues in which women can develop their leadership skills and forge strong bonds with one another. Cutting across this controversy are tensions surrounding social class, with sororities often accused of being elitist, exclusionary, and politically and socially conservative. Like claims about women's colleges themselves, claims and counterclaims about the extent to which sororities are characterized by different kinds of gender and social-class traditionalism are investigated in this book.

The second set of contradictions with which this book is concerned is encapsulated in the term *careerism*. While occupational careerism is often regarded as a component of emancipation for women, educated women have traditionally been channeled into occupations considered suitable for women, a practice that may be less common today but continues to exist. In addition to the issues of emancipation and traditionalism surrounding women's careers, there are also major controversies among educators concerning the appropriateness of careerism, especially in its more vocational forms, as the major goal of higher education. Many today bemoan the eclipse of the general, liberal arts form of education by what they see as a more utilitarian, less intellectual, and too-narrow program of study. This controversy echoes a long historical debate about the linkages between higher education and the job market, a debate that has usually exhibited gender biases, albeit often in the form of gender obliviousness.

Yet another controversy about careerism grows out of a concern that students are not being careerist enough. From this viewpoint, the careerist student is the serious student who has well-formed goals and is willing to work hard to achieve them. This student's opposite is the "party animal" who seeks to avoid as much academic work as possible, cares little about grades and less about learning, and devotes much more time to sociability than to studies. Although party animals come in both sexes, for women the emphasis has often been on their participation in the culture of romance. Husband-hunting has been seen as an activity of undergraduate women that undermines their commitments to academe and occupational careers, although some have suggested that this has been and continues to be less true at women's colleges than at coeducational institutions. This suggestion, along with other controversies surrounding careerism for women, is investigated in this book.

Community has emerged as a major metaphor for envisioning higher education, and those who advocate that colleges become better communities usually assume that this means developing greater unity of purpose and mutual caring. Like gender traditionalism and careerism, however, community is embedded in controversies about its meaning and implications. Will unity of purpose stifle individual creativity? Will mutual caring prevent community members from fully developing their personal autonomy? One argument of this book is that such questions do not lend themselves to simple, one-sided answers because communities, by their very nature, offer both opportunities and constraints simultaneously and often by the same social mechanisms.

One way to understand community as an empirical reality, rather than an ideal, is to examine the ties that bind members to one another as well as the forces that divide and disconnect them. Within the college context, this requires an examination not only of how and why the college as a whole constitutes an attractive, supportive community for at least some of its students but also of the extent to which students are tied to the college by their participation in such intermediate structures as extracurricular clubs, teams, and organizations. For women, in particular, friendship networks, including sororities, are also likely to be important sources of community ties. Finally, account needs to be taken of the fact that college students come from other communities. Most will retain ties to their families and hometown friends, and events that occur in those communities of origin have the potential to undermine even a high level of academic and social integration in the college community.

This book tells the story of how a cohort of undergraduate women at a small women's college experienced and coped with the contradictions of gender traditionalism, careerism, and community that formed the context in which they received their college education.

CENTRAL WOMEN'S COLLEGE: WHAT'S IN A NAME?

The institution of higher education described in this book traces its origins to a residential Female Academy founded in the middle of the 19th century by a Protestant religious denomination. Over time, it evolved into a secular institution of higher education for women, gaining accreditation for its junior college division just prior to World War I, eventually dropping its high school department, and awarding its first baccalaureate degrees in 1964. The focus of this book is on the institution's final years as a women's college, 1991 to 1997.

I named this institution Central Women's College (CWC) because I want to call attention to three of its defining characteristics. First, I put the term *women* at the center of the name because women were the only undergraduates at CWC during the years of our study, and they and their experiences are at the center of this book. In actual fact, the term *women* did not appear in the name of the college we studied nor does it appear in the names of most of the institutions of higher education for women. Of 76 such institutions listed in a recent report by the Department of Education (Harwarth, Maline, & DeBra, 1997), only four incorporated the word *women* into their names. This limited use of a gender designation in the names of contemporary women's colleges and universities is in sharp contrast to naming practices throughout the United States prior to the Civil War when most educational institutions for women, like CWC itself, proclaimed themselves as "female" seminaries, academies, or colleges.

The second characteristic of Central Women's College emphasized by its name is its composition as a college. In the United States, the term *college* is most commonly applied to institutions of higher education that grant a bachelor's degree at the completion of a course of study, and women's colleges today typically are 4-year institutions of this kind. In contrast, universities typically grant advanced degrees, such as master's degrees or doctorates, in addition to bachelor's degrees. Universities are also considerably larger than colleges, with the result that they encompass not only graduate or professional schools but also multiple undergraduate colleges, such as colleges of business, education, arts and letters, engineering, agriculture, and sciences. Because of the ever larger numbers of Americans who have enrolled in higher education during the second half of the 20th century, almost all 4-year public colleges have evolved into universities. In contrast, many private colleges have remained small and have not subdivided into multiple colleges and schools. As a result, when applied to a total institution, the term *college* increasingly connotes a small, private, 4-year institution.

Central Women's College, like most women's colleges today, was an institution of this type when our study began in 1991. Total enrollment that fall was less than 800. During the course of our study, CWC added some graduate programs and restyled itself a university, but these developments had no direct impact on the undergraduate college or its students. Most of the graduate courses were taught off campus, and no programs were introduced to bring graduate students and undergraduates into contact with one another. Although the graduate students increased and diversified the student body of the institution by adding men, mature-age adults, and part-time students, no evidence of this diversification could be seen on campus where the small, undergraduate college continued throughout our study to enroll only women, most of whom were young, full-time students who lived on campus. Our study ignores the graduate programs and their students and focuses only on the undergraduate college.

I chose the term *central* to call attention to the fact that Central Women's College is located in the central part of the United States. In contrast, most contemporary women's colleges are located in the Northeast or the South, and these have been the more popular sites for women's colleges throughout U.S. history. Regardless of region, however, historical evidence (e.g., Farnham, 1994; Gordon, 1990; Newcomer, 1959; Schwager, 1988; Woody, 1929) suggests that all women's colleges have had to deal with the contradictory and controversial issues surrounding gender traditionalism, careerism, and community.

A fourth important characteristic of Central Women's College is not suggested by its name. CWC is a nonelite college. The term *elite* is usually applied to colleges and universities that have high admission standards, social prestige, and reputations for academic excellence. Bachelor's degrees from such institutions increase their recipients' chances for good jobs and for admission to the top graduate and professional schools. Not surprisingly, the elite colleges and universities often benefit from the successes of their graduates with the result that many have large endowments. Because of their reputations and despite the fact that they are often very expensive, elite colleges and universities generally attract more student-applicants than they need or want. As a result, they are able to limit the student body to those best able to meet expectations for outstanding performance, and these students are highly likely to come from elite backgrounds as indicated by the socioeconomic status of their parents and by the prestige of the secondary schools they attended. Scholarship funds are usually available and are used to attract outstanding students from less wealthy backgrounds.

In contrast, nonelite private colleges rarely can afford to be choosy. They have small or no endowments and are primarily dependent on student tuition for their survival. As a result, they must attract and retain enough students to remain fiscally solvent. To do so, they often lower admission standards. During the period of our study, Central Women's College admitted more than 90% of all applicants. This rate of acceptance is not unusual according to Astin and Lee, who reported in 1972 (before the current fiscal crisis in higher education) that more than one half of all private colleges had admission standards like those that existed at CWC. As David Riesman (1981) has pointed out, however, many colleges mask their lack of selectivity in order to depict themselves as valuable and scarce opportunities.

Although CWC's administration put their admissions rate on the public record by revealing it to the American Council on Education, the rate seemed not to be known to the CWC students whom we studied, some of whom wrote application essays expressing hopes of being admitted and fears of being rejected despite the reasonable academic records they had compiled in high school. Perhaps these applicants wanted to avoid what Riesman (1981) has dubbed the Groucho Marx syndrome: If admissions requirements "seemed too lenient, students might come to feel that their brave new institution resembled the kind of club Groucho Marx would not join because, as he put it, any place that would take him couldn't be any good" (p. 115).

Many of the studies that have been done of women's colleges have focused on elite institutions. Particular attention has been paid to the Seven Sisters—Barnard, Bryn Mawr, Mount Holyoke, Radcliffe, Smith, Vassar, and Wellesley. Although these elite colleges occupy an important position in the history of women's education and have often functioned as models for other institutions, it is not clear how many of the campus experiences and educational outcomes of their students can be generalized to students at nonelite institutions such as CWC. As I suggest in the following chapters of this book, among the institutional characteristics that affect the ways in which the themes of gender traditionalism, careerism, and community are constructed and play themselves out in women's colleges are the academic and social status of the institution.

Although I consider the nonelite status of CWC to be a major defining characteristic of the college, I did not include the term *nonelite* in the college's name for two reasons. First and most obvious, Central, Nonelite Women's College is an awkward-sounding name. Second, but most important, the students we studied either chose to ignore or were oblivious of the nonelite status of the college. In contrast, they all recognized that CWC was a small, private, undergraduate college for women located in the central part of the United States. Although their praise for and criticism of the college often touched on its size or location, and sometimes on its gender composition, its nonelite status was rarely mentioned. The few comments made about the academic standards of the institution were just as likely to fault them for being too high as for being too low, and even those who left CWC for other academic institutions showed little, if any, understanding of the prestige system that characterizes American higher education or of the place of CWC in that system. Omitting "nonelite" from the name of CWC symbolizes its absence from the frames of reference of most of the students we studied.

STUDYING CENTRAL WOMEN'S COLLEGE

In spring of 1991, Harriet and I decided to do a longitudinal study of the next class of entering first-year students at CWC. That class consisted of 201 women, but 16 of them were enrolled in a 2-year vocational program. We decided to focus on the remaining 185, all of whom were enrolled full time in the college programs leading to baccalaureate degrees. Demographically, the composition of this class was about the same as the composition of the previous entering classes still attending CWC. They were young, mostly White, and Christian. Although the entering students ranged in age from 16 to 30, their average age was 18, and only four were more than 20 years old. Only 10 students indicated racial identities other than White or Caucasian. Of these, four were African Americans, three were Asian Americans, two were Hispanics, and one described herself as an American Indian. Of the 144 students who were willing to express a religious preference, the largest single denominational group was Roman Catholic, but those who mentioned specific Protestant denominations or said, simply, that they were Protestant outnumbered Catholics by a ratio of more than 2 to 1 ($n = 88$ to $n = 38$). One said she was Greek Orthodox, one was Mormon, one was a nondenominational charismatic, and 15 indicated only that they were "Christian."

An examination of the states from which the 1991 entering class came to CWC revealed that the college serviced, primarily, a regional student market and, secondarily, a national one. More than half of the class ($n = 100$) came from the state in which CWC was located, but only a few of these came from within commuting distance, and even those few tended to live on campus. Another 51 students came from states that bordered the state in which CWC was located, one student came from Europe, and the remaining 33 came from an additional 16 states stretching from Maine to Hawaii.

Evidence for the nonelite status of the entering class came from information about their entry-level qualifications. As is true at most American colleges and universities, applicants at CWC were expected to provide both their transcript from high school(s) indicating their overall grade point average (GPA) and their results on one of the national tests of academic achievement, usually the American College Test (ACT) or the Scholastic Aptitude Test (SAT). Using a 4-point scale for GPAs in which a grade of D = 1, C = 2, B = 3, A = 4, and anything above 4 indicates an A+ or advanced placement credits, the high school GPAs for the CWC class ranged from 1.5 to 4.5, with an average of 2.9. This average is not only considerably below the A– average one would expect to find at an elite women's college, but it is also considerably below the grades reported by a large national sample of first-time, full-time freshmen surveyed in the fall of 1991 by the Cooperative Institutional Research Program. That survey found that more than 70% of the freshmen women had high school GPAs of B or higher (Astin, Dey, Korn, & Riggs, 1991), a level achieved by fewer than half of the first-year students at CWC.

During the undergraduate careers of the class we studied, an article by Patricia Beard (1994), an alumna of Bryn Mawr, appeared reporting the SAT scores of undergraduates at the Seven Sisters Colleges. For the five of these colleges that had remained women-only institutions into the 1990s (Barnard, Bryn Mawr, Mount Holyoke, Smith, and Wellesley), the median or middle SAT scores ranged from a low of 1130 for Mount Holyoke to a high of 1320 for Wellesley. In contrast, the SAT scores for students entering CWC in 1991 ranged from 480 to 1150, with a median score of 890. Only 6% of entering CWC students who had taken the SAT (rather than the ACT) had scores at or above the median score for Mount Holyoke undergraduates.

To provide a framework for our study of the 1991 entering class at CWC, we surveyed a representative sample of the students enrolled at CWC the previous spring. Responses to that survey provided us with a portrait of the student culture at CWC that the next class would be joining. Survey questionnaires were distributed to the new class in the summer of 1991, just prior to their matriculation at CWC; in spring semester of 1992 before the end of their first year; and during 1994 and 1995 to both those who had left the college and those who eventually graduated. In addition, three sets of interviews were conducted, two with samples of those students who remained enrolled at the college (in 1992 and 1995) and one with students who had left (in 1994 and 1995). The survey questionnaires and interviews were supplemented with information about the same students obtained from CWC records and documents.

Information was also collected about the organizational structure and official school culture of CWC by examining opinions and decisions of college personnel. A survey of faculty who were at CWC at the same time as most of the students (1991–1995) was conducted in 1997. Information from official college documents published during this decade were assembled and analyzed. These documents included school newspapers, yearbooks, catalogs, promotional materials, alumnae magazines, and announcements of campus events. Informal interviews with administrators and faculty were also conducted.

More detailed descriptions of the samples that completed each survey and formal interview are contained in Appendix A at the end of the book. Appendix B contains excerpts from the survey questionnaires that are relevant to this book, and descriptions of additional survey questions are presented in Chapters 2–7 as they become pertinent to the topics and research questions on which each chapter focuses. To avoid cluttering the text with statistical notations, the same procedures were used throughout the book to determine whether a research finding was significant and how strong it was. These conventions are described in Appendix C, which also contains information about the statistical manipulations used to create the multi-item scales that are analyzed in the book. Appendix D contains relevant parts of the three interview schedules referred to above.

GENDER TRADITIONALISM, CAREERISM, AND COMMUNITY AT CWC

Although the contradictions surrounding gender traditionalism, careerism, and community are interrelated, each of the next five chapters focuses primarily on one of them. Chapter 2 examines the extent to which traditional and emancipatory themes were institutionalized at CWC and were expressed in the norms and values of students and faculty. Based on existing literature, a theory is presented to predict the conditions under which college contexts will maintain or change student values and norms, and this theory is tested using data collected at CWC. Finally, the mixture of traditionalism and emancipation found in the norms and values of CWC students over time is validated and elaborated by analyzing the information the students provided about their views of feminism and their (un)willingness to identify themselves as feminists.

Chapter 3 explores the possibility that the effects reported in Chapter 2 might be different among sorority members and independent women. Two major claims characterizing historical and contemporary writings about sororities are tested at CWC. The first is the charge that sororities are elitist and exclusionary. The second is the claim that sororities are bastions of gender traditionalism. Some research evidence supports this second claim, but some does not. By, first, distinguishing among several kinds of traditionalism and, then, examining the kinds of traditionalism endorsed or rejected by sorority members and independents at CWC, I am able to show that this seeming contradiction may depend on how traditionalism and emancipation are defined and measured.

Whereas the theme of traditionalism has one major countertheme (emancipation), careerism has two. One of these is an academic orientation. Many contemporary publications about higher education contrast careerism, or its vocational and professional components, with academic values, a liberal arts orientation, the quest for knowledge, or intellectualism. Both the students who attend college and the colleges themselves are said to differ in the extent to which they exhibit one or the other of these two orientations, and careerism is said to have increased greatly in the last three decades of the 20th century. This increase tends to be viewed as a negative development. To some it is a necessary or inevitable evil, and to others it is the abandonment of the noble traditions of American higher education and Western intellectual life.

The fact that careerism has always been part of American higher education for women, especially outside of the deep South, challenges the sharp distinction that is often made between careerism and academic traditions as well as claims about the recency of "the threat of careerism." More support for these challenges is presented in Chapter 4 in the context of an argument that the mix and meanings of careerism and the liberal arts have differed not only across historic periods but also across gender. Against this background, I present information about the academic and careerist commitments of matriculating CWC students and of the college itself, with particular emphasis on the ways in which these commitments affected students' academic performance and career choices. Throughout the chapter, I suggest ways in which both the liberal arts and careerism have promoted gender traditionalism at CWC and elsewhere, and I close with a vision of a more emancipatory education for women.

A second countertheme to careerism, and to the academic orientation as well, is what some writers have identified as the collegiate culture. Clark and Trow (1966) call the collegiate culture "the most widely held stereotype of college life" and define it as a "world of football, fraternities and sororities, dates, cars, drinking, and campus fun" (p. 20). This culture flourishes on, but is not confined to, residential campuses of big state universities. Although students cannot continue their participation in the collegiate culture unless they pay some attention to faculty and courses and grades, "serious intellectual or professional interests on the part of students and faculty work against the full flowering of a collegiate subculture" (p. 21).

Helen Lefkowitz Horowitz (1987) traces the origins of the collegiate culture, or "college life" as she calls it, to the late 18th and early 19th centuries when wealthier and worldlier undergraduate men revolted against the demands and restrictions of college presidents and faculty. Although the first generation of women to attend coeducational colleges tended to be "outsiders" with serious, academic goals, Horowitz (1987) suggests that later generations of "coeds" were much more likely to embrace the male-dominated and male-defined college life. Like the college men, these coeds came to college for fun. "They did not see college as a steppingstone to a career, but as a way station to a proper marriage" (p. 201). A similar depiction of contemporary women undergraduates emerges from the research of Holland and Eisenhart (1990) who were interested in the question of why so many women who entered "Southern University" with strong academic backgrounds and firm career goals left with dramatically scaled-down ambitions. The answer to this question, they suggest, is that the women get caught up in a peer-dominated culture of romance in which being attractive to men and having appropriate romantic and sexual partners count for more than academic success.

Can Horowitz's portrait of coeds and Holland and Eisenhart's research findings from Southern University be generalized to women's colleges? Research reviewed in Chapter 5 provides some reasons to think the answer to this question might be "no." Given the differences in findings reported for women's colleges versus coeducational institutions, it seemed possible that the culture of romance and the broader collegiate culture might have had relatively weak effects on the career orientations of undergraduates at CWC. In Chapter 5, I test this possibility by determining the form that the collegiate culture took at CWC in the 1990s and by investigating the ways in which students' academic achievements and career plans were affected both by the collegiate culture and by the relative importance they assigned to "the college life."

The focus of Chapter 6 is on community and the effects of various forms of community involvements on student persistence at CWC. These involvements include relationships both on the campus and in the students' hometown, as well as participation in campus-based academic, athletic, and social communities. In addition to examining the ways in which these involvements are related to one another and to students' commitments to CWC, the chapter also examines the conflicting tensions that characterized communal life at CWC and some of the implications that such contradictions may have for the search for community renewal and student involvement on American campuses.

Finally, in Chapter 7, a brief summary of findings about gender traditionalism, careerism, and community at Central Women's College is presented. The findings are examined in light of the major claims that surrounded the administrative decision, announced in 1996 and implemented in 1997, to admit men to CWC. These claims focused on the women-centered nature of CWC and the importance of student diversity. Evidence relevant to these claims is examined within the contexts of both contemporary debates about women's colleges and historically embedded contradictions in higher education for women in the United States.

CHAPTER 2

Traditionalism and Emancipation: Socialization at CWC

A large literature, describing thousands of research projects, has appeared on the topic of how college affects students. Excellent reviews and syntheses of this literature have also appeared (especially Feldman & Newcomb, 1969/1994; Pascarella & Terenzini, 1991). Although only a tiny proportion of this literature has been concerned with the effects of college on gender traditionalism, information relevant to that topic can be obtained from examining studies concerned, more broadly, with college effects on prescriptive and proscriptive norms and on values. In particular, such studies suggest three circumstances that are likely to determine whether and to what extent college will produce changes in norms and values. For convenience, I refer to these circumstances as college culture, prior agreement, and residential isolation.

College culture includes the norms and values that are stressed at a college by the administration, faculty, and students. The greater the stress on particular norms and values by one or more of these groups, the greater the likelihood that incoming students will form (or retain) norms and values consistent with those in the college culture. Also, the greater the consensus among administration, faculty, and students about what appropriate norms and values should be, the greater the likelihood that incoming students will form (or retain) those norms and values.

Prior agreement refers to the extent to which an entering student, or group of students, has norms and values that are similar to those characteristic of the college culture. An obvious example is a fundamentalist Christian who enters a fundamentalist Bible college. The greater the prior agreement, the less change one would expect to find in the students' norms and values. The less the prior agreement, the more room there is for change. Whether that change will or won't occur depends, at least in part, on residential isolation.

Residential isolation refers to the extent to which the living arrangements for students at a college isolate them within the college culture.

13

Obviously, living on campus produces more residential isolation than does living off campus. Commuting from one's family home to college on a daily basis probably produces the least amount of residential isolation. Even for those living on campus, the extent of residential isolation depends on the location and design of the campus and the amount of contact with "outsiders." On the basis of existing research comparing students living on campus with commuters (reviewed in Pascarella & Terenzini, 1991, pp. 399–402), one would expect colleges at which students experience relatively high levels of residential isolation to have more influence on their norms and values than colleges at which the residential isolation of students is low.

College culture, prior agreement, and residential isolation are discussed in more detail below. Although this discussion draws from the broader literature concerned with norm and value changes at college, particular emphasis in this chapter is given to gender traditionalism and women's emancipation and to Central Women's College. In what ways and to what extent were the college culture, the prior agreement level of the entering students, and the degree of residential isolation at CWC likely to produce increases or decreases in gender traditionalism among entering students? After discussing each of these three circumstances and their likely effects, I address the central question of how much change in gender traditionalism actually occurred during the undergraduate careers of the class that entered CWC in 1991. Were the amount and kind of changes the same as those predicted on the basis of CWC's culture, the prior agreement levels of the 1991 entering class, and the residential isolation levels of CWC students? Or, were the kind and amount of change different from what was expected?

Regardless of the kind and amount of change during the undergraduate years, such changes may or may not be due to the college itself. Residential isolation at colleges never reaches a level that leaves students unaware of external influences. Mass media, telephone calls from parents, e-mail exchanges with friends at other colleges, and trips home are only a few of the multitude of penetrations into students' campus lives. For this reason, I examine whether changes in gender traditionalism among CWC undergraduates were due to external influences of this type or to the college itself.

If changes seem to be due to the college, is it the general college culture that produces them, or are they due to specific influences internal to the college? Although it is not possible to examine all the many internal conditions to which students were exposed, one difference among women students that is likely to have a strong effect on whom they live, interact, and identify with is sorority membership. In Chapter 3, I examine the sorority system at CWC and report the results of efforts to determine the impact of that system on the socialization of students at the college. In contrast, this chapter keeps its focus on the college as a whole and examines the extent to which the college culture successfully encouraged or discouraged gender traditionalism and women's emancipation.

CULTURES OF WOMEN'S COLLEGES: FROM BENNINGTON TO CWC

Arguably, the best known study of the impact of college on students is the study of Bennington College during the years from 1935 to 1939 by Ted Newcomb (1943, 1958) who was then a member of the Bennington faculty. The senior class in 1935 was the first to graduate from Bennington. Newcomb's study both compared that class to the other classes and followed that year's entering class through their senior year. Newcomb (1943) framed his research problem in the following way:

> Each year some ninety young women . . . leave families whose opinions about contemporary public issues are, as the term is currently used, definitely conservative. . . . Both home and school influences have been such that there was little or no necessity for them to come to any very definite terms with public issues. . . .
> From such backgrounds and with such predispositions they come to a college where community life is intense; . . . where there is more pressure to come to terms with public issues, and where there are people of intelligence and good breeding (upper-class students and faculty, in the main) who do *not* agree with their families and their families' friends regarding contemporary public affairs.
> And so some form of adaptation must be made. (pp. 9–11)

For most of the students, this adaptation meant an increased interest in public affairs and a shift in political opinions from conservative to liberal or even radical.

Although Newcomb's study of Bennington is often cited for demonstrating "the liberalizing effect" of a college education, less attention has been given to the unique characteristics of the college culture that were responsible for this effect. Bennington was a new women's college without campus traditions but with a firm commitment to progressive education. During the years of Newcomb's study, the student body consisted of only 250 students. The college had recruited an exceptionally young, attractive faculty, with "not more than two or three instructors whose ages exceeded forty, and none over fifty. . . . The faculty . . . was almost universally described by those familiar with the college as 'liberal'" (Newcomb, 1943, p. 8). Most of the faculty of approximately 50 members lived on or near the campus, and they were expected to establish close relationships with students not only in the classroom but also in the student–faculty committees that constituted the governance structure of the college. Given these expectations, it is not surprising that most of the faculty "were selected with an eye to capacity for smooth community relationships as well as to their professional qualifications" (p. 8). Horowitz (1987) argues that these characteristics of Bennington produced a unique campus culture: "In the 1930s Bennington was *sui generis*. Few other colleges had faculty as consistently liberal. No other college had students, even female students, so vulnerable to professorial influence" (p. 216).

In contrast to Bennington in the 1930s, Central Women's College in the 1990s did not have a uniquely progressive political climate. Even with regard to gender traditionalism and women's emancipation, college documents and practices failed to reveal a strong, consistent stance. The student-recruitment brochure used in 1991 leans more to the side of emancipation than traditionalism. Highlighted throughout its 16 pages are 10 quotations from 19th- and 20th-century women. Some of these quotations would be entirely appropriate in the brochures of men's colleges or coeducational institutions. Mary Wells Lawrence, for example, is quoted as saying: "I was taught to think you can always do anything you want to do if you work hard enough." In contrast, more than half of the quotations express strong emancipatory, nontraditional views of women and their education:

> Women's colleges are places that take women seriously. They are places where you can be sure that the thinking going on is how to best serve women students.—Marcia K. Sharp
>
> It's important for women to have a place where they are given every opportunity, not just equal opportunity.—Nannerl O. Keahane
>
> Women's colleges teach women to think in terms of possibilities for their lives, rather than in terms of their limitations.—Mary S. Metz
>
> Women are the real architects of society.—Harriet Beecher Stowe
>
> Now we are becoming the men we wanted to marry. Once women were trained to marry a doctor, not be one.—Gloria Steinem
>
> It's the women who make decisions. Women are strong, women are the doers, that's the way it is.—Eugenie Clark

These resounding rejections of gender traditionalism stand in sharp contrast to the curriculum and extracurriculum of CWC, which contained little that could be called emancipatory or feminist. The 1990–1992 catalog listed 46 programs from which students could choose majors, but women's studies was not among them. Nor did the curricula of traditional departments, such as English, history, or psychology, list courses centrally concerned with women or gender. Although the extracurriculum included a broad array of student organizations, none of them had a name or mission that was feminist in nature. In contrast, both the extracurriculum and curriculum included many exemplars of gender traditionalism, including four sororities, a home economics association, five different education majors, and courses in such traditionally female subjects as child and family development, family economics and management, foods and nutrition, and clothing construction. In fairness, the curriculum also included majors and minors in fields that have not been considered traditionally female subjects, such as business administration and coaching, and administrators frequently encouraged students to develop their leadership skills while working toward their academic degrees. Thus it would be unfair to characterize the official school culture as solidly traditional, but there is little evidence to support the proposition that the college was either innovative or strongly emancipatory in its approach to women's roles in contemporary society.

What about the student culture? Could it more fairly be described as emancipatory? To find out, I examined the answers that CWC students in the spring of 1991 gave to questions about their gender norms and personal values. The questions about gender norms asked students to indicate the extent of their agreement or disagreement with 13 statements about how women should or should not behave or be treated (see Appendix B, Figure B.1). A statistical technique called factor analysis, described in Appendix C, revealed that the 13 statements could be divided into four different clusters or scales (see Table C.1). I named these scales Traditional Family Norms, Propriety Norms, Gender Equality Norms, and Self-Oriented Norms.

The statements on the Traditional Family Norms scale measured the extent to which students thought that women and their careers should take second place to husbands and children. The statements on the Propriety Norms scale measured the extent to which students thought that women should engage in proper or conventional behavior such as not swearing and waiting for male partners to propose marriage. There was a positive correlation between scores on these two scales, which can be interpreted to mean that high scores on both the Traditional Family Norms and Propriety Norms scales indicated high amounts of gender traditionalism, and low scores on these two scales indicated nontraditional gender norms. Although statistically significant, the correlation between the two scales was weak, indicating that they measure somewhat different aspects of gender traditionalism.

The statements on the Gender Equality Norms scale measured the extent to which men and women should either perform the same behaviors (e.g., share housework) or be treated equally (e.g., in class, in the work force). The statements measuring Self-Oriented Norms assessed the extent to which women should pursue their own personal goals instead of being oriented to their friends or to sociability more generally. There was a significant, positive, but weak correlation between scores on these two scales, which can be interpreted to mean that high scores on both the Gender Equality Norms and Self-Oriented Norms scales indicated high advocacy of women's emancipation; low scores on these two scales indicated low advocacy of women's emancipation; and the two scales tap different components of women's emancipation.

When average scores on the four scales were compared to one another, scores on the Gender Equality Norms scale were found to be significantly higher than scores on the other three scales. Students strongly endorsed gender equality. In contrast, students gave only slight endorsement, on average, to the Self-Oriented Norms scale and the Propriety Norms scale, and both scales received about the same level of endorsement. The lowest level of endorsement was given to the Traditional Family Norms scale, with which students slightly *dis*agreed. Although this latter finding suggests low levels of gender traditionalism among students at CWC, that conclusion is contradicted not only by their endorsement of propriety norms but also by what they said about their personal values.

To measure those values, students were presented with an alphabetically ordered list of 10 values or goals that people might have for their lives (see Appendix B, Figure B.2). They were asked to rate each goal on the basis of how important it was to them personally. Again using factor analysis, it was found that these 10 values could be grouped into four clusters or scales (see Appendix C, Table C.2). I named these scales Achievement Values, Autonomy Values, Traditional Family Values, and True Friendship.

The Achievement Values scale consisted of four values: a prosperous life (financial security), sexual fulfillment, social approval (admiration), and a successful career. They represent achievements in four different domains: economic, sexual, social, and occupational. The more students valued one of these achievements, the more they were likely to value the others. The Autonomy Values scale consisted of only two values, freedom (independence, free choice) and self-respect (self-esteem), and the more that students valued one of these values, the more they valued the other.

The Traditional Family Values included a happy marriage, loving children, and salvation. Although salvation was rated less highly, on average, than the other two values in this cluster, ratings of all three of these values were positively and significantly correlated with one another. The fourth scale consisted of only one value, True Friendship. Because it lacks a clear meaning with regard to questions about gender traditionalism and women's emancipation, it is not discussed in this chapter.

When average scores were compared on the remaining three measures of values, a large, significant difference was found between Autonomy Values, on the one hand, and Traditional Family Values and Achievement Values, on the other. Whereas Autonomy Values were rated as very important, on average, the other two value scales were considered only somewhat important, and ratings of these two scales did not differ from each other.

When the findings about values and norms were combined, they revealed a student culture that seemed to be a mix of emancipatory and traditional norms and values with more emphasis on the former than the latter. This conclusion is based on the assumption that a strongly emancipatory culture would give high ratings to Gender Equality Norms, Self-Oriented Norms, Autonomy Values, and Achievement Values and would give low ratings to Propriety Norms, Traditional Family Norms, and Traditional Family Values. In contrast, CWC students gave their highest ratings to Gender Equality and Autonomy, gave moderate ratings to Propriety, Self-Oriented Norms, Traditional Family Values, and Achievement Values, and gave low or negative ratings to Traditional Family Norms. The mixture of emancipatory and traditional norms and values with moderate ratings meant that the student culture of CWC—unlike that of Bennington in the 1930s—did not provide students with a strong, unambiguous prescription of what opinions they should adopt to be fully accepted and approved in the undergraduate culture. Although those with more emancipatory norms and values might feel somewhat more comfortable with their peers, those with gender-traditional norms and values, unlike conservatives at Bennington, would not feel like outsiders.

CWC students with emancipatory norms and values probably also felt more comfortable with CWC faculty than did gender-traditional students. The faculty had been asked to respond to the same measures of norms and values as the students. Like the students, the faculty gave their highest rating ("very important") to Autonomy Values and gave significantly lower and approximately equal ratings to Traditional Family Values and Achievement Values. The pattern of faculty ratings of Gender Equality Norms and Traditional Family Norms was also the same as the pattern of student ratings, with strong agreement, on average, expressed for Gender Equality Norms and slight disagreement, on average, expressed for Traditional Family Norms.

In contrast, the faculty ratings for Self-Oriented Norms and Propriety Norms were unlike the student ratings in three different ways. First, the faculty rated Self-Oriented Norms significantly more favorably than did the students. Second, the faculty rated Propriety Norms significantly less favorably than did the students. Third, the faculty rated Self-Oriented Norms significantly higher than Propriety Norms. Unlike the students, who indicated slight agreement with these two kinds of norms, the faculty gave moderate endorsement to Self-Oriented Norms, and they disagreed slightly with Propriety Norms.

Although these findings about faculty ratings of norms suggest that the CWC faculty advocated more emancipation than did the CWC students, one of the findings about value ratings seemed to suggest otherwise. There was a large and significant difference between faculty and student ratings of Achievement Values, and it was faculty who gave those values a *lower* rating. This finding was contradicted, however, by the finding that the faculty also gave significantly lower ratings to Traditional Family Values than did the students. Interestingly, these findings about values, as well as those about norms, held true for both male and female faculty; there were no significant effects of gender on any of the seven measures of faculty norms and values.

In order to interpret the seeming contradiction between ratings of norms and values, it's important to remember that the normative questions concerned what women should and should not do and how they should be treated, but the values questions concerned the importance of the values to each rater personally. As a result, the finding that the faculty gave more consistent endorsement to emancipatory norms and more consistent rejection to traditional norms than did the students probably had more consequences for how faculty treated students than did the finding that faculty gave lower ratings than students did to Achievement Values for themselves. In addition, subsequent findings, presented in Chapter 3, suggested that the kinds of achievements included in the Achievement Values scale may not have been entirely emancipatory.

Taken in combination, the findings summarized in this section reveal some differences, but no major conflicts, between faculty and students about gender traditionalism and emancipation. Students entering CWC could expect to find a culture in which most people valued marriage and family for themselves, but did not advocate women's subservience to husbands or children. Entering students would also find a heavy emphasis on gender equality and personal autonomy among both faculty and students with a considerably weaker stress on women's self-orientation and their emancipation from conventional proprieties.

PRIOR AGREEMENT ABOUT GENDER TRADITIONALISM

What norms and values did students bring with them to CWC? According to the information students provided the summer before they matriculated, their pattern of ratings was the same as that found for faculty. Incoming students gave the highest ratings to Gender Equality Norms, next highest to Self-Oriented Norms, third highest to Propriety Norms, and lowest to Traditional Family Norms. Highest value ratings were given to Autonomy Values with about equal ratings given to Traditional Family Values and Achievement Values. Thus the pattern of ratings of incoming students differed from that of the existing students in only one respect. Like faculty, matriculating students rated Self-Oriented Norms significantly higher than Propriety Norms, whereas existing students rated the two types of norms equally.

Although the *patterns* of ratings for norms and values showed considerable prior agreement between incoming students, on the one hand, and existing students or faculty, on the other, there were some significant differences in the actual *levels* of the ratings. These differences occurred for three of the four measures of norms—Gender Equality, Self-Orientation, and Propriety—and for two of the three measures of values—Autonomy and Achievement. No significant differences were found between the ratings of Traditional Family Norms or Values given by incoming students and existing students or faculty.

Of the five significant differences that were found, there were important differences in the consistency, size, and direction of these differences. The largest and most consistent difference was found for Gender Equality Norms. Incoming students scored moderately and significantly lower, on average, than both faculty and existing students on this measure. Incoming students also scored lower, on average, than both faculty and existing students on the measure of Autonomy Values, but the size of the differences was small and the difference was significant only for the comparison between the two groups of students. Incoming students scored moderately and significantly lower than the faculty on Self-Oriented Norms, but their average scores on this measure were not different from those of existing students. Incoming students scored moderately and significantly higher than the faculty on Achievement Values, but, again, their average scores were not different from those of existing students. For Propriety Norms, incoming students had an average level of ratings that fell between the average ratings of faculty and existing students. The incoming students' ratings were moderately and significantly higher than those of the faculty, but they were slightly and significantly lower than those of the existing students.

Taken together, these findings suggest that the socialization pressures on incoming students varied across different kinds of norms and values. Most pressure was in the direction of more gender egalitarianism and more autonomy because there was a more emancipatory consensus between faculty and existing students about these issues. Least pressure on incoming students was directed toward their traditional family norms and values because their opinions were already in agreement with those of faculty and existing students. Predictions concerning Self-Oriented Norms, Achievement Values, and Propriety Norms depended on whether incoming students would be more influenced by faculty or by existing students. If the former, then their ratings of Self-Oriented Norms could be predicted to increase and their ratings of Achievement Values and Propriety Norms should decrease. If they identified with other students, however, then one would expect no changes in their Self-Oriented Norms or Achievement Values and an increase in their ratings of Propriety Norms.

RESIDENTIAL ISOLATION

Central Women's College is located on an attractive, 160–acre campus in a small town of about 12,000 in a rural county. One of the most striking things about the campus during the period of our study was the way in which its design, the configuration of its surrounding terrain, and fencing created barriers that limited vehicular and pedestrian access to the campus. No through traffic could cut across the central parts of the campus, and the main entrance to the campus gave visitors the impression that they were entering an isolated enclave from which they could most easily exit using the same roadway on which they entered. The physical organization of the campus definitely communicated a sense of safety.

Adding to this sense of safety during the period of our study was a security office located at the main entrance to the campus. Students entering the campus after specified closing hours were expected to stop and show their college identification card to the security officer. If students were accompanied by male escorts, the security guard would give a pass to that man, but he was expected to return the pass and exit the campus within 30 minutes. The Student Handbook for 1991–1992 lists the closing hours as 1 a.m. Sunday through Thursday and 2 a.m. on Friday and Saturday.

The 40 buildings on the campus included 13 residence halls. Although sororities referred to their residences as chapter houses, they were actually on-campus residence halls assigned to the sororities by the college. During the period of our study, all residence halls were locked at 10 p.m., after which they could be entered only by residents using a combination lock. Residents were instructed not to give out their residence hall combination, and they were not allowed to bring guests into the building after it was locked.

All students were expected to live on campus unless they were at least 23 years old, were single mothers, or lived with parents, guardians, or husbands within commuting distance from the college. Of the 185 students who began baccalaureate programs in August of 1991, only 11 lived off campus during their first year. Because sorority rush did not start that year until after the semester was under way, none of the entering students lived in the chapter houses. Instead, they were scattered across eight residence halls, all of which also housed returning students from other classes. These housing arrangements, coupled with the physical isolation of the campus and the restricted contacts with "outsiders," probably did more to facilitate than to interfere with interaction and mutual influence among incoming students and between them and existing students.

Unlike faculty at Bennington, those at CWC did not live on campus and did not participate with students in college governance committees or in the kinds of evening programs described by Newcomb (1943). Thus it seems likely that the residential isolation of CWC had little effect on student–faculty interaction. This isolation probably increased the influence of students on one another more than it increased the influence of faculty on students.

CHANGES IN GENDER TRADITIONALISM

To determine whether existing students or faculty had more influence on incoming students, I compared students' levels of endorsement of norms and values in summer 1991 with their levels of endorsement 4 years later. Because it seemed likely that the college would have its greatest effect on those students who remained the longest, I limited this comparison to those who eventually graduated from CWC. Within this group, the evidence for student peer influence was stronger than the evidence for faculty influence. The average ratings of Self-Oriented Norms and Achievement Values were the same at graduation as they had been when the students entered in 1991, which means they remained the same as those of existing students and significantly different from those of the faculty.

In contrast, scores on the Propriety Norms scale did not increase in the direction of the norms of existing students, but the scores also did not decrease in the direction of the Propriety Norms of faculty. Instead, the average ratings of Propriety Norms remained about the same over the years from matriculation to graduation. Although it is possible that this finding resulted from a compromise on the part of incoming students between the norms of existing students and faculty, it is also possible that the findings of no change in Propriety Norms, as well as findings of no change in Self-Oriented Norms and Achievement Values, simply mean that the college experience had no effect on CWC students. This conclusion is contradicted, however, by findings concerning the effects of the college years on Gender Equality Norms and Autonomy Values.

As expected, there was a significant, moderate increase in the average level of endorsement of Gender Equality Norms between the summer of 1991 and the time that those incoming students graduated from CWC. The increase was even greater for those students whose entry-level endorsement of Gender Equality Norms was below the average level of endorsement of the existing students. For these "below average" students who later graduated from CWC, there was a *large*, significant increase in the average level of endorsement of Gender Equality Norms. In contrast, students whose entry-level endorsement of Gender Equality Norms was above the average level of endorsement of the existing students did not change their average level of endorsement between entry to CWC and graduation. These findings are consistent with the conclusion that the norms of Gender Equality held by students who entered in 1991 and remained to graduate was affected by the existing culture of CWC. The strong commitment to gender equality characteristic of the culture of CWC produced an equally strong commitment in the class that entered in 1991.

For Autonomy Values, the findings were similar but not identical. Students who entered with Autonomy Values lower than the average of the existing students and faculty exhibited a large, significant increase in their ratings of Autonomy Values by the time they graduated. In contrast, the students who entered with Autonomy Values higher than the average of the existing students and faculty exhibited a significant, moderate decrease in their ratings of Autonomy Values by the time they graduated. In other words, both the low scorers and the high scorers changed their Autonomy Values in the direction of those most characteristic of the campus culture. As a result, by the time they graduated, there were no longer any differences between Autonomy Values of the group that had entered in 1991 and those of the students and faculty who were already at CWC when they arrived.

As expected, there were no changes over the 4 years in the ratings students gave to Traditional Family Norms and Values. The average ratings of these two scales were the same at matriculation and graduation and, as noted above, they were the same as the ratings given to these scales by existing students and faculty. On average, a happy marriage, loving children, and religious salvation were considered somewhat important personally, but Traditional Family Norms that would place women's interests below those of their husbands and children were rejected, but not vehemently.

Taken together, the findings suggest that the norms and values of the students we studied were influenced by the culture of CWC. If the students entered with norms and values that were, on average, the same as those preexisting among students at CWC, the undergraduate culture served a maintenance function and there was stability, rather than change, in those norms and values. Little change also happened when entering students found themselves caught between the Propriety Norms of existing students and faculty. If the students entered with norms and values that were, on average, different from norms and values that preexisted at CWC, especially among students, they tended to move their norms and values in the direction of the college culture. As a result of these changes and nonchanges, the average norms and values of the students who entered in 1991 became more emancipatory but no less (or more) traditional by the time they graduated.

EXTERNAL INFLUENCES ON GENDER TRADITIONALISM

Could the changes in entering students' norms and values be due to events that were external to the college, rather than to socialization experiences at CWC? Evidence in favor of this possibility concerning norms comes from research reviewed by Pascarella and Terenzini (1991) showing that "during the college years students become increasingly more egalitarian, or 'modern,' in their views on the equality of the sexes with respect to educational and occupational opportunities" (p. 282). Astin (1993) asked a large national sample of college students in 1985 and again in 1989 whether they thought that "Women should receive the same salaries and opportunities for advancement as men in comparable positions," a question similar to one on the Gender Equality Norms scale used at CWC (see Appendix C, Table C.1). He found a significant increase in agreement with this statement over the 4 years of college.

Although these findings are consistent with the possibility that the changes in Gender Equality Norms found at CWC have more to do with increases in the amount of education than with the particular culture of CWC, there also are findings in the research literature that contradict this possibility. In the same national study mentioned above, Astin (1993) asked students whether they believed that "The activities of married women are best confined to the home and family," a question similar to those appearing on the CWC measure of Traditional Family Norms (see Appendix C,

Table C.1). Astin reports a large and significant increase in *dis*agreement with this statement during the four undergraduate years of college. Similarly, Pascarella and Terenzini (1991) report that most of the research studies they reviewed found a negative correlation between the amount of college education and gender traditionalism as measured by questions about the distribution of responsibilities in marriage and family relations. If the CWC students had been affected by the same socialization experiences as the students in Astin's research and the studies reviewed by Pascarella and Terenzini, their scores on Traditional Family Norms should have decreased instead of remaining the same during their years at CWC.

The lack of change found for the CWC students who entered in 1991 on the measure of Traditional Family Norms coupled with their changes in Gender Equality Norms suggests that they were influenced more by the culture of CWC than by the number of years of education they completed or by American society more generally. When the entering norms of students were consistent with norms advocated by more advanced students and faculty, as was true for Traditional Family Norms, no significant changes occurred in entering norms over students' years at CWC. When the entering norms of students were not consistent with norms advocated by more advanced students and faculty, as was true for Gender Equality Norms, significant changes occurred in entering norms, and these changes moved entering students' norms in the direction of those already existing at the college.

As far as autonomy is concerned, it has often been dealt with in the theoretical literature as an ideal of human character that is fostered by education and is essential to the maintenance of a free society (Callan, 1988). The general argument in developmental theory (e.g., Chickering & Reisser, 1993) is that autonomy increases during adolescence and young adulthood, including during the years spent in college. The research evidence is not entirely consistent with this argument, however. Heath (1968), for example, found that entering freshmen scored higher on various measures of autonomy and emotional independence than they did 7 months later. Also, whether autonomous behaviors and feelings increase or decrease during college says little about the extent to which autonomy is *valued*, and our study at CWC was concerned with changes in norms and values rather than with changes in psychological development.

The researcher who has probably done the most extensive studies of the relationship between education and the kinds of values we studied at CWC is Norm Feather (1975). Like the American students at CWC, the students whom Feather studied in several other countries highly valued autonomy, especially freedom. When Feather examined a group of students over time, however, he found no significant changes in the evaluation of freedom during the time period from enrollment at university until 2½ years later. Like us, Feather compared students who remained at the same institution, but the students he studied were Australians rather than Americans, and his research was done more than 25 years ago. Nevertheless, his research does suggest that the increases in autonomy values that were found for students who enrolled at CWC in 1991 and remained there to graduate are not inevitable for all cohorts of entering and remaining students at all institutions of higher education. As I suggested in my discussion of norms, the characteristics of the institution itself shape the kinds of socialization that take place—or fail to take place—in the values of its students.

SUMMARY OF FINDINGS AT CWC

Our findings lend credence to the theoretical framework we used to organize this chapter. According to that framework, the extent to which the college experience will change the outlook of students depends on how much stress the college culture puts on certain values and norms, how much consensus there is about those values and norms within the existing college culture, how much prior agreement there is between the norms and values of that culture and those of the entering students, and how much entering students are embedded or isolated in the college culture. At CWC, residential isolation was high and the college culture put more stress on gender equality and autonomy values than did the entering students. The dominant views within the college culture concerning the other norms and values we studied were either mixed (as in the cases of propriety norms, self-oriented norms, and achievement values) or very similar to those of the entering students (as in the cases of traditional family norms and values). As our framework predicted, students who entered CWC in the fall of 1991 increased their endorsements of gender equality norms and autonomy values, but they retained, rather than changed, the norms and values that already matched those of the college culture, as well as the norms and values about which there was disagreement between existing students and faculty.

Our findings also support the conclusion that the administration, faculty, and students of CWC were neither a vanguard of gender emancipation nor a rearguard of gender traditionalism. Although their norms and values clearly and consensually supported gender egalitarianism and personal autonomy, they were only moderate advocates for self-orientation among women and for personal achievements. Although students and faculty tended to reject the position that women should subordinate their interests to those of husbands and children, this rejection was only mild, and most of them assigned a moderately high value to marriage and loving children in their own personal lives.

CONCLUSION: WERE CWC STUDENTS FEMINISTS?

The gender traditionalism of the CWC curriculum and extracurriculum may be one of the reasons most of the students whom I interviewed in 1995, during their senior year, rejected or were ambivalent about the label "feminist." Fewer than 8% of them gave an unequivocally positive response to the question about whether they considered themselves to be feminists (Appendix D, Interview III). In contrast, almost 60% gave an unequivocally negative response to the question, with the remaining third giving either a highly qualified response or a response indicating that they did not know if the label was appropriate for themselves or not.

Regardless of which of these four answers a respondent gave, however, she was likely to endorse gender equality. When a student I've named Barbie was asked why she considered herself to be a feminist, her entire response was: "Because I believe in equality of the sexes." And she answered "no" when asked if there were any other reasons she would call herself a feminist. Laurel, who gave a highly qualified "yes" to the question about being a feminist, went on to say: "Umm, I just feel like women deserve the same kind of treatment as males . . . they shouldn't be put down because of their gender but rather be on a totally equal basis with men." And, Francie, who said, "No, not at all," when asked if she was a feminist, went on to say: "I think that men and women, I think that they're equal in almost every aspect."

Of all women interviewed, almost 60% volunteered their support for women's rights or gender equality, including more than half of the respondents who rejected the label "feminist." None of those interviewed volunteered values opposing women's rights or norms advocating unequal treatment of men and women. This pattern of interview responses is clearly consistent with the strong emphasis on autonomy values and norms favoring gender equality that was found in our survey data. The interview findings also suggest that most of the students at CWC felt free to endorse gender equality even if they rejected or were ambivalent about the label "feminist."

Unwillingness to use this label is certainly not unique to CWC. It has been documented in a number of recent books and articles about feminism (e.g., Beck, 1998; Bellafante, 1998; Findlen, 1995; Fox & Auerbach,

1983). In her introduction to an edited volume of essays by young women "of the next feminist generation," Barbara Findlen (1995) writes:

> As is made clear by several of the writers in this book, some young women do fear the feminist label, largely because of the stereotypes and distortions that still abound. If something or someone is appealing, fun or popular, it or she can't be feminist. Feminists are still often assumed to be strident, man-hating, unattractive—and lesbian. (pp. xiv–xv).

None of the women we interviewed at CWC mentioned unattractiveness, lesbianism, or a lack of fun as correlates of feminism, and only two said that man-hating was characteristic of feminists. Instead of the stereotypes stressed by Findlen and others (e.g., Beck, 1998), the CWC students were more likely to focus on the political commitments of feminists. As a result, when students talked about the angry style of feminists (none used the word *strident*), they were likely to see that style as a means toward the ends of protesting existing gender relations and fostering social change.

The theme of feminist commitments came out in two different ways. On the one hand, there were comments focused on the activism of feminists, on their commitment to using their time and energy to promote the welfare of women. Ginger, for example, could not decide if she was a feminist because "I'm not totally active in promoting women's equal rights or equal pay or whatever." Similarly, Francie, whose defense of gender equality was quoted earlier, gave as her reasons for *not* being a feminist, "I'm neutral to everything . . . and I'm not into the feminist movement at all."

A less positive view of feminist commitments came from those who felt that feminists were extreme or radical. Sometimes these opinions referred to the style of feminists' cognitions, as when Kinsey described them as "rigid in their beliefs" or Opal said:

> When I personally think of a feminist I think of somebody who is almost radical in their thoughts and their views! I mean, yes, I'm a feminist in that I believe in equality and things like that, but when I think of that label I think of extremes.

Sometimes feminists' extremism seemed to lie in their style of behavior, as when Paulette said that feminists "go overboard," and Bernice said that feminists take things "a little too far or want a little too much." Sometimes the extremism seemed to lie in the word *feminism* itself, as with Opal, who was quoted above, and with Carol, who refused to label herself a feminist because:

I'm not always pushing to get things for me. I feel equal to men, but I'm not always saying, "Well, he got it because he's a man." I think that I can get things, too, but I'm not "yea ERA" or anything like that. It just seems like a strong word (pause) I just don't like it.

Even Edie, who did consider herself a feminist because "I'm just very aware of and interested in women's issues and that kind of thing, women's education and just being equal and not stereotyped," began her answer to the question of whether she would call herself a feminist by saying, "It may sound radical, but yeah, I think I would."

Although comments stressing radicalism have sometimes been interpreted as antifeminist, the interviews at CWC gave more evidence of ambivalence and defensiveness than of total hostility to feminists and feminism. As noted above, the endorsement of gender equality was widespread, and several students seemed almost apologetic about their personal unwillingness to champion women's rights more forcefully and actively. As if to compensate for her current lack of independence and activism, Georgia thought she might become a feminist when she was "out in the real world trying to make it on my own with my own job and stuff."

While it is certainly true that most of the students who entered CWC in 1991 did not emerge from college as strong feminists who advocated women's emancipation, it is also true that they were not strong advocates for gender traditionalism. Nor were their implicit and explicit comments about the activism, independence, strong commitments, and radicalism of feminists totally negative, even in their own estimations. Perhaps Louise best expressed both the ambivalence of the majority and their halting attempts to find a middle ground:

I didn't come here to an all-women's college because I'm a feminist or anything. It gave me the opportunity that I wanted, you know, academically and athletically, I mean, I am [a feminist] because you know, yes, I'm a woman; so, you know, I think we should have our rights, but . . . I don't feel, you know, like I'm gonna go out and march in anything for a feminist parade or anything and stuff. I mean, I might be kind of interested, but I probably wouldn't take a very active role in it and stuff. So, I mean, I don't know if I'm a very active feminist, but I'm not, you know, I'll go for our rights and stuff, but I'm not gonna go out and do anything really about it, I guess.

CHAPTER 3

Traditionalism and Emancipation: Sororities at CWC

This chapter begins with a discussion of the major criticism of sororities nationally and throughout American history, namely, that they are highly exclusive and snobbish, and then examines the extent to which this criticism applied to sororities at CWC. Next, the chapter reviews contemporary literature about sororities that has tried to determine whether they foster traditionalism or emancipation among their members. Within this literature, five different kinds of traditionalism are identified. They include not only gender traditionalism in the kinds of norms, values, and feminist identities discussed in Chapter 2, but also political conservatism and the traditional concerns about social approval and appearance that some writers consider to be the sine qua non of contemporary sorority life. After each of these different forms of traditionalism is described, research findings are presented indicating the extent to which sorority women at CWC exhibited each of them. The chapter closes with a discussion of the emancipatory "goodness" of sororities.

SELECTIVITY AND EXCLUSIVENESS

In contemporary society, most Americans, including educational researchers, associate the national system of Greek-letter sororities with both fraternities and coeducational institutions of higher education. Thus it may come as a surprise to learn from historian Christie Farnham (1994) that the first sorority in the nation was founded on May 15, 1851, at Wesleyan Female College in Macon, Georgia. Originally called The Adelphian Society, it came to be known later as Alpha Delta Pi. Even though some societies of college women did not switch to Greek-letter names until the 20th century and the term *sorority* did not come into general use until the 1920s, Farnham (1994) tells readers that the following defining characteristics of sororities and fraternities were well established by the end of the antebellum period:

31

selective membership in secret orders, which included elaborate rituals based on explicitly stated Christian principles as perceived through the prism of nineteenth century gender conventions; and badges, mottos, grips, and secret passwords, which established a boundary between the initiates and the rest of the student body. (p. 154)

Such boundaries were often opposed by both educators and college women. At the turn of the 20th century, for example, the dean of women at the University of Chicago based her decision to ban secret societies of women from campus on her conviction that they would promote snobbery and exacerbate social-class divisions among the students (Gordon, 1990). At Wellesley College, during the first decade of that century, students and faculty waged an unsuccessful campaign against sororities, with Professor Katherine Coman asserting that "a college community should be an intellectual democracy" (Solomon, 1985, p. 108). A more successful effort to abolish sororities was initiated during World War I in the Barnard College student newspaper, where student-council leader Freda Kirchwey declared that the exclusiveness of sororities, known then as fraternities, was their defining characteristic:

> Without secrecy and petty regulations, without exaggerated loyalty and artificial bonds, without social distinctions and the snobbery that inevitably accompanies them, without a certain unavoidable amount of politics—without all these, no fraternity can exist and be a fraternity. (Horowitz, 1993, p. 256)

Such arguments continued throughout the 20th century. Describing American campuses in the 1980s, for example, Helen Horowitz (1987) found elitism and exclusiveness everywhere:

> Students divide themselves into groups based on wealth, ethnicity, and social status. Few undergraduates need confirmation of this in a club structure. However, in many places the Greek system still provides a highly visible framework of discrimination. (p. 275)

Despite decades of such arguments and despite the decisions of many institutions of higher education, especially smaller colleges, to eliminate sororities and fraternities, there seems to have been no hesitancy about the establishment of sororities at CWC during the second half of the 20th century. Just 3 years after the college made the transition from a 2-year to a 4-year institution, and only one year after it awarded its first baccalaureate degrees, three national sororities established chapters at CWC. The fourth national sorority on campus opened its CWC chapter 12 years later.

Like the sororities described by Farnham, Kirchwey, and Horowitz, each of those at CWC had a club structure replete with rituals, emblems, collective secrets, and petty regulations that set them apart from other sororities and, even more so, from the "independent" students who did not join sororities. Like sorority members elsewhere, those at CWC also tended to come from higher status backgrounds than did the independent students at CWC, but the differences were not large. Among those who entered CWC in 1991, 89 joined sororities during their first year and 96 did not. When asked to describe their parents, sorority members reported that their fathers had significantly, but only slightly, more formal education than the education levels that independents reported for their fathers. In addition, the occupations reported for fathers of sorority members had significantly, but only slightly, higher status-rankings, on average, than did the occupations of the fathers of independents. No differences were found between the educational or occupational levels of the mothers of these two groups of students, but the students' ratings of their own social-class standings were moderately and significantly different. For those who pledged sororities, more than half described themselves as coming from the upper middle class, but among those who did not join, the most popular self-description was middle class. Also, three times as many independents as sorority members described themselves as working class.

Did these social-class differences translate into perceptions of superiority and snobbishness among sorority women? Responses to questionnaires administered in spring of 1992 and to interviews conducted during that same semester provided some answers to this question. The questionnaires asked students whether, at CWC, it was better to be a sorority member or an independent. About half of the students (44.9% of sorority members, and 47.3% of independents) chose the response that said: "It doesn't matter. Greeks and independents are equal." Among sorority women, however, the most popular response—chosen by 53.9%—was "Being a sorority member is better." In contrast, only 37.8% of independents chose the response that said: "Being an independent is better." Whereas only one sorority member said that she thought being an independent was better, 15% of independents said that being a sorority member was better. Taken together, more than 90% of all first-year CWC women tended to see their own status (sorority member vs. independent) as equal to or superior to the other status, but sorority members were significantly and substantially more likely to claim and to be accorded superiority than were independents.

Unlike the survey questionnaires, the interviews were designed, in part, to determine what had been the major issues of concern to those interviewed and to other first-year students during the 1991–1992 academic year (see Appendix D, Interview I). With regard to sororities, students were asked: "Do you think that CWC freshmen are concerned about the differences between being a Greek and an independent?" In response, almost half insisted that the distinction was not an important one, and most of these supported their claim by describing the distinction as a matter of personal choice and by noting that they personally had friends who were both sorority members and independents. Dara's comments were typical of this group:

> Well, I'm an independent, and I don't seem to, like, clash with people a whole lot who are in sororities. I mean, sure, there's a difference, you know. They have their little group, and they do things, but I do have some friends who are in a sorority and we do get along, and it's not a big deal.

In contrast, slightly more than half of those interviewed not only considered the distinction between sorority members and independents to be an important basis for personal and social identity at CWC but also felt that there was considerable tension between the two groups. A few of these respondents distanced themselves from the tension, as did Mandi, a sorority member, who told the interviewer that Abbie, an independent, was her best friend at CWC, and then went on to say:

> I'm sure there's some Greeks that look down on independents and independents that look down on the Greeks. So I think that's a two-way street. But, like with [Abbie] and I, there's no problem because, first of all, because I knew her before I went through rush and everything, you know, at the beginning of the year. And we both have open minds about it and it doesn't matter, you know . . . But there is tension, I think. There, there's quite a bit of tension.

In contrast to this student who saw the tension between sorority women and independents as "a two-way street," most sorority women attributed tensions between the two groups to independents. Tabitha, for example, reported:

> One of my girlfriends turned on me, stopped hanging around me. I used to get along with her really well, and she just started putting me down and putting my friends down because it started when I joined a sorority and she didn't. That was really negative.

A similar experience was related by Sandy: "I'm the only Greek on my floor, and it's hard because they're all anti-Greek and they are MAJOR anti-Greek, and it makes me mad sometimes."

Independents, on the other hand, were considerably more likely to attribute the tension between the groups to sorority women, as the following quotations demonstrate:

> I think that if you're an independent, then everyone else looks down on you because, because you're not in a sorority. (Georgia)

> Some of them [sorority women] are real stuck up and if you're not in their sorority or not in a sorority, you're nothing. (Theo)

> Some people won't be friends with other people because they joined a certain house . . . once that one person gets into a sorority, she kind of just hangs with those people and doesn't really hang with anyone else. (Billye)

These quotations also show that the age-old association between sororities and exclusivity was present at CWC, but my review of all the interviews suggests that this association was not as strong as researchers have found it to be at other places and other times. Two characteristics of the CWC context may account for this relative muting of the image of sorority women as snobs. First, the sororities at CWC accepted most of the women who wanted to join them. In 1991–1992, only four of the students who went through the sorority recruitment process and wanted to join a sorority failed to receive a "bid" or invitation to join, and all of those who received a bid got to join the sorority that was their first choice among the four. This low level of rejection may account for the large number of students at CWC who viewed sorority membership as solely a matter of personal choice.

Second, housing arrangements for first-year students at CWC were quite different from those at many other campuses. On some of those campuses, more of the women who joined sororities could move into sorority houses during their first year, an option less available to CWC women. On many other campuses, Greek-letter organizations hold their recruitment week ("rush") before classes start, and those who want to join sororities and fraternities are housed in separate dormitories from those who plan to remain independent and arrive on campus a week later. In contrast, rush at CWC in 1991 occurred a month after classes had started and after most first-year students had settled into dormitories that housed a mix of those who later joined sororities and those who did not.

A few of the students at CWC indicated an awareness of the ways in which housing arrangements affected relations between sorority members and independents. Marie used housing arrangements to contrast these relations in her first-year class and other classes at CWC:

> Our hall is kind of mixed. There's only a few on our side of the hall that have gone Greek. Most of us are independents, and we tease the Greeks quite a bit. But I don't know that it would be a concern, you know. I've noticed that the Greeks are, their attitudes toward the independents are quite stand-offish. But, I mean, the freshmen Greeks and the freshmen independents are still really close. They haven't separated yet.

Her sentiments were echoed by Theresa: "I think our freshman class really gets along really well . . . we're all in the dorms together and every night we're always together. I think we're pretty much all friends." Although it is clear that not all first-year students would agree with Theresa, it also seems clear that the boundaries between sorority members and independents during their first year at CWC were not as sharp as those that could be found on other campuses, particularly at large, coeducational universities.

IN WHAT WAYS ARE SORORITIES TRADITIONAL?

Writings about women's colleges have linked them to *both* gender traditionalism and gender emancipation, a linkage Schwager (1988) calls "the central paradox in women's educational history" (p. 164). In contrast, writings about sororities tend to be formulated in either/or terms. Either sorority pledges are more traditional than those who do not participate in rush or they aren't. Either sorority members become more traditional than independents over time or they don't. Underlying this approach is the more fundamental question of whether sororities are good or bad. In general, "good" means that the sororities foster emancipatory goals of some kind, and "bad" means that sororities foster traditional, male-centered behaviors, retard women's development, and/or undermine the educational goals of the college or university in which the sororities are located.

This concern with the overall goodness or badness of sororities (and fraternities) often leads to sweeping condemnation. A good example is an article by Maisel (1990), which is entitled "Social Fraternities and Sororities Are Not Conducive to the Educational Process" and contains the following thematic statement: "Fraternities and sororities are exclusionary by practice, sexist in nature, and gender specific by design. They reinforce, without reexamining, the values their members possess upon entering" (p. 8). Her condemnation is echoed by Risman (1982), who writes:

> An eighteen-year-old girl is not imprinted "traditional" for life; the experiences she has and the people with whom she interacts will contribute to her continuously evolving sense of self. What happens to sorority girls, however, is that they are shielded from alternative perspectives by the comfortable, conservative Greek world. (p. 250)

Defenses of sororities that are as adamant as these attacks are hard to find in the professional journals, but it is not uncommon to find articles and books stressing the positive potential of sororities (and fraternities) even when the research evidence shows that they are not having positive effects (e.g., Strange, 1986; Winston, Nettles, & Opper, 1987). In addition, some publications stress the contributions or potential contributions of sororities to leadership training and careerism among women (e.g., Fisher, 1991; Sermersheim, 1996), but Spitzberg and Thorndike (1992), who studied 18 institutions of higher education, point out that these leadership opportunities are rarely used for emancipatory ends. Sororities, they write, tend to be characterized by "traditional male-centered values and behavior" (p. 53) and have failed to take a lead in the fight against sexism and violence against women on campus.

Although most of the research about sororities and their members tends to find them more traditional than emancipatory, some studies have supported the opposite conclusion (e.g., Lottes & Kuriloff, 1994). One possible reason for this difference is the fact that so many different definitions and measures of traditionalism and emancipation have appeared in this research. It seems probable that the women who go out for sorority rush may be more traditional than other students in some ways but not in others. It also seems probable that sororities as organizations might foster some kinds of traditionalism while discouraging others. To assess these possibilities, five different forms of traditionalism (vs. emancipation) are distinguished in this section of the chapter, and findings are presented indicating the extent to which sorority members at CWC exhibited each of them.

Traditionalism as Gender-Relevant Norms

Of the four kinds of norms examined in Chapter 2, three have received attention in the literature concerned with sororities and fraternities. One of these is Propriety Norms. The other two are Gender Equality Norms and Traditional Family Norms, although they are usually combined into measures of traditional stereotypes about male and female behaviors. Self-Oriented Norms, or comparable measures, have not received prior research attention. As a result, there was no basis on which to make a prediction about the scores on Self-Oriented Norms of sorority members and independents at CWC.

Predictions about Gender Equality Norms and Traditional Family Norms were also hard to make because prior research has yielded contradictory findings. In support of more gender traditionalism among sorority women, Kalof and Cargill (1991) found that sorority members held more conventional stereotypical views about male dominance and female submissiveness in interpersonal relations than did independents, and Malone (1996) found that women who were active in Greek organizations were significantly more likely than other undergraduates to hold traditional gender attitudes regarding dating and marriage. In contrast, Lottes and Kuriloff (1994) found that future sorority women reported significantly more feminist attitudes than first-year female students who remained independent.

Evidence concerning Propriety Norms is more consistent and tends to support the conclusion that sororities place a heavy emphasis on proper deportment. Risman (1982), for example, reports that a sorority woman's reputation is a key to her success. This stress on reputation refers to the expectation that sorority women should conduct themselves in ways that produce or defend a positive reputation for themselves as individuals and for their sorority as an organization. This positive reputation is not based on emancipation but rather on propriety, conventionality, and discretion. Arthur (1998) found that sororities sent a controlling message to their members: "Be feminine and be a lady" (p. 89), instead of advocating freedom to make one's own decisions. Similarly, Scott (1971) notes the ways in which alumnae and current leaders of sororities stressed "proper behaviors" for members, especially behaviors thought to be appropriate to the upper strata of society, and Horowitz (1987) describes sororities as "conservative and cautious" organizations that "insisted on social distinctions and feminine behaviors" (p. 17).

Did sorority women at CWC also put more stress on Propriety Norms than did independents, and what kinds of effects, if any, did sorority membership have on Gender Equality Norms, Traditional Family Norms, and Self-Oriented Norms? To answer these questions, I used the same four measures of norms described in Chapter 2 (see also Appendix B, Figure B.1; Appendix C, Table C.1). Scores on these measures were compared for sorority members and independents at three points in time.

Of the 287 students who answered our question about sorority membership in spring of 1991, about half ($n = 145$) said they were sorority members and about half said they were not ($n = 142$). As expected, sorority members scored significantly higher than independents on the Propriety Norms scale, but there were no significant differences between the two groups on the measures of Gender Equality Norms, Traditional Family Norms, and Self-Oriented Norms. Like the existing students, those who entered CWC in 1991 and intended to pledge a sorority (or later did so) scored significantly higher on the Propriety Norms scale than those who did not intend to pledge a sorority, but there were no significant differences between the two groups of entering students on the other three measures of gender-relevant norms.

When the scores of the two groups of entering students were compared with those of the existing sorority members and independents, the patterns of similarities and differences were the same as those reported in Chapter 2. Matriculating students who intended to pledge a sorority (or later did so) had scores on the measures of Self-Oriented Norms and Traditional Family Norms that were about the same as those of existing sorority members, but their scores on the Propriety Norms scale and Gender Equality scale were significantly lower than those of existing sorority members. Similarly, entering independents scored significantly lower than existing independents on the Propriety Norms scale and Gender Equality scale, but they did not differ from existing independents in their scores on the other two measures of norms.

Over time, the patterns of stability and change in the norms of sorority members and independents were also similar. No significant changes occurred for either group in Traditional Family Norms or Self-Oriented Norms, and both groups showed a significant increase in their willingness to endorse Gender Equality Norms. These patterns are the same as those reported in Chapter 2 and provide no support for arguments for or against sorority traditionalism.

The norms with the greatest potential for being affected by CWC sororities were Propriety Norms. Given the finding that existing sorority members were significantly more likely to endorse Propriety Norms than were pledges and the finding that pledges had significantly stronger Propriety Norms than those who remained independent, it seemed reasonable to predict that pledges would increase their endorsements of propriety over time, thereby becoming nonsignificantly different from the other sorority members. This is *not* what happened, however. Over their 4 years at CWC, sorority members evidenced a decline in their ratings of Propriety Norms. The decline was slight and not significant, but it was enough to eliminate the significant difference found in the summer of 1991 between those who would and those who would not pledge sororities. By the time they graduated, sorority women had moved their endorsement of Propriety Norms in the direction of the *lower* endorsements by independent students and away from the previously existing, higher endorsements of sorority members.

Taken together, these findings provide no evidence that sororities at CWC had significant effects on the gender-relevant norms of their members. Although the data support the likelihood that propriety was a basis for selective recruitment into sororities at CWC, the only significant change among sorority members in gender-relevant norms was an increase in their endorsement of gender equality. Because this increase was the same for independents as it was for sorority members, it seems reasonable to reaffirm the conclusion of Chapter 2 that this change was caused by socialization of the entire student body at CWC.

Unlike some of the sororities described in the literature, sororities at CWC did not socialize the women who joined them in 1991–1992 toward greater propriety. Instead, these women were socialized by the independent students (and faculty) on their campus toward putting less emphasis on Propriety Norms. Although the measures we used may account for the difference between these findings and the depiction of sororities as contexts that stress proper, feminine behaviors (Arthur, 1998; Risman, 1982; Scott, 1971), it also seems plausible that the findings about Propriety Norms support and extend the conclusion about the importance of campus context reached at the end of the previous section of this chapter. The homogenizing effect of small, residential colleges with relatively open sorority recruitment, such as CWC, may not only prevent the development of significantly different norms between sorority members and the rest of the student body but also decrease over time some of the differences in the norms that the students bring with them.

Traditionalism as Gender-Relevant Values

Do these conclusions about gender-relevant norms also apply to gender-relevant values? To answer this question, I used the same three measures of values examined in Chapter 2 (see also Appendix B, Figure B.2; Appendix C, Table C.2) and examined ratings of these values across the same three surveys that produced the findings about norms. I began with the assumptions that *if* sorority members had more traditional values than did independents, then they would score lower than independents on Achievement and Autonomy Values and higher on Traditional Family Values. This assumption was based on my interpretation of the three measures of values, one of which proved to be questionable. What was also questionable before I began the analyses of values at CWC was whether sorority members were likely to have more traditional values than independents.

Prior evidence bearing on this question is either limited or contradictory. The largest number of relevant studies have focused on autonomy, usually defined as independence. The general finding is that students who join Greek-letter organizations score lower on measures of independence and autonomy than do other students (Baier & Whipple, 1990; Eddy, 1990; Hughes & Winston, 1987; Scott, 1965; Wilder, Hoyt, Doren, Hauck, & Zettle, 1978; Wilder, Hoyt, Surbeck, Wilder, & Carney, 1986). Although Hughes and Winston (1987) report that those who joined Greek-letter organizations came to value independence less over time than did nonmembers, Scott (1965) reports the opposite change over time, and other researchers (Baier & Whipple, 1990; Wilder et al., 1978) report that the difference between Greeks and independents in this form of traditionalism was due more to selective recruitment than to either negative or positive changes over time. Most of these studies are limited to fraternities, and none focuses on a women's college. In addition, Pascarella and Terenzini (1991) point out that many of these studies fail to control for precollege levels of autonomy or for residential locations of the independents and Greeks whose autonomy levels were examined.

At CWC, no significant differences were found in the Autonomy Values of sorority members and independents. Existing sorority members and independents gave Autonomy Values almost identical ratings in spring 1991. Those who entered CWC the next fall and joined a sorority also rated Autonomy Values the same as did entering students who remained independent. As noted in Chapter 2, entering students scored significantly lower on the Autonomy Values scale than did existing students (or faculty), but this was true of both sorority members and independents. Also, over time, both groups significantly increased their scores on the Autonomy Values scale.

These findings are consistent with the claims made in Chapter 2 concerning the socialization of Autonomy Values at CWC. No evidence was found to indicate that sororities either enhanced or impeded this socialization process. Nor did the data support the notion that sororities selectively recruited the less autonomous students. Although it is possible that the differences between these findings and some of those in the existing literature may be due to different ways of measuring autonomy or to differences between fraternities and sororities, it also seems likely that the campus context makes a difference. At small, residential colleges where sororities are relatively nonexclusive, as was true at CWC, the college culture may exert a homogenizing effect on sororities that prevents the development of major differences between sorority members and the rest of the student body.

This homogenizing effect can also be seen in what happened to students' Achievement Values and Traditional Family Values. Interestingly, sorority members enrolled at CWC in spring 1991 rated *both* Traditional Family Values and Achievement Values as slightly, but significantly, more important than did independents. Students who entered CWC in 1991 and later joined sororities also rated *both* Traditional Family Values and Achievement Values slightly higher than did independents, but the difference between the two groups was significant only for Achievement Values.

The significant difference between ratings of Achievement Values persisted through graduation but did not undergo a significant increase or decrease in size. Although these findings are consistent with the conclusion that sororities selectively recruited members who valued achievement more highly, on average, than did independents, there is no evidence to support the conclusion that sororities socialized their members toward a higher (or lower) evaluation of achievement.

Nor did they change the average ratings their members gave to Traditional Family Values. The size of the nonsignificant difference between ratings of those who entered in 1991 and joined sororities and those who entered that year but did not join decreased slightly over the undergraduate careers of the students who remained at CWC, but the decrease was nonsignificant.

What accounted for the significantly higher scores of sorority women over those of independents on the Achievement Values scale both at matriculation and graduation? Surprisingly, this difference was *not* due to the higher social-class origins of sorority women. For the CWC women we studied, social-class background had no significant effect on ratings of Achievement Values, and the effect of sorority membership on Achievement Values continued to be positive and significant when the social class of the students was controlled. This finding means that sorority members would have scored higher on Achievement Values even if they came from the same social class as did the independents.

Another possible reason for the higher Achievement Values of sorority women may lie in the multifaceted nature of our measure of these values. Normally, when one hears that a group of women value achievement, one thinks of them as oriented in favor of nontraditional goals. It was this interpretation that led me to the questionable assumption that higher scores on our Achievement Values scale would indicate a more emancipatory, less traditional orientation. I now see this assumption as questionable for three reasons. First, sorority women who scored higher than independents on the Achievement Values scale also scored higher on Traditional Family Values. Second, as noted earlier, sorority women valued their membership status more, on average, than independent women valued being independents. Third, as reported in Chapter 2, the Achievement Values scale included achievements in traditionally male domains (economic prosperity, sexual fulfillment), achievements in a traditionally female domain (social approval), and an achievement (a successful career) that could be either traditionally male or female. Ratings of all of these achievements were positively correlated and constituted a single measure of values (see Appendix C, Table C.2). Taken together, these findings suggest that sorority women at CWC were selectively recruited from among those who assigned more value to all kinds of success, including *both* traditional and emancipatory forms of achievement.

As was true of Propriety Norms, sororities did not socialize the women who joined them in 1991–1992 toward stronger Achievement Values. Nor did the sororities strengthen (or weaken) any of the other gender-related norms and values held by the students prior to joining. When significant changes did occur over students' college careers at CWC, as was true of both Autonomy Values and Gender Equality Norms, these changes were the same for sorority women as for independents. Thus all of the evidence reported so far in this chapter supports the conclusion that it was the campus cultural environment, rather than sorority membership, that had the major socializing effect on the gender-relevant values and norms of students at CWC.

Traditionalism as the Rejection of Feminist Identities

Lottes and Kuriloff (1994) use the term *feminism* as the antonym of traditionalism, and the measure of gender-related norms they employed in their study is known as the Attitudes Toward Feminism scale. Despite this usage, studies of the opinions and attitudes of sorority women have rarely, if ever, asked them whether they consider themselves to be feminists. Because this question was asked of those CWC women who were interviewed during their senior year (Appendix D, Interview III), it is possible to compare the answers given by sorority members and independents to this direct measure of feminist identification.

Unlike values and norms, however, feminist identities were not assessed prior to matriculation at CWC. So, it is not possible to determine whether these identities had more effects on recruitment or socialization by sororities. What is clear is that more sorority women than independents refused to label themselves feminists. Seventy-three percent of the sorority women interviewed, compared with 40% of the independents, clearly rejected the feminist label. Despite this large difference, the comments sorority women made about feminists and feminism were no more negative, on average, than those made by independents, and both groups were highly likely to endorse gender equality.

Traditionalism as Political Conservatism

In his now classic study of Bennington College, Newcomb (1943, 1958) was less concerned with *gender* traditionalism than with *political* traditionalism. As noted in Chapter 2, it was his hypothesis that the experience of attending Bennington with its politically liberal, even radical, faculty would move students away from the conservative, even reactionary, politics of their families. Although Newcomb was aware of the left-leaning political climate of the college he studied, many of the researchers who followed his lead failed to link the liberalism acquired by so many Bennington students with the fact that Bennington was a unique and highly politicized women's college. Instead, it has often been assumed that most college students—male as well as female—come from family and community contexts that are more conservative politically than those to be found on most college campuses. On the basis of this assumption, it has frequently been hypothesized that attending college, especially while living on campus, will exert a liberalizing effect on students' political attitudes.

Within the context of this argument, Greek-letter organizations have often been viewed as enclaves of conservatism that selectively recruit their members from the least liberal of the college entrants and help those members to maintain, if not increase, their conservatism during their years in college. Evidence to support these arguments is mixed. Although some studies report smaller increases in liberalism among sorority and fraternity members than among independents (Astin, 1977; Longino & Kart, 1973; Wilder et al., 1986), other studies report no Greek versus independent differences in these changes over time (Lottes & Kuriloff, 1994; Miller, 1973; Wilder et al., 1978).

Not only the mixed findings but also the research methods employed made it difficult to use these studies as a basis for predictions about political liberalism at CWC. Some studies focused only on fraternities, and others failed to analyze data for women and sororities separately from those for men. In addition, different researchers used different measures of political opinions, despite the fact that they all called what they measured "liberalism." The danger of this latter practice is nicely demonstrated by Peterson, Altbach, Skinner, and Trainer (1976), who compared a sample of sorority pledges at the University of Wisconsin to various national samples, including a sample of all freshman women at public institutions. In contrast to the national samples, the sorority pledges were more likely to label their political views as conservative and were more likely to favor the Republican presidential candidate over his Democratic opponent, findings that would seem to support the conclusion of less liberalism among sorority women. That conclusion was called into question, however, by the findings that these same sorority women were *more* likely than participants in the national surveys to endorse both legalization of marijuana and the freedom to choose abortions, positions widely regarded as liberal.

The possibility that sorority women might be more conservative than independent women on some political issues, but more liberal on others, was examined at CWC using responses to three different measures of political conservatism. The first to be discussed here are answers to an interview question about political labels. The second are responses to a survey question about political party preference, and the third are responses to a set of political policies included on some of our survey questionnaires.

Political Labels. In the same interview in which CWC students were asked about being a feminist, they were also asked what political label they would give themselves (Appendix D, Interview III). About 18% of the sorority women interviewed and 40% of independents described themselves as uninterested in politics. A typical response in this category was given by Bernice: "I don't care about it. I really don't. I take no interest in politics whatsoever. I'm like, I know nothing about politics. I should, but I don't. I just don't care."

With only one exception, the women who voiced no interest in politics or political labels did not feel it necessary to justify their disinterest. The exception was Paulette, whose answer suggests that the reasons for students' political apathy included their disillusionment with the political process and their lack of a sense of political efficacy.

> Mostly I don't care. I'm not into politics at all. I don't much care.
> I don't see personally that I can change anything, and I've never
> gotten into it just because it's just, I mean, a bunch of lies. And I'm
> just sick of politicians, and, so, no matter what you do they're still
> going at the same thing, and I've seen it for years and years and
> years, and it's, like, why go into that, you know? I feel like I can't
> ever change anything, and I don't see any differences being made,
> you know. It seems like a kind of hopeless situation. So, I don't
> care. I'm just going to put my energies into something else.

Although sorority women were significantly more likely than independents to embrace political labels, accepting a label did not mean that a student knew what it meant or that she had a clear, coherent political ideology. Georgia, for example, called herself a political independent who "agreed with a lot of what the liberals say." When asked, "What kinds of things do you hear liberals saying that you agree with?" Georgia replied:

> Well, just like I heard them talk about, like, the welfare issue, and I think that if you really want to work, you know, you should have a set time on welfare, you know. If you can't get off it by then, that's fine, but if you have a way to get a job, go get it. I don't think it should just be a free for all. I've heard them talk about it on TV and stuff, and I have to agree with that. That's the way I see it.

When asked whether there were any other "liberal" positions that had caught her attention, Georgia continued to display her confusion about political issues:

> Not really. That's just what sticks out in my mind the most because that's what I sit there and listen to, that kind of thing. And they were talking about whether they were going to offer the lower class people to be able to buy the land they're living on. They can barely afford to pay the rent where they're living. How are they ever going to afford to save up and buy the land they're on—which doesn't make much sense. It would be a good opportunity and stuff, but if they're struggling to make rent, how do they expect them to buy, you know? That doesn't make sense to me. (laughter)

Among students who did apply a political label to themselves, students who were not members of sororities were more likely to call themselves "middle-of-the-road" or political independents, and sorority women were more likely to call themselves conservative with most sorority members who said "middle-of-the-road" also saying that they leaned to the conservative side or would probably vote Republican. Like "liberal leaning" Georgia above, few of the "conservative" students could articulate an informed or coherent political position. And "middle-of-the-road" referred less to positions on political issues than to political ignorance, as this quote from Ginger clearly indicates: "I'm not quite sure. I think I'm pretty much, like, middle-of-the-road maybe, because I'm not that aware of the political avenues, of what's going on, what everybody's saying about everyone else."

Only two students, Edie who belonged to a sorority and Barbie who had never pledged, labeled themselves "liberal." Barbie was able to defend this label with reference to her political positions on race issues, homosexuality, the environment, and abortion. In contrast, Edie used the term "liberal" to refer more to open-mindedness than to political policies. In addition, she qualified her acceptance of this label by claiming also to be "middle-of-the-road":

> Liberal means that I'm open to a lot of different things, I guess. Middle-of-the-road because I can see both sides of the issues. I'm definitely not conservative, just more liberal. I think it's more open-minded. I try not to be closed minded about things.

Given the high levels of political disinterest and ignorance among CWC seniors, it seems unlikely that either the sororities or the college context had provided students with much political education. At the end of their first year at CWC, not a single student mentioned party politics when asked what issues had been of concern to their first-year class, and in their senior year, most students gave no indication that they had been involved in discussions of political issues with other students. A review of campus newspapers published from 1991 to 1995 revealed a focus on the campus and college-sponsored activities with little attention given to off-campus politics at local, state, or national levels. Two of the students interviewed did mention that, as education majors, they had been given considerable information by faculty members about a statewide referendum that would negatively affect school funding, if it were to pass, but no other political education by faculty was mentioned.

Political Party Preferences. A well-articulated political position has never been a prerequisite for voting in American elections. All sorts of people vote for political candidates because of their party affiliation, without having much understanding of the policy positions those candidates endorse. What political parties did CWC students endorse when all they had to do was "vote," and were the votes of sorority women more or less traditional than those of independents?

To answer these questions, the students who entered CWC in 1991 were asked, just prior to both their matriculation and their graduation, to indicate which political party they preferred in national politics. Both the sample of students surveyed in spring 1991 and the faculty were also asked to indicate their political party preference. Thus it was possible to determine if the party preferences of the students who entered CWC in 1991 and later graduated from CWC changed over the time they spent at the college and whether these changes might have been affected by the party preferences of existing students or the faculty.

Of the students who "voted" for a particular political party in the spring of 1991, 64.0% of sorority members and 51.8% of independents chose the Republican Party. In contrast to this significant difference, the difference in votes for the Democratic Party was slight, with 30.9% of sorority members and 34.0% of independents choosing what is generally regarded as the more liberal party. None of the students voted for a third party, although this was one of the choices they were given, and 5.0% of sorority women compared with 14.2% of other students indicated that they were political independents or didn't have a preference. The preferences of these students were in sharp contrast to those of the faculty, 66.7% of whom "voted" Democratic, 21.2% Republican, and 12.1% Independent.

The class of students who entered in 1991 "voted" Republican at about the same level as CWC students had in the spring of that year. Almost two thirds (64.4%) of those who intended to join a sorority indicated that they preferred the Republican Party in national politics, compared with 45.8% of incoming students who did not intend to join a sorority. Of this latter group, 28.8% indicated a preference for the Democratic Party, and 25.4% said they were politically independent or had no preference. Of those intending to be sorority members, 22.2% opted for the Democratic Party, and 13.3% said they were politically independent or had no party preference.

Because there were no significant differences between the voting patterns of the new students and of their counterparts already on the campus, there was no reason to expect very much change in the party preferences of students during their years at CWC. This expectation held true for women who remained independent of sororities. Although there was a tendency for the number of these students with no party preference to decrease, most of the change went toward the Democratic Party, with only a slight increase in the number of women choosing the Republicans. As a result of these shifts, the voting pattern in 1995 of graduating students who were independent of the sorority system—51.4% Republican, 35.1% Democratic, and 13.5% with no preference—was almost identical to what the voting pattern of independents had been in spring of 1991. For this group, there were only minor, nonsignificant changes in political party preferences during their years at CWC, and there was nothing to indicate that their choices had been strongly, or even moderately, affected by the more liberal political-party preferences of the faculty.

In contrast to independents, sorority members underwent a significant shift in party affiliation. By the time of their graduation, 53.3% of the women in this group indicated that they preferred the Republican Party, 37.8% preferred the Democrats, and 8.9% indicated no party preference. This impressive shift is even larger if the group of graduating sorority members is compared only to themselves 4 years earlier. When the political-party preferences of those who entered CWC in 1991 but dropped out before graduation are omitted from the summer 1991 data, those data show that 71.1% of the students who subsequently graduated from CWC preferred the Republican Party at matriculation and only 17.8% voted Democratic.

What can account for these dramatic shifts in the party preferences of sorority members during their years at CWC? Clearly, the answer does not lie in any socialization process occurring *within* the sororities. Although the possibility that the faculty may have had some effect cannot be ruled out, it seems unlikely that faculty would have "liberalized" only those students who belonged to sororities and not, as mentioned earlier, those who did not. So it seems more likely that the sorority women were being influenced by nonsorority women in their own class and in the other classes at CWC. And, perhaps, they were also being influenced by national politics and by the success of the Democratic candidate for U.S. President in 1992.

Political Policies. The tendency for sorority members to change their political views more than other students was true not only for political-party preferences but also for some of the 15 political and social issues about which these students were asked (Appendix B, Figure B.3). With one exception, all of these issues can be considered matters of political policy in that they involved a judgment about what laws should be passed or how laws should be interpreted. Twelve of the statements measured five types of political liberalism that have been identified by scholars, politicians, and journalists: lifestyle liberalism (more permissive laws regarding marijuana, drug dealers, drinking age, abortion), economic liberalism (progressive taxation, availability of health care for all), civil rights liberalism (affirmative action for race-ethnic minorities, equality under law for homosexuals), secularism (opposing prayer and religious instruction in public schools), and civil libertarianism (permitting flag-burning and pornography as forms of free speech). One additional item measured lifestyle liberalism in the form of sexual permissiveness, but it had no explicit legal ramifications. There also were two items asking about federal funding priorities, one advocating military spending as the top priority (at the time, a more conservative position) and the other stating that the top spending priority should be cleaning up and protecting the environment (a more liberal position).

An examination of the summer 1991 responses of entering students to the 15 items revealed that those who would join sororities were neither more liberal nor more conservative than those who would remain independent. On *none* of the 15 items was there a significant difference in the average answer of these two groups of students. This finding may seem to be inconsistent with the finding that sorority women were significantly more likely to prefer the Republican Party at that time, but these findings are inconsistent only if one assumes that party preferences carry with them coherent, integrated political ideologies. Not only is this not true among professional politicians in the United States who often "cross party lines" when voting on legislation, but it seemed particularly untrue among CWC students who often did not know or care whether their positions on political matters were consistent or not.

A good example of the willingness to embrace inconsistency emerged in my interview with Dahlia, a senior who labeled herself an extreme conservative. When asked why, she replied:

> I believe in capital punishment. I believe in not taxing the rich so much because the rich create the jobs. . . . And I believe in most of the things that the Republicans believe in: Pro-choice, which not all Republicans are pro-choice, but I'm going to say I'm on the extreme conservative side and pro-choice . . .

Just to be sure I had understood her correctly, I asked Dahlia whether by pro-choice she meant that she was pro-choice on the abortion issue, and she said she was.

Whereas Dahlia signaled that being pro-choice might actually be inconsistent with her other political views, no such understanding could be found in the interview with Francie, who said, "I will always be a Republican and not vote Democratic. I despise Clinton. I just think he needs to be out of there." When asked whether there was anything in particular that she found objectionable about President Clinton, she replied: "Everything. I just don't agree with really anything he does. I don't agree with his health care plan. Isn't he against pro-choice?" When told that Clinton was pro-choice on the abortion issue, Francie said, "He is for it?" When assured that he was, she said, "OK, I didn't think he was. Umm. I just don't think he's good." Although Francie was bemused to discover that a politician she loathed agreed with her on an important political issue, she was definitely not alone in her willingness to endorse a political party that was on the public record taking policy positions with which she disagreed.

The fact that entering students who intended to pledge (and later joined) sororities had the same opinions about political policies as independent students suggests that political views were not a basis for selective recruitment into sororities. Unfortunately, this suggestion cannot be tested directly because existing sorority members and independents in spring 1991 were not asked to give their opinions concerning the same set of political issues about which the entering students were asked.

Faculty were asked about these same issues, but no evidence emerged to suggest that they exerted a consistent, effective influence on the political opinions of the students who remained at CWC through graduation.

Of the six issues on which entering students held views that were significantly different from those of faculty, students moved in the direction of the more liberal faculty views on three issues (marijuana use, penalties for drug dealers, and tolerance of homosexuality) but showed no change during their college careers on the other three (flag-burning, military spending, and the legal drinking age). In addition, students showed significant changes during their time at CWC on four issues (abortion, the environment, sexuality, and health care) about which they had initially agreed with faculty, and their opinions on a fifth issue (progressive taxation) underwent a nonsignificant change that was large enough so that by the time they graduated the average opinion of students on this issue was significantly more conservative than that of the faculty.

Although the patterns of stability and change among student opinions provided no evidence for systematic faculty influence, they did reveal two striking similarities between sorority women and independents. The first of these was the finding that on each of the six political issues for which sorority women showed no significant changes during their years at CWC, independent women also showed no significant changes. These issues were affirmative action for minorities, the two measures of civil libertarianism (free speech), the two measures of secularism (vs. religiosity), and support for military spending.

The other striking similarity was the finding that on five of the remaining political issues, both sorority women and independents showed the same pattern of significant changes. On the progressive taxation issue, both sorority women and independents became significantly less in favor of higher tax rates for the rich. Both groups also became significantly less in favor of making environmental protection the major funding priority of the U.S. government. In contrast to these declines, there were significant increases in tolerance among both sorority and independent women for marijuana use, drug dealers, and homosexuality.

In addition to these similarities, there were also some major differences between sorority members and independents. One of them had to do with the size of the changes just discussed. Two of these changes—the greater tolerance of drug dealers and homosexuality—were significantly larger for sorority members than for independents. Similar differences in the size of changes were found for the issues of health care, abortion, and sexuality. Although both sorority members and independents became less in favor of making good health care available to all Americans, regardless of their ability to pay, and became more in favor of legal abortions, the shifts in average opinion on these issues was twice as large for the sorority women as for the independents, and only the change of the sorority women's opinions was statistically significant. On the issue of sexual permissiveness, there was actually no change in the average endorsement given by independent women from matriculation to graduation, but the increased endorsement of the sorority women was sufficiently large to produce a significant switch in the average sexual permissiveness of the entire class.

Despite differences between sorority members and independents in the sizes and significance levels of their shifts in political opinions during their undergraduate years at CWC, at the time of graduation there was only one of the 15 measures of political and social liberalism on which the two groups obtained significantly different scores. Due to slight shifts over time, graduating seniors who were independents gave significantly more support than did graduating sorority members to the more conservative position of making 21 the legal drinking age throughout the United States.

The findings about political-policy opinions support the conclusion that the major differences between sorority members and independents were the larger increases in lifestyle liberalism of the sorority women. Like their independent counterparts, these women became more tolerant of marijuana use, less punitive toward drug dealers, and more in favor of legal abortions, and on two of these issues (drug dealers and abortions) the changes among sorority women were substantially greater than among independents. In contrast to independents, sorority members also became significantly more permissive sexually, and they were significantly more permissive with regard to the legal drinking age by the time they graduated.

These findings about the increases in lifestyle liberalism, especially among sorority women, provide a contrast to findings produced by the two measures of economic liberalism. CWC students, especially sorority women, became significantly less likely to endorse affordable health care, and they decreased their endorsement of progressive taxation to the point where it was significantly lower than that of the faculty. Like the support for economic liberalism, support for environmental protection—usually regarded as a liberal position—eroded during the time that students were at CWC, and this erosion was the single instance in which change among independents was greater than among sorority women.

Summary of Findings About Political Conservatism. Taken together, these findings support the conclusion that it would be a mistake to talk about whether students at CWC became more or less liberal and whether sorority members were more or less liberal than nonmembers without specifying the kind of liberalism that is at issue. In general, both sorority members and independents rejected the "liberal" label. Compared with independents, sorority members were significantly more willing to embrace the Republican label when they entered CWC and were slightly more willing to describe themselves as "conservatives" when they left. But labels can be misleading if they are expected to provide a basis for predictions of all forms of political liberalism. Although they didn't want to be called liberals, the average opinion of CWC women on religion and prayer in schools was one of opposition and, by the time they graduated, their average support for legal abortions and the civil rights of homosexuals was very strong. Most political pundits would consider these opinions to be very liberal.

Given the many inconsistencies within the political cultures of both the campus and its sororities, what accounts for the changes in political opinions found at CWC? Although I cannot prove it beyond the shadow of a doubt, I think most of the answer lies in the personal and group experiences of the students at CWC (and at other colleges across the country). College is a time of lifestyle experimentation with drugs, alcohol, and sexual behaviors. Not every young woman does all of this experimenting on her own; sometimes she is an observer of the experimentation of others. According to researchers and people who work in the field of student services (e.g., Alva, 1998; Cashin, Presley, & Meilman, 1998; Nuwer, 1999; Tyler & Kyes, 1992; Walker & Avioli, 1991), this experimentation is particularly rampant in the Greek system, where it sometimes reaches dangerous levels. At less than dangerous levels, however, students who participate in or observe various forms of lifestyle experimentation may develop greater tolerance for behaviors that come to be seen as "no big deal." And this tolerance should be greater in those groups, such as sororities and fraternities, where the experimentation is greater. This line of reasoning would explain why sorority women at CWC in the 1990s, like those at the University of Wisconsin in the 1970s (Peterson et al., 1976), coupled preferences for conservatism and the Republican Party with high levels of tolerance for abortion and marijuana.

Personal experience might also explain why CWC students, especially sorority women, became less economically liberal during their years at the college. More than 70% of graduating students had mothers who had not completed baccalaureate degrees. Not only were these students upwardly mobile on the basis of education but, as they indicated in response to survey questions about their plans for the future, they had financial and occupational aspirations that, if fulfilled, would eventually raise their economic level far above that of their parents. Since economic liberalism is known to be inversely related to social class (Lipset, 1960; Gilbert, 1998, pp. 219–249), the decline in this form of liberalism from their first to their last year at CWC may have reflected both the upward mobility and anticipated upward mobility of these young women.

If these speculations are correct, they suggest a major modification to the assumptions in the literature about the "liberalizing effect" of higher education. Unless the faculty of a college deliberately try to politically liberalize students, as was the case at Bennington in the 1930s, it is unlikely that their own political views will have much effect on the students. The faculty at CWC were clearly more liberal (except on the drinking age) than the students, but there is no compelling evidence to suggest that *they* liberalized the students. Instead, it was the students' own experiences and interactions with one another that produced more lifestyle liberalism and, probably, less Republicanism and more tolerance of homosexuality as well. And it was probably their growing identification with college-educated and more prosperous American women that made them more economically conservative. Being at CWC as opposed to some other campus probably made little difference, and being in a sorority mattered only because sororities were both sponsors of more lifestyle experimentation and organizations whose members assigned a high value to economic (and other) achievements.

Traditionalism as Concern for Appearance

No discussion of sorority traditionalism would be complete without giving some attention to the heavy emphasis these organizations give to appearance. Although there actually are studies (e.g., Atlas & Morier, 1994) claiming that women who choose to join sororities are more physically attractive than those who don't, the stress on "looks" seems to have less to do with living up to some universal and everlasting aesthetic principles of beauty than with a willingness to expend the time, effort, and money necessary to make one's appearance conform to the socially approved images endorsed by a given set of Greek organizations at a particular time and place. Even the most casual perusal of college yearbooks over a few decades reveals that these images are ever-changing. What seems not to change, however, is the relatively high stress sororities place on socially approved appearances (Arthur, 1998; Carroll, 1985; Risman, 1982).

In the same year that Harriet and I began our study of CWC, Naomi Wolf (1991) published her national bestseller called *The Beauty Myth*. Central to Wolf's book was the following argument:

> We are in the midst of a violent backlash against feminism that uses images of female beauty as a political weapon against women's advancement: the beauty myth. . . . The contemporary backlash is so violent because the ideology of beauty is the last one remaining of the old feminine ideologies that still has the power to control those women whom second wave feminism would have otherwise made relatively uncontrollable. (pp. 10–11)

Although Wolf's book had nothing to say about sororities, her argument combined with the evidence that sororities put a heavy emphasis on "pride in appearance" when selecting pledges (Carrol, 1985) suggests that sororities prevent the full emancipation of women by reinforcing the beauty myth. How true was this at CWC?

The first step to answer this question was to construct two instruments, one to measure the need for social approval and another to measure concern for appearance (see Appendix B, Figure B.4). The first of these presented students with statements such as "I worry about what other people think of me" and "I want people to like me" and asked them to indicate how true of themselves each statement was. Concern-for-Appearance was measured by the same scale, but all the items referred to appearance, such as "Looking good is very important to me" and "I try to look as attractive as I possibly can." These measures were included in all of the surveys of CWC students.

Answers to the spring 1991 survey supported my expectation that sorority women would express significantly more need for social approval and more concern about appearance than would independent women. In addition, there was a strong, significant correlation between responses to the two measures within both groups, suggesting that attention to one's appearance was seen by these young women as a way to gain approval.

Answers to the summer 1991 survey were consistent with those given in the spring. Women who were likely to join a sorority after matriculating at CWC expressed significantly more need for social approval and more concern about their appearance than women who had no intention of joining. The correlations between Need-for-Social-Approval and Concern-for-Appearance scores were even stronger in these two groups than they had been in the sorority and independent groups surveyed the previous spring. This strong association between approval seeking and concerns about appearance continued throughout the 1991–1992 academic year for the first-year students we studied. Also, by the end of that year, women who had joined sororities continued to score significantly higher on both the Need-for-Social-Approval and the Concern-for-Appearance scales than did women who had remained independent.

One of the issues about which some first-year students were asked in spring of 1992 was "their weight and their bodies" (Appendix D, Interview I). Of the 40 students who were asked this question, three independents said that there was little or no concern about bodies among first-year students. All the rest—21 sorority women and 16 independents—thought weight and bodies were major concerns. A few of these women—all independents—were quick to point out that they personally were not concerned about their own weight or body shape but knew lots of other women who were. When asked if some groups on campus were more concerned than other groups about their weight and their bodies, the most frequently identified group was sororities.

Although most students were not asked *why* they thought members of their first-year class were concerned about weight, a few were, and some who weren't volunteered reasons. Echoing Naomi Wolf (1991) and other writers (e.g., Hesse-Biber, 1996), Marilyn cited the pressures of American culture: "Well, overall the United States of America has a view of the slim, trim, firm-bodied woman. And it's just everybody here, well not everybody, but most of the girls I know are watching their weight and trying to exercise and do things."

Other students cited more specific causes for concerns about weight, such as Sandy's remark that "everybody's formals are coming up so everybody's on Slim Fast" and Darlene's observation that "swimming suit season is coming up; so, everybody's going on a diet and exercising and stuff." The college had also received a grant that year to fund a program designed to promote good health practices among the students. As part of this program, students were given opportunities to have the fat levels in their bodies assessed. Marilyn was one of four students who suggested that this program may have increased students' concerns with their weight:

> We have the fat testing [which] has come through twice now, and the majority of the girls I know have gone and had it done. And they get really upset over it when their fat percentage is higher than they think it should be or where they thought it was going to be, but didn't want it to be there.

At the end of the same interview in which students were asked about weight and bodies, they were also asked whether they thought first-year students at CWC had been concerned that year with "their grooming and attire, such things as clothes, cosmetics, hairdos, etc." In contrast to the concerns about weight which most women described as pervasive and ongoing, the concerns about grooming and attire were seen as largely contextual. Almost all of the respondents echoed the comments of Timmie, who said:

> [First-year students are concerned with grooming] when they're off campus or if they have someplace to go. When they're on campus, they look like shit. We all do. You see so many sweat shirts, it's like, "Sweats on Campus." It's scary. I've never seen so many girls look so shitty in my life. But, when they go off campus, they fix themselves up . . . well, when they've got someplace to go.

I have a class with guys [from nearby "Canterbury" College], and you can tell. You can tell as a girl walks across campus [that] she's got class with a guy. She'll be wearing a skirt and she'll be, you know, she'll have make-up on. You can tell.

One of the few contradictions of Timmie's comments was made by Marianne, who, after describing herself as someone who "usually runs around in sweats or cutoff sweats and a T-shirt," went on to say: "I know there's guys walking around on campus that take a few classes here, but if they look at you out of all the girls, you know, they're not gonna like you, anyway. So, it doesn't matter if you look bad or not."

Although more of the interviewed students agreed with Timmie than with Marianne about whether CWC women dressed up when they expected to encounter college men in classes, Marianne was far from alone in saying that she rarely dressed up on campus. In contrast, everyone agreed that most of the CWC women dressed up when they left the campus or for special occasions, as Sandy explained:

It's an all-girls school, and if you see somebody dressed up, like in the morning, you're like, "Is your mom coming?" or "Do you have a lunch date?" Because normally people just—oh, there are certain people, but almost everybody just gets up. I know sometimes I have 8:00s every morning except for Friday, and I just get up at 7:50 and get my hair brushed and my teeth and leave, and you go to class. And, you know, it's really funny. We had, like, a benefit dinner, and I went, and one of our professors spoke to us, and we were all dressed up, and he goes: "I don't recognize any of you." (laughter) And, it's true.

Aside from the occasional parental visit or special event, the major stimuli for attending to one's appearance were men and, as Sandy's comments indicate, not just any man (such as a professor) but a man whom they would consider to be a potential dating partner. And the most convenient place to find such men was at Canterbury College, located in the same town as CWC. Over and over again, the CWC students told us about dressing up to go there, even if they were only going to drive through the Canterbury campus.

Sororities were also mentioned as having an effect on grooming and attire. Several students said that they thought sorority members were more concerned than independents about appearance. Ronna told her interviewer: "I don't ever wear make-up unless the [sorority] house tells me I have to dress up." Echoing the linkages Carroll (1985), Risman (1982), and Arthur (1998) have made between personal appearance and the reputation of sororities, Dara remarked:

> I've noticed that, like, most of my friends aren't in the sororities; so, they're not really worried about how they're looking. But the girls who are in sororities always need to be dressed up because the higher people in the sororities are looking at them and making sure that they're not putting down the sorority name or doing something that would affect the sorority in a bad way.

Despite this pressure, however, some sorority members, like Ronna and Marianne who were quoted above, clearly indicated that they rarely dressed up on campus.

Given the grooming practices described in the interviews, it is not surprising that surveys of CWC students revealed that the Concern-for-Appearance scores of both the sorority members and the independents declined from the summer before they started college until the end of their first year. This decline was significant for independents but was smaller and not significant for sorority members, additional evidence for the greater stress placed on appearance in the sororities. Nevertheless, being at an all-women's college gave independent students, and even some sorority members, a context in which they didn't have to worry very much or very often about what they looked like, at least as long as they stayed on campus.

The survey that students took at the end of their first year also presented them with a list of 20 characteristics and asked them to indicate how important each of them was "to your evaluation of yourself" (see Appendix B, Figure B.5). Included among the 20 characteristics were three that are relevant to this discussion about concern for appearance: "the shape of your body," "your weight," and "how physically attractive you are." Whether considered separately or in combination (i.e., totaled and averaged), the importance assigned to these three characteristics by sorority women was significantly higher than the importance given these three characteristics by independents. On average, the sorority women said that body, weight, and attractiveness were *very* important to them, but the independent women, on average, considered these characteristics only *somewhat* important.

This stress on body, weight, and attractiveness as very important components of the self-evaluations of sorority women continued throughout their stay at CWC. In the survey conducted shortly before graduation, sorority women continued to rate body, weight, and attractiveness as significantly more important, on average, than did independent women. What continued over time for *both* sorority women and independents were significant positive correlations among these self-ratings, their scores on the Need-for-Social-Approval measure, and their scores on the Concern-for-Appearance scale. Throughout their college careers, CWC students saw concern for appearance as a way of gaining both social approval and better self-evaluations.

Despite these continuities, senior-year interviews revealed that a new set of goals and activities was increasing the amount of attention some CWC women were giving to their appearance and grooming. When asked whether they were more or less concerned with their appearance than they had been when they first came to CWC, about 20% of those interviewed responded that their concerns had followed a curvilinear pattern, first decreasing but now increasing. Martha, an independent, gave one reason for this pattern:

> I think that [appearance] was more of a concern as an incoming freshman than it was my sophomore and junior years. And, it's more of a concern now than it was my sophomore and junior years. More now because I'm a student manager, and I need to look half-way decent.

And a more elaborate version of this explanation was given by Georgia, another independent:

> My freshman year [appearance] was important. Now I don't care, you know. I mean, that's another thing about it being a women's college. You're not going to class to try to pick up somebody. (laughter) But, it's become important this year just because I have my intern[ship] and my job. . . . It's getting more important because I know in the future I'm going to have to shape up or ship out when it comes time to get that [post-graduation] job. (laughter) But over the past 4 years, I mean, I know we've discussed it with—I've discussed it with a lot of my friends, and it's just not important to put on makeup and throw your hair together for class. That's not why you're going [to class].

Perhaps because they were more likely than sorority members to have taken jobs while at CWC, the independent women were more likely to describe this curvilinear pattern. And, perhaps because of this pattern, the difference in average concern for appearance between the two groups that had been significant in summer of 1991 and spring of 1992 was slightly smaller and no longer significant by the time of graduation. Nevertheless, sorority women continued to express more concern for appearance than did independents, and there were no findings from our study of CWC that contradicted the widely accepted proposition that sororities give a high priority to "pride in appearance."

The differences between the two groups were moderate or small, however, probably much smaller than one would find on a large, coeducational campus. Also, the differences became smaller, rather than larger, from matriculation to graduation and from the end of students' first year at CWC to the end of their last year. These findings suggest that selective recruitment into sororities, rather than socialization by the sororities, played a larger role in creating a concern for appearance among their members. The "Sweats on Campus" that Timmie and Marianne and so many other students described was probably too well established and accepted *on campus* for sorority women to resist, and most had developed no reason for doing so aside from special events or the appearance of male students in one of their classes.

To say this is not to say that Wolf's (1991) "beauty myth" had no power on the CWC campus. The more CWC women wanted social approval, the more concerned about their appearance they were and the more emphasis they placed on the shape of their body, their weight, and their attractiveness in their own self-evaluations. This was true of both sorority members and independents, and it was true from when they entered CWC until they graduated. Being at a women's college did not eliminate the tyranny of the beauty myth, but it did give these young women—even those who joined sororities—considerable respite from the constant pressure to look their best.

CONCLUSION: HOW "GOOD" ARE SORORITIES?

Readers who want evidence for the emancipatory "goodness" of sororities can take little comfort from the findings presented in this chapter. Although sororities seem not to have *caused* the high levels of concern their members showed for propriety, their physical appearance, social approval, and other kinds of statusful achievements, sororities did nothing to undermine these concerns, and their recruitment practices reinforced them. The major "liberalizing effect" of CWC sororities over the 4 years was in precisely those areas—alcohol and drug use, sexual permissiveness and abortion—that have produced most of the criticisms of the Greek system nationwide. The significant moves that sorority women at CWC made toward what feminists would applaud as desirable forms of gender emancipation—increased endorsement of Gender Equality Norms and Autonomy Values and decreased concern with Propriety and Appearance—were found to be due to the college culture and not to the sororities themselves. Indeed, there is no evidence that CWC sororities were able to socialize their members into norms, values, identities, or opinions that ran counter to those of the independent students. The most that they accomplished was to maintain some (but not all) of the differences from independent students that sorority pledges brought with them.

Given the exclusionary tensions they were perceived to create by more than half of the students and the emphases on status striving and socially approved appearances that they reinforced, would the college and its students have been better off without sororities? I will duck this question for now, but return to it at the end of the book after examining the roles sororities played with regard to careerism and community, the concerns of the next three chapters. With regard to traditionalism and emancipation, it seems clear that what effects sororities did have (apart from the effects of the college itself) favored a combination of gender traditionalism (seek social approval and adjust your "looks" to please the men), achievement orientation (but not necessarily achievements accomplished through one's own hard work), conservative economic positions, and lifestyle emancipation.

CHAPTER 4

Careerism and Academic Traditions

This chapter focuses on the distinction that is often made between an academic orientation and a careerist orientation toward higher education. Although the distinction is now deeply embedded in educational discourse, the fact that it has had and continues to have different implications for college women and men is often ignored. The first section of this chapter explores the gendered nature of the relationships between academic pursuits and careerism throughout the history of American higher education.

Against this historical background, I then examine academic and careerist orientations at CWC, looking first at the attitudes of entering students, next at the official and student cultures of the college, and then at the effects of these cultures on students' academic choices and achievements. Finally, I advance an argument about the way in which both the liberal arts and careerism have been linked to gender traditionalism.

THE GENDERED HISTORY OF CAREERISM

School-teaching was the first occupational career for which American women were intentionally trained by institutions of higher education, although it was widely accepted—and sometimes legally required—that they would give up their teaching careers when they married. Women who devoted themselves to housewifery and motherhood were not seen as having "wasted their education," however, since it was assumed that the same education that prepared them to be good schoolteachers also prepared them to be polished and intelligent companions to their husbands and competent mothers to their children. For women attending female academies and women's colleges during much of the 19th century, this education was a classical one that had as its primary goals the development of mental discipline and the elevation of moral character. The achievement of both goals was considered a major asset for any woman, whether or not she ever taught school or pursued any other occupational career.

Men were not exempt from this emphasis on moral character. The classical education they were given at institutions of higher education from the colonial period well into the 19th century was the model for the mental discipline and moral elevation stressed in women's academies and colleges. The training of ministers, rather than teachers, was considered a major goal of men's colleges, and those who aspired to this career were expected to undergo even more rigorous mental and moral training than the college men who sought other careers. For all men, however, little distinction was made in these early years between training for occupational careers and training for life. The same stress on developing mental discipline and moral character that would make you a good lawyer or physician would also make you a better person.

What differentiated the messages given to men and women was that preparation for a disciplined, moral life for men came to mean preparation for careers and for the public life of a citizen. Although there was some stress on the "father as moral overseer" of the family (Pleck, 1987) during the colonial period, the ideal role for men had shifted by the 19th century to being a good provider, and the emphasis on improving home and family life that was so strong in discussions of women's higher education was far less common in discussions about the education of men. Absent from both of these discourses was the now familiar distinction between an academic curriculum or orientation, on the one hand, and careerism, on the other. Instead, it was argued that a prescribed and narrow college curriculum emphasizing classical languages and ancient history would discipline the mind and serve as the basis for subsequent intellectual or vocational achievement.

Major challenges to this argument emerged during the second half of the 19th century. Although controversial at the time, these challenges would eventually succeed in transforming the classical curriculum of American higher education into what we now call the "curriculum of the liberal arts and sciences" or, more briefly, a "liberal" education. Not only did the sciences, modern languages, and contemporary history and literature find respected places in the curriculum, but so also did studies of the political economy, such as sociology, political science, and economics. Instead of a fixed and classical course of study for all, students were encouraged to elect a broader variety of courses consistent with their own interests and life plans.

The transformation was not without its problems. In a speech to the Association of Collegiate Alumnae, Elizabeth Kemper Adams (1912) bemoaned the "haphazard and trivial motives for selection [of courses] now influencing a large number of college students" (p. 261). Adams's speech is noteworthy less for its criticism of the elective system, a critique already developed by others (e.g., McCosh, 1888; Thomas, 1908; Wendell, 1904; West, 1884), than for the solution she proposed. Unlike those who argued that what Adams called the "evils of an unregulated elective system" (p. 261) could best be redeemed by returning to the classical curriculum or by reorganizing the curriculum into what we now call majors or areas of concentration, Adams suggested a greater emphasis in the college curriculum on preparation for vocations. By this, Adams did not mean a curriculum of narrowly defined courses emphasizing skills required by specific occupations but rather, as the title of her speech made clear, an emphasis upon "The Vocational Opportunities of the College of Liberal Arts."

Adams's defense of the academic curriculum of the liberal arts college as an adequate, and even superior, training for a broad range of occupations continued throughout the 20th century (see, e.g., Figler, 1989), but it did not serve as an effective alternative to the rising vocationalism of the Progressive Era that became both a cause and a consequence of the "reaction against coeducation." This reaction was a response to two developments in higher education. One was the large increase in the numbers of women students who were outnumbering men students by a considerable margin at some institutions (Van Hise, 1908). The second was the growth of career-oriented programs designed for men. These programs were in both older, established fields, such as medicine and law, and newer ones, such as business and engineering. Even in medicine and law, the courses became more specialized, technical, and vocationally oriented than they had been in earlier years. Men could no longer aspire to such careers on the basis of only a classical education that would "discipline their minds."

Because women of that era were still discouraged from entering the public worlds of men's vocations and professions, they came increasingly to dominate enrollments in the older, more prestigious liberal arts curriculum even on campuses where they constituted a minority of total enrollments. The "reaction against coeducation" was basically an attempt to find a way to reduce the competitive threat that these women posed for college men. It was too late to expel women from higher education on grounds of their intellectual shortcomings. Numerous (male) professors had already testified to the high quality of scholastic performance demonstrated by their women students, even in the hardest subjects. So the preferred proposal was not to abolish coeducation entirely but to search for ways to segregate women and men within existing institutions.

One successful plan was advocated by President Charles Van Hise (1908) of the University of Wisconsin, who suggested in 1907 that the best form of segregation was the "natural segregation" that occurred because of choices "freely made" by the students:

> At the present time, provision has been made for nearly complete segregation on a large scale by the establishment of courses and colleges which are practically for the one sex or the other. The colleges of engineering, law, commerce, agriculture, and medicine are essentially men's colleges. While open to women, their opportunities have been taken advantage of only to a very limited extent. Similarly courses for training the heads of household have been established for the women. Whether such courses be called home economics, household science, or domestic science, they are the first of the professional schools for women. (p. 41)

He called on all colleges and universities to "provide for natural segregation by the development of professional courses" that would appeal to one sex but not the other (p. 44).

Home economics was not the only set of career programs "for women" to become established on university campuses during this era. Others included social work, library science, and nursing. The establishment of colleges or departments of education, separate from programs in the liberal arts, also contributed to gender segregation and changed the nature of teacher training. Gone was the vision of M. Carey Thomas (1908), president of Bryn Mawr, who wanted women to take a bachelor's degree based on rigorous training in the liberal arts and sciences followed by specialized, professional training in teaching or home economics or medicine or law or some other respected career field. In place of the kinds of career preparation envisioned by both Thomas and Adams (1912) was a set of "female" undergraduate programs, usually poorly regarded and poorly funded, that would provide "professional" training for women seeking employment in "appropriate" fields.

Even after separate curricula in "women's fields" were established, women continued to pursue degrees in the liberal arts at higher rates than men. In her astute analysis of the reasons for this fact during the post–World-War-II period of 1945 to 1963, Fass (1997) documents the heavy emphasis that was placed upon the value of a liberal arts education as a "training for life." Like earlier justifications of classical education for women, this defense of the postwar liberal arts curriculum presented it as a suitable education for women who would never work for pay outside the home, for those who would move in and out of the labor force or volunteer work, and for those—expectedly few—who would pursue lifelong occupational careers.

The negative effects of this linkage of liberal arts education for women with marriage and the family have been documented by Mervin Freedman (1956), whose study of students at Vassar College in the 1950s revealed that graduating students who had concentrated solely in the liberal arts were experiencing a greater conflict between their intellectual and academic pursuits, on the one hand, and their upcoming marriages, on the other, than were students who had career interests and professional ambitions. Even though this latter group of women were also more likely to marry than to participate in the labor force, they had an identity vested in a possible future career and a belief that they could do something important. This belief, and their career identity, was something that they could cling to when they became wives and mothers. In contrast, the students who had concentrated solely on the liberal arts had been involved in a curriculum that emphasized becoming and being a particular kind of person—rational, creative, disciplined, freed from prejudice and blind adherence to convention.

This emphasis failed to prepare students for their futures, wrote Freedman (1956), because:

> The emphasis in our society is, in short, on doing, not being; and unfortunately, the doing involved in being a wife and mother often brings little recognition, no matter how demanding the tasks involved, no matter how creative the participation. . . . One may well wonder if a more equal admixture of professional and liberal schooling may not at the present time, given the current status of the housewife in our society, be more effective in "liberating" women than is the current liberal arts philosophy with its secondary emphasis on professional training. (pp. 26–27)

Despite Freedman's misgivings, evidence exists to support the contention that women's greater emphasis on a liberal arts education as preparation for all of life's contingencies continued into the early 1980s. Katchadourian and Boli (1985) found that undergraduate women attending Stanford University from 1977 to 1981 were considerably more likely than comparable men to endorse academic values such as "a general liberal education" and "learning to think critically" above careerist values such as "specialized preparation for a future career" and "acquiring technical/preprofessional skills."

By dividing all the Stanford students they studied into those who rated academic values and careerist values above or below the average, the researchers were able to identify two groups they called the Intellectuals and the Careerists. The Intellectuals were those who rated academic values high and careerist values low, and Careerists were those who rated academic values low and careerist values high. Katchadourian and Boli (1985) report that among the students they studied:

> *Gender* is probably the single most important variable influencing academic and career orientations. . . . Our finding that women place greater emphasis on liberal education, and men on career orientation, is hardly surprising, but it is revealing to find that women outnumber men more than two to one among Intellectuals, while the ratio is even greater in the opposite direction among Careerists. (p. 230)

Such findings are not unique to elite universities like Stanford. Throughout America today, women are considerably more likely than men to enroll in liberal arts colleges, both small ones and those that exist as part of large universities. This century-long commitment of women to the liberal arts is not without its ironic twist. Because undergraduate degrees in the liberal arts became stepping-stones to graduate professional schools, college women were well-positioned to enter those schools once opportunities to do so were fully opened to them, something that did not happen until quite recently. Only 20 years ago, Katchadourian and Boli (1985) found that women Intellectuals at Stanford were less likely than Stanford men—including intellectual men—to seek careers in law or medicine. It is unlikely that this finding would be replicated today. By 1996, the proportion of American women entering undergraduate colleges who intended to become physicians, dentists, or lawyers had increased by 430% from what it had been 30 years earlier and had surpassed the proportion of male freshmen in 1996 who intended to pursue careers in those same three professions (Astin, Parrott, Korn, & Sax, 1997).

Even 20 years ago, many women students did not clearly separate their ratings of academic and careerist values. In addition to the Intellectuals and Careerists who did so, Katchadourian and Boli (1985) also identified two other types of students: Strivers and the Unconnected. Whereas Strivers were defined as those who gave above average ratings to both academic and careerist values, the Unconnected were those who rated both types of values below the average scores of all the Stanford students who participated in the study. Like their findings about Intellectuals and Careerists, those for the Unconnected revealed gender differences, but those for Strivers did not. Katchadourian and Boli (1985) concluded that these findings challenged traditional gender stereotypes:

> The equal proportion of the sexes among Strivers belies the common perception that men are more ambitious and hard-driving. By the same token, the overrepresentation of men among the Unconnected contradicts the

notion that women are more likely to be undirected in their career interests and less involved with the institution as a whole. Among today's college students, women may be different from men in their orientations toward [academics] and careers, but they are not less concerned to develop at least one of these two important aspects. (p. 230)

ACADEMIC AND CAREERIST ORIENTATIONS AT CWC

I begin this section of the chapter by examining the extent to which women entering CWC had academic and career orientations similar to those found at Stanford and elsewhere. Next, I examine the extent to which these orientations were embedded in the official and student cultures of the college. Finally, I look at the extent to which these cultures affected the orientations—and academic performance—of entering students during their years at CWC.

Orientations Among Entering Students

One page of the survey given to entering CWC students in summer 1991 asked them to indicate how important to them personally were 19 different opportunities that going to college might offer (see Appendix B, Figure B.7). Using, once again, the statistical technique called factor analysis (see Appendix C, Table C.3), I examined whether responses to these 19 opportunities organized themselves into clusters or scales. Five scales emerged from this analysis. The two that are relevant to this chapter are the Academic Orientation scale and the Career Orientation scale.

The Academic Orientation scale measured the importance to entering CWC students of the following six different academic opportunities: to gain a better understanding of the world; to study and learn new things; to take interesting classes; to develop my reading and writing skills; to meet people of different races and backgrounds than my own; and to learn more about the great art, music, and literature of the world. As is generally true of clusters identified by factor analysis, there were moderate or strong, significant correlations among the ratings students gave to all combinations of the six opportunities included in the Academic Orientation scale. The scale score for each student consisted of the average ratings she gave to the six academic opportunities.

How academically oriented were the entering CWC students? More than one third of them (35.3%) rated academic opportunities as very or most important, and only 6% rated academic opportunities as less than somewhat important. How do these responses compare to those reported in other studies? To the best of my knowledge, no other researchers have asked entering students exactly the same questions about college opportunities that we asked at CWC. This means that claims about similarities or differences between the academic orientation of CWC students and students at other colleges or universities must be accepted with caution.

Nevertheless, some plausible comparisons are provided by Astin et al. (1991), who surveyed a national sample of American freshmen in fall of 1991. They asked these students to rate the importance of 11 reasons for attending college including two academic reasons that are similar—but not identical—to opportunities on the Academic Orientation scale used at CWC. One of these reasons was "to improve my reading and study skills," and Astin et al. report that 43.5% of women (and 35.8% of men) entering 4-year colleges rated this as a very important reason for attending college. In comparison, 60.1% of entering CWC students rated "the opportunity to develop my reading and writing skills" as either very or most important.

Astin and his colleagues also included "to learn more about things that interest me" on their list of reasons for attending college, and they report that 76.9% of women (and 68.8% of men) entering 4-year colleges gave a "very important" rating to this reason. In comparison, an impressive 92.3% of entering CWC students rated "the opportunity to study and learn new things" as either very or most important. Taken together, these findings indicate that the entering CWC students were no less—and possibly more—academically oriented than their counterparts at other colleges.

The Career Orientation scale that emerged from the factor analysis of the CWC responses (see Appendix C, Table C.3) consisted of the average importance ratings of four opportunities: to get qualified for an interesting career; to develop my leadership skills; to get ahead in the world; and to train for a higher paying job. Two of these ratings can be compared to ratings by the national sample surveyed by Astin and his colleagues (1991), although the questions asked were not identical. The list of reasons for attending college in the national survey included "to be able to make more money" and "to be able to get a better job." Among students who entered 4-year colleges in 1991, Astin et al. (1991) found that 68.3% of the women (and 75.3% of men) gave very-important ratings to making more money, and more than three quarters of both women and men rated a better job as very important (76.7% and 75.8%, respectively).

Women students entering CWC in 1991 were even more career oriented than the national samples of students entering other 4-year colleges that same year. The proportion who rated training for a better paying job as very or most important was 79.5%, and the proportion rating the opportunity to get qualified for an interesting career as very or most important was a huge 97.4%. The ratings for the remaining two opportunities included in the Career Orientation scale were not this high, although the four ratings were significantly intercorrelated. When the ratings of all four opportunities included in the Career Orientation scale were averaged together, 69.2% of respondents had rating scores at the very-important level or above it. Only 1.9% of respondents thought the four career opportunities were less than somewhat important, with the remaining 28.9% of respondents rating these opportunities, on average, from somewhat to just below very important.

Katchadourian and Boli (1985) report that the correlation between intellectualism and careerism scores among Stanford students was small and nonsignificant. In contrast, the correlation between scores on the Academic and Career Orientation scales among CWC students was strong and significant. This strong correlation plus the high ratings given to both academic and career opportunities by the CWC students meant that it would be misleading to divide students into four equal-sized groups, on the basis of scores above and below the median on the two scales, as Katchadourian and Boli (1985) did at Stanford. Instead, I defined Intellectuals as those students who reported that academic opportunities were very or most important, on average, but whose average ratings of career opportunities were less than very important. Careerists were defined as those students whose average ratings of career opportunities were very or most important, but whose average ratings of academic opportunities were less than very important. Strivers were those whose ratings of both academic and career opportunities averaged very important or above, and the Unconnected were those whose ratings of both sets of opportunities averaged below very important.

Using these definitions, I found that CWC students were more likely to be Careerists or Strivers (38.5% and 30.8%, respectively) than to be Intellectuals or Unconnecteds (4.5% and 26.3%, respectively). This unequal distribution across the four categories reflects the stronger scores of CWC students on the Career Orientation scale, compared with the Academic Orientation scale. As noted above, however, this difference should not be interpreted to mean either that CWC students were less academically oriented than their counterparts across the country or that career aspirations among CWC students were negatively related to academic aspirations. Instead, the orientations of entering CWC students reflect two tendencies among American college students. The first is the long-standing tendency among both college men and women to justify higher education not as an end in itself but rather as a means to being a better person and to leading a better life. The second is the increasing tendency among college women, following the path of college men, to define that better self and better life in occupational terms.

These tendencies were also apparent in the information entering students gave on the CWC application form they completed in spring or summer of 1991. Among other things, this form asked students to write an application essay consistent with the following instructions:

> The essay is designed to give you the opportunity to present yourself to the Admissions Committee. Please indicate your reasons for applying to [CWC], your educational goals, career aspirations, and the role which you hope [CWC] will play in your future.

The form also asked students to select a major. Of the 185 entering students, 45 chose academic majors, 134 chose vocational majors, and the remaining six indicated that they were undecided.

The students who selected academic majors did not present themselves as purists interested in learning only for learning's sake. More than a third of them ($n = 16$) clearly indicated their career plans by selecting the academic majors of prelaw or premedicine. Several of the others also made clear in their application essays how they intended to link their academic major with a specific career. Dusty wrote, "I am interested in being an English major because my career aspirations lean toward writing," and Alice, who planned to major in history, wrote:

> Since history and political science have always been my favorite subjects and I hope to develope [sic] these interests into skills that will prepare me for law school, it is my desire to utilize what [CWC] has to offer and combine it with my interests and become the best prosecuting attorney possible.

It is possible, of course, that this mentioning of career plans was prompted by the instructions students were given for their application essay. Students choosing academic majors who were less certain of their career plans than Alice or Dusty, still expressed concern about careers, as this excerpt from the application essay of Deanna, a political science major, reveals: "My career aspirations are not clear at this point in my life. I hope through [CWC's] leadership and direction that I will know what my career aspiration will be."

If the instructions concerning the application essay explain why so many students—even those with academic majors—mentioned careers, then one could reasonably expect that most students would also discuss their educational goals, another topic they were instructed to address. This proved not to be the case, however. Aside from mentioning their choice of a major, which most did, few had anything else to say about academic matters. About 10% of all application essays mentioned the fact that CWC was a liberal arts college as one reason it was attractive, but these comments were as likely to come from women with careerist majors as from those whose majors were more academic. Not a single student drew a clear distinction between a liberal arts education and vocational training.

The heavier stress that CWC applicants put on careers, rather than academic matters, in both their choices of majors and their essays is consistent with the stronger endorsement they gave to the Career Orientation scale in comparison to the Academic Orientation scale. All three sources of research findings support the conclusion that entering CWC students were highly careerist, and that their commitment to careers was stronger than their interest in academic matters. Even those few who were categorized as Intellectuals had not developed a stable, integrated, set of academic commitments. As a group, the Intellectuals were no more likely than other students to choose academic majors, and they were just as likely as other students to stress career interests and concerns in their application essays. And the students who chose academic majors actually had higher average scores on the Career Orientation scale, albeit nonsignificantly higher, than did students who chose majors in vocational fields of study.

Perhaps it should not be surprising that the academic commitments of entering students had not yet crystallized. At the time that these data were collected, the students were applicants who had not yet matriculated at CWC. They were often ambivalent about the major they had chosen, and they exhibited little understanding of the academic traditions associated with the liberal arts. Before turning to the question of what effect CWC had on the poorly organized academic commitments of the entering students and on their stronger careerist commitments, I examine the extent to which the college these students were about to enter—both in its official culture and in its student culture—was a place that would offer them academic and careerist opportunities and challenges.

Official and Student Cultures

On the application forms used in 1991, CWC listed 48 majors that students could emphasize in their studies, and entering students chose 31 of them. These majors did not correspond to separate departments on the campus. Instead, they represented often overlapping areas of concentration available within the CWC curriculum or in cooperation with other institutions. Of the 48 concentrations, almost half ($n = 21$) were academic fields and slightly more than half ($n = 27$) were vocational specialties. During the following 4 years, the number of majors was reduced to 43. Although academic majors were slightly reorganized, their number remained at 21, whereas the vocational specialties were more extensively reorganized and reduced in number to 22. Most of the majors that disappeared were vocational specialties that relied heavily on cooperative arrangements between CWC and other colleges or universities.

In *American Universities and Colleges*, a guide for applicants and their parents published by the American Council on Education, CWC described itself in the early 1990s as "a professions-oriented liberal arts college for women." This blending of careerism and liberal arts was also evident in the degree requirements established by the college. Four degrees were offered: bachelor of arts (BA), bachelor of fine arts (BFA), bachelor of science (BS), and bachelor of social work (BSW). Whereas the BFA and BSW were offered only to majors in the division of fine arts and the social work program, respectively, most of the other major areas offered students the choice of programs leading to either the BA or BS degree.

Regardless of the degree they sought, all students were required to complete two courses in English composition with a grade of C or higher. In addition, all students were required to take some courses in "The Liberal Arts Component," which consisted of the behavioral and social sciences, humanities, fine arts, and mathematics and sciences. As a result of these requirements, no students graduated from CWC without some exposure to courses in the curriculum of the liberal arts and sciences, but both the breadth and depth of coverage varied across degree programs and across students within programs.

To find out more about the relative stress on academics and careers at CWC, I examined the evaluations made by both faculty and students of 19 different characteristics of the college (see Appendix B, Figures B.8 and B.9). Faculty were asked to describe CWC as it was from 1991 to 1995, and students were asked to answer these questions either after leaving CWC or shortly before their graduation. Three of the evaluated characteristics of CWC were averaged into a Liberal Arts Emphasis scale, two formed an Academic Rigor scale, and four were combined into a Career Emphasis scale.

The characteristics included in the Liberal Arts Emphasis scale were improved understanding of the world; good opportunities to develop reading and writing skills; and encouragement to learn more about the great art, music, and literature of the world. The truer a faculty member or student thought it was that CWC promoted these outcomes for students, the higher that person scored on the Liberal Arts Emphasis scale.

As was true of classical education, one of the rationales used to promote a liberal education has been the belief that a proper form of this education will promote a trained or disciplined intelligence. In other words, it is not only the content of the curriculum—its attention to great literature, for example—but also the academic focus and effort demanded of the students that define a good liberal education. To measure these demands at CWC, students and faculty were asked to indicate how true it was that CWC "put a strong emphasis on studying and learning" and "had low academic standards." To create the Academic Rigor scale, responses to the second (but not the first) item were reverse-scored, so that the *less* true students and faculty thought it was, the higher their scores on the scale.

The four evaluations included in the Career Emphasis scale were ratings of how true it was that CWC provided good opportunities to get qualified for interesting careers; was a good place to develop leadership skills; encouraged students to become work and career oriented; and was a good place to train for high-paying jobs. The truer a faculty member or student thought it was that CWC promoted these outcomes for students, the higher that person scored on the Career Emphasis scale.

What do responses to these scales tell us about the academic climate at CWC? The average scores of faculty and students on the Liberal Arts Emphasis scale were almost identical, as were their average scores on the Career Emphasis scale. Both faculty and students were significantly more likely to agree that CWC emphasized careers than that the college emphasized the liberal arts, although the differences in scores on the two emphasis scales were not large. Interestingly, there were no significant differences between the average scores on each of these two scales obtained by the students who dropped out of CWC and those who remained to graduate. Both dropouts and graduates also described the college as placing more emphasis on careers than on the liberal arts.

Students who left CWC and those who remained to graduate also obtained similar scores on the Academic Rigor scale. Scores on this scale, unlike those on the Liberal Arts and Career Emphasis scales, were moderately and significantly different for students and faculty. On average, students were more likely than faculty to think that CWC was characterized by a rigorous academic emphasis. On none of the three scales did either faculty or students have average scores that were at the extremes of agreement or disagreement. Thus the findings revealed a campus climate that tilted toward career preparation rather than the rigorous pursuit of the liberal arts, but neither the survey data nor the degree requirements support the conclusion that the college had completely abandoned either the content or the rigor of the traditional liberal arts.

Although the faculty gave the college fairly low marks for academic rigor, no evidence ever emerged of administrative pressure on faculty to give better grades or to lower academic standards. Instead, the explanation for the faculty's assessments lay in the open admissions practices of the college. The large proportion of students who entered CWC with average or poor academic records limited the academic competition experienced by the better students and reduced the efforts they needed to make in order to gain good grades and academic honors. One faculty member told me that, compared with the other three colleges at which she had taught, CWC seemed to have fewer students who were intellectually curious enough to do more than the faculty required of them. Then, reflecting on what she had just said, she opined that she really wasn't sure that she had met *any* students of this type at CWC. Her opinion seems to have been widely shared. When CWC faculty who participated in our survey were presented with a list of topics and asked how important each of them would be to most of the CWC students (Appendix B, Figure B.10), the majority of the faculty (61.8%) said that "how much they were learning in their classes" was only slightly or somewhat important to students. In contrast, 73.5% of the faculty said that "their future jobs and careers" were very or most important to these students.

Effects of CWC Cultures on Students' Majors and Grades

Given the strong careerism of the student culture at CWC and the tilt toward careerism of the official college culture, it would have been surprising if the students who entered in 1991 had abandoned their own careerist orientations and had made stronger academic commitments. As a group, they didn't. Graduates of CWC who had entered with plans to major in vocational fields were five times more likely to graduate with a vocational major than with a liberal arts major. In contrast, only about one third of graduates entering with academic majors still had such majors 4 years later; almost two thirds had switched to vocational majors.

In addition, there is some evidence that the college climate may have interacted with the academic and careerist orientations of entering students to determine who would change majors by the time of graduation. Proportionately, the group least likely to change from vocational to academic majors were the Careerists, and they were twice as likely as Strivers and the Unconnected to change from academic to vocational majors. These findings suggest that the campus cultures may have provided Careerists with the support necessary to bring their commitments into greater conformity with their orientations than they had been able to do before matriculating.

Unfortunately, the small number of Intellectuals who entered CWC makes it difficult to be certain if such students suffered from a corresponding lack of support. It seems noteworthy, however, that Intellectuals were proportionately more likely to drop out of CWC than students in the other three groups, and all of the Intellectuals who later graduated from CWC switched majors, with more switching in a vocational than in an academic direction.

Taken together, there is nothing in these findings to suggest that attending CWC decreased the vocational commitments of entering students and some evidence to suggest that attendance may have increased those commitments. Whereas almost one fourth (24.3%) of the first-year students who entered CWC in 1991 intended to major in the liberal arts, the proportion of graduates from that same cohort who actually did so was less than one fifth (18.3%), and some of them had minors or second majors in vocational fields. Conversely, whereas three fourths (75.6%) of entering students intended to pursue vocational majors, more than four fifths (81.7%) actually did so. Although these shifts are not large or significant, they provide additional evidence that CWC was a place where careerism was supported and fostered.

The emphasis that the college climate—especially the peer culture—placed on careers rather than the liberal arts affected not only students' choice of major fields but also their academic performance, as measured by their grade point averages (GPAs). When students entered CWC, their high school GPAs were unrelated to their levels of academic and career orientation and to their choice of either a vocational or liberal arts major. Although students' academic and career orientations continued to have no significant effects on their GPAs during their years at CWC, their choice of majors did have a significant effect on grades. The liberal arts majors who remained at CWC to graduate had an average high school GPA of 3.01 and an average GPA at CWC of 3.06. In contrast, the vocational majors who remained at CWC to graduate had a significant increase in their GPAs from an average high school GPA of 3.05 to an average GPA at CWC of 3.28.

Could this significant increase in GPAs of students with vocational majors have been caused by lower academic standards held by faculty teaching vocational courses compared with faculty teaching courses in the liberal arts? Because our study did not include a systematic investigation of faculty grading procedures, we cannot entirely rule out this possibility, but most of our data suggest that this explanation for the significant increase in the grades of vocational majors is either wrong or, at most, only a partial explanation. A check of scores on the Academic Rigor scale revealed only a minuscule difference between scores of students with academic majors and scores of students with vocational majors. Students with vocational majors were all required to take liberal arts courses, and there was almost no difference between the GPAs of students who opted for the

BA and BS degrees, even though the former degree required more inten-sive work in "The Liberal Arts Component." If we accept these findings as indicating that the significantly lower GPAs of students with liberal arts majors were not due to any greater difficulty in the courses they took at CWC, then we are left with the question of what happened at CWC to cause these different GPA outcomes for students with different majors.

Two interrelated factors seem to have been at work, one suggested by the literature reviewed earlier in this chapter and the other suggested by findings about the campus cultures at CWC. The dilemma facing lib-eral arts majors at Vassar College that Freedman (1956) identified 40 years earlier may have been even worse at CWC in the 1990s, by which time the pressures on women to develop career-based identities had become stronger than ever. In contrast to earlier periods when liberal arts degrees were considered suitable for women who would become full-time home-makers (Fass, 1997), few women today feel that they have the choice of assuming those family identities on a full-time, long-term basis. This was certainly true at CWC, as findings presented in Chapter 5 will show.

In a careerist context, being a liberal arts major is acceptable *if,* like the college men, college women use that major as a means toward a pro-fessional goal. But this was not true of most of the liberal arts majors at CWC. More than one third (35.7%) of them answered our final survey by saying either that they did not plan to continue their education or that they were uncertain whether they would. Even though a majority planned to seek some additional education, the comments of the graduating seniors I interviewed indicated that the linkages between these educational plans and specific occupational goals were not very clear. In addition, *none* of the liberal arts graduates planned to go to a professional school that would lead directly to a career in an elite profession.

In contrast to the students who had selected vocational majors, the students with liberal arts majors graduated into a more uncertain future. This is not to say that all the vocational majors would get jobs in their chosen field, or that they would do well at those jobs, but while they were at CWC, the vocational majors seemed to become increasingly certain of their goals and the liberal arts majors did not. Although I cannot be certain, it seems to me that it was this goal commitment that made the students with the vocational majors more comfortable, motivated, and academically suc-cessful than their peers.

These individual outcomes were probably the result of the greater supportiveness students felt for careerism than for the liberal arts. Thus the same explanation I gave for the choices of majors students made *after* arriving at CWC can also be used to explain the greater increase in GPAs among students with vocational majors. To affect a student's grades, how-

ever, supportiveness and help had to come from the faculty and not just
the peer culture. Evidence that it did can be found in analyses of the survey completed by graduating seniors. When asked to indicate how true it
was that CWC had a caring faculty, students with vocational majors scored
higher than students with liberal arts majors. Similarly, students with
vocational majors were more likely to *dis*agree with the statement that
CWC had an uncaring administration. This evidence is weak, however,
since the differences between the scores of the two groups of students were
small and not significant.

Somewhat more convincing—but not conclusive—evidence comes
from the interviews with graduating seniors who were asked to talk about
their positive and important experiences at CWC (Appendix D, Interview
III). Of those interviewed, only one fourth (26.9%) mentioned anything
directly related to their academic work and outcomes.

The two liberal arts majors included in this group made only brief
comments about having learned a lot or having received a pretty good
education. In contrast, among the students in this group with vocational
majors, more than half volunteered information about how much academic help and support they had received from faculty. Edie was one of
the students in this group, and she began her answer to my question as
follows:

> Several things [have been positive]. Probably my professors. I've
> had some very good ones. They've always been the kind of people
> that will pull you aside and say, "That was good," you know, or
> "Good job." They always have been available if you wanted to talk
> to them about school. . . . That was a good experience. I mean, it
> was nice to hear that you were doing well. I always think, you
> know, good comments will help give an extra push whenever you
> need it or kind of a little jerk back to try to get on track.

Later in the interview, when asked whether, all things considered,
her experience at CWC had been positive, negative, or a balance of both,
Edie revealed the likely link between faculty support and students' grades:

> [My experience has been] more positive, I think, and I think that's
> attributed a lot to the professors that I have had. They made the
> experience unbelievable. It has been wonderful. It really has. I've
> done a total turn around from what I was in high school. I make
> the grades that I never thought were possible, and they make me
> work harder.

Neither Edie's testimony nor the finding that vocational majors generally made more favorable comments about faculty support should be taken to mean that faculty who taught in vocational programs were, in fact, more supportive of students than were liberal arts faculty. As noted earlier, all students in vocational programs had to take liberal arts courses, and their perceptions of faculty supportiveness would likely have been affected by these faculty as well as those in their major fields. Instead of attributing the grades of the students to differences in faculty standards, the theory that I am developing here suggests that the process was an interactive one. Students with clearer career goals might reasonably be expected to seek out faculty who can help them achieve those goals. Students who feel that they are "on track" and doing what is expected become more comfortable with themselves and with other people. And, surely, the more comfortable a student is, the more willing and able she is to welcome faculty compliments and listen to faculty advice. And the more open and teachable a student is, the more faculty attention she is likely to attract.

If this theory is correct, then it was not so much the major that a CWC student selected that—with faculty help—enhanced her academic performance. Instead, it was the clarity of her career plans and her motivation to pursue them that got her more involved with faculty and increased her academic success. Vocational majors were more successful than liberal arts majors at CWC because, on average, they had more focused career plans. In a careerist culture, not only is "doing" valued, as Freedman (1956) pointed out, but so also is "knowing what you're doing."

LINKING GENDER TRADITIONALISM, CAREERISM, AND THE LIBERAL ARTS

Historically, occupational careers for women have often been planned to be consistent with the ideology of gender traditionalism. In this section of the chapter, I first examine the extent to which this was still the case at CWC in the 1990s. Then I contrast the traditionalism that has characterized both the liberal arts and careerist education with a more emancipatory vision of women's education.

Sex-Typed and Untyped Career Planning at CWC

Both entering students and those who were about to graduate were asked whether they planned to be employed 20 years from the time of the survey and, if so, what occupation they planned to have at that time. Subsequently, I used U.S. Census data to determine if the students who planned to be employed had chosen predominantly women's occupations, which I defined as those jobs whose occupants in 1991 were 60% or more female, according to the U. S. Bureau of Labor Statistics.

At both matriculation and graduation, more than 95% of CWC students planned to be working 20 years later. Of those who had decided on a future occupation, 33.1% at matriculation and 31.5% at graduation planned to be working in predominantly female occupations, and the traditional women's professions of teaching and social work accounted for half of their choices at matriculation and slightly more than half (56.5%) at graduation.

Only a few of the students selected occupations that were predominantly male occupations, which I defined as occupational titles for which the job holders in 1991 were less than 40% female, according to the U.S. Bureau of Labor Statistics. Of matriculating students who reported an occupation that they planned to hold 20 years later, 18.0% selected a predominantly male occupation. Among students who graduated from CWC with a definite occupational choice, this number had fallen to 9.6%. Part of this decline was due to a slightly greater tendency among those who chose predominantly male occupations to drop out of CWC, but even among those who stayed, the 9.6% choosing these occupations at graduation represented a decline from the 15.4% who had made that choice at their matriculation. About half of all the CWC students who chose a predominantly male occupation indicated that they wanted to be lawyers. In 1991, only 19.0% of U.S. lawyers were women, but this has become an increasingly popular career choice for college women, and, as a result, women's representation among lawyers and judges increased to 29.7% in 2000.

At CWC, about half of all matriculating students (48.9%) and more than half of graduates (58.9%) planned to work in occupations that, in 1991, were neither predominantly male nor predominantly female in their U.S. labor force composition. Most popular among both matriculating and graduating students were business-related occupations, many of which were predominantly male occupations until fairly recently but now have a composition of 40%–60% female nationwide. Not surprisingly, given the heavy emphasis on business, liberal arts majors who graduated from CWC were far less likely than vocational majors to select occupations in this less-gendered category. Only 23.1% of the former versus 68.3% of the latter made these selections.

What is more surprising is the finding that not a single liberal arts major selected a predominantly male occupation. Usually, students who plan to become lawyers take bachelor's degrees in the liberal arts, but this was not true at CWC where, among graduating seniors, future lawyers were either business majors or majors in a paralegal program. The liberal arts majors who sought advanced degrees planned to enter professions that were either traditionally female, such as education, or had become predominantly female by 1991, such as psychology. In addition, there were liberal arts majors who planned to become teachers or counselors even though they had not majored in education.

Despite the small number of liberal arts majors among our graduating cohort, these differences in choice of careers were statistically significant, and they were certainly large. Seventy-five percent of the students who graduated with a liberal arts major planned to enter predominantly female—mostly traditional—occupations compared with only 20.0% of the students who graduated from CWC with a vocational major. In light of the theory developed in the previous section of this chapter, it seems entirely possible that the career choices of the liberal arts majors may have resulted more from their lack of planning than from traditional values. Indecisiveness may have prompted them to resort to the more familiar, common, and comfortable professions for women. Whatever the reason, the historical connection—for women—between a liberal arts education and gender traditionalism persisted into the 1990s at CWC even though the emphasis on full-time homemaking had all but disappeared.

Traditional vs. Emancipatory Education for Women

If Elizabeth Kemper Adams (1912) had visited CWC in the early 1990s, she probably would have been disappointed to discover that the college was not placing more emphasis on rigorous education in the liberal arts and that it had, instead, made so many concessions to "the clamor for the introduction of vocational courses." Despite this disappointment, Adams would probably have recognized that the need to prepare women for the labor market was even more important at the end of the 20th century than it had been when she concerned herself with this need in the early years of that century. This concern sets Adams apart from the many other critics of vocationalism in higher education (e.g., Hutchins, 1936; Scott, 1991a; Veblen, 1918) who, for the past hundred years, have seen the emphasis on elective courses and careerism as an unmitigated evil that lowers academic standards and turns liberal arts colleges into trade schools.

This "evil" is widespread in contemporary higher education. Using *Peterson's Guide to Four-Year Colleges* for 1993, which provided profiles and in-depth descriptions of 779 institutions, Michael DeLucci (1997) determined that 327 (42%) had mission statements—like the one at CWC—that stressed the liberal arts. Despite this claim, more than two thirds of these "liberal arts" colleges (68%) gave most of their degrees in "professional fields," such as business, criminal justice, education, engineering, health, and human services. Employing the same either/or mentality that afflicts so much writing about academic traditions and careerism, DeLucci views his findings as evidence of a major deception by 4-year colleges. He suggests that they cling to their "liberal arts" mission statements as promotional devices evocative of elite institutions.

Although I cannot rule out the possibility that some administrators and recruiters at CWC held the cynical view that DeLucci attributes to them, the degree requirements were explicitly designed to prevent students from obtaining only a trade school education. Unlike DeLucci and many critics of careerism, CWC administrators and faculty viewed the liberal arts and "professional education" as complementary, and they took pride in the fact that they were helping young women prepare themselves for the job market. In this regard, their orientation was a continuation of the emphasis on "useful employment" that has always characterized higher education for women in America. The major discontinuity with earlier years was not the careerism but rather the deemphasis at CWC on preparation for homemaking as one form of "useful employment." Although home economics was listed as a possible major on the application forms used in 1991, and the college catalog for the 1991–1992 academic year described a program in "Human Environment" that included courses in child and family development, family economics and management, and foods and nutrition, both the major and the program were being phased out and had disappeared by 1994.

The link that DeLucci (1997) makes between the liberal arts and elite institutions probably has some truth to it. Liberal arts degrees remain a major stepping-stone to graduate and professional schools, and one would expect more students from elite colleges than from CWC to take this step (Schleef, 2000). Nevertheless, as indicated earlier, the use of a liberal arts education as a first step to entering an elite profession is no less careerist than the use of a bachelor's degree to become a teacher or social worker.

In addition, evidence has been available for more than a hundred years to show that even the most elite institutions have made accommodations to careerism. Forty years before DeLucci did his study, the Institute of Higher Education at Columbia Teachers College undertook a study of liberal arts colleges. In an early report of this undertaking, Earl McGrath (1958) summarizes their review of both the mission statements and curricula of these colleges by asserting that "the programs of even the most conservative liberal arts colleges have been revolutionized in the past several decades through the addition of programs with specific vocational objectives" (p. 12). And, more recently, Scott (1991b) has documented several ways in which the "corporation–college connection" has been promoting career education throughout the United States, even in the elite Ivy League institutions and at what many consider to be the best liberal arts colleges.

For nonelite college students—especially for the women in this category—calls for a return to a more rigorous liberal arts education are based on a misleading promise. The long-standing claim for a rigorous liberal arts education is that it will make you a better person by helping you to develop what used to be called "mental discipline" and would now be called analytic or problem-solving ability. The dangers for women of a curriculum that emphasizes "being" a particular kind of person in a socio-cultural milieu that emphasizes "doing" seem to be even greater in this era of women's careerism than they were when Freedman (1956) described them in the 1950s.

The promise that the liberal arts will make one a more rational, thoughtful, and moral person also becomes misleading when efforts to teach students *how* to think disguise efforts to teach students *what* to think. Historically, much teaching in the liberal arts has been sexist, as well as classist and racist. The goal of the pioneering women's colleges to make women's liberal education as good as men's often meant developing a curriculum of courses in which women's experiences and accomplishments were either ignored or belittled. As a result, the liberating potential of the liberal arts, rooted in a critique of the social and cultural status quo (see Scott, 1991a; Wolff, 1992), has been even less likely to be realized by women than by men. Instead, the consequence of a liberal arts education for women has often been, either deliberately or unexpectedly, to strengthen gender traditionalism.

Unfortunately, careerism is not necessarily the antidote to gender traditionalism. Instead, careerism makes two promises that ignore both historical and contemporary realities for women. The first is the promise that a vocational or professional education will lead to a good job. If "good job" means one that is high-paying, prestigious, and powerful, then it is obvious that most women who graduate from college with vocational or preprofessional degrees—and especially graduates from nonelite schools— will not achieve "good jobs." Instead, as documented by many analysts (e.g., Thornborrow & Sheldon, 1995; Tomaskovic-Devey, 1993), jobs in the United States continue to be highly segregated, and most women continue to be employed either in traditional women's occupations or at lower level jobs in nontraditional fields.

The second misleading promise of careerism is that a good job will be the key to a good life. This promise ignores the major responsibility so many women continue to have for children and family life. An extensive research literature (e.g., Hochschild, 1989; Vannoy & Dubeck, 1998) documents the fact that both women who achieve "good jobs" and those who don't are finding it difficult to combine motherhood, family life, and occupational careers in ways that constitute what the women themselves would call a "good life."

Like many feminist educators (e.g., McCoy & DiGeorgio-Lutz, 1999), I believe that an emancipatory education would be one that helps women develop a sophisticated critique of the gender status quo in American society and enables them to make analytic linkages between this critique and their own biographies. Such an education is unlikely to come either from a return to a traditional liberal arts education in which paths to careers are unclear and male perspectives are universalized or from the kind of careerism that continues to make assumptions—even if they are occasionally updated—about what jobs are appropriate for women. What is needed, instead, is a gender-conscious education that encourages women to move beyond male-dominated models of what it means to be a good person with a good job and a good life. Unfortunately, this was *not* the educational vision that existed in the 1990s at CWC.

CHAPTER 5

Careerism Versus the Collegiate Life

Do women's colleges have collegiate cultures, and if so, what form do these cultures take and with what consequences? I begin this chapter by reviewing the answers given to these questions by other writers and researchers. Then I use information provided by both faculty and students to sketch a portrait of the collegiate culture at CWC. Next I examine the students who entered that culture in 1991 to determine how receptive they were to a collegiate culture and how that culture affected their social lives, academic achievements, and plans for the future. Finally, I discuss homosociality and heterosexuality as two major themes of collegiate cultures, and I assess the ways in which these themes were developed by the students at CWC.

COLLEGIATE CULTURES AT WOMEN'S COLLEGES

In contrast to her portrayal of "the college life" at men's colleges and co-educational institutions of the 19th and early 20th centuries, Horowitz's (1987) depiction of campus life at women's colleges is considerably more favorable:

> At Vassar and at the other Northern women's colleges, female undergraduates had a chance to define themselves on their own terms. They quickly developed a collective culture that they, too, called college life. It shared the independence and the exuberance of male college culture, but it lacked the hostile edge of its masculine counterpart. Women had not participated in the conflicts of the late eighteenth and early nineteenth centuries. They did not see themselves at war with their professors. Thus, though their self-assertion and hedonism conflicted with institutional goals, students in the women's colleges generally took their studies seriously. (pp. 195,197)

Much of the independence, hedonism, and exuberance to which Horowitz (1987) alludes took the form of activities that women students

initiated for themselves and their female peers. These included both im-
promptu and organized parties in dormitories; trips off campus for theater,
shopping, museums, and musical events; the formation on campus of a
variety of cultural, civic, political, and literary clubs; and even the formation of team sports (Inness, 1993).

By the 1920s, collegiate social activities were more likely to involve
men, and the "weekending habit" became a regular part of the routine at
women's colleges (Fass, 1977). Much of the weekending consisted of trips
by men to women's colleges and by women to men's colleges to attend
special social events. As a result, students at women's colleges, like the
women attending coeducational institutions, became increasingly involved
in what sociologist Willard Waller (1937) would later describe as "the rating
and dating complex." This complex is somewhat different from the courtship rituals that Farnham (1994) found to be central to student culture at
Southern women's colleges in the 19th century. Dating in the 1920s and
in the following decades sometimes led to courtship, but it was often a
different process designed to avoid marriage. Dating was more casual, more
public, and more under the control of men than the courtship rituals it
replaced.

One effect of the emphasis on dating was the disruption of some of
the homosocial activities at both men's and women's colleges. As the
Princetonian student newspaper noted in 1924, "The [male] students no
longer look forward to a weekend with [male] friends at Princeton as they
used to. They are much more interested in establishing friendly relations
with [women at] Vassar, Bryn Mawr and Spence" (quoted in Fass, 1977,
p. 205). Nevertheless, it would be a mistake to assume that dating became
a substitute for same-sex socializing and friendships. Instead, especially at
the women's colleges, the homosocial friendship networks and the heterosexual dating networks became increasingly intertwined. Women ar-
ranged dates for their friends, advised one another on dating etiquette,
evaluated each other's dates, and often accompanied one another on out-
ings with two men ("double dates") or with larger groups of dating couples.
Being a popular date gave college women prestige in their same-sex friendship networks, but these friendships were also used by college women to
facilitate dating. According to Lisa Handler (1995), this symbiotic relationship between friendship and dating has continued to the present time,
especially in sororities where "the sorority sisters' friendships, although
vulnerable to relationships with men, are, nevertheless, at least as important as their relationships with men" (p. 252).

Although dating rituals did not necessarily lead to courtship, marriage
rates for graduates from women's colleges accelerated greatly during the
20th century. A precise accounting was never kept, but both alumnae sur-

veys and national studies (e.g., Havemann & West, 1952) suggest that more than a third and possibly more than two thirds of all the students who graduated from women's colleges prior to World War I never married. Even in the period between the two World Wars, when the marriage rates for college-educated women increased, graduates were more likely than other women to delay marriage and to have a small number of children.

Most of the differences in marriage rates, age at first marriage, and family size between graduates of women's colleges and other women had disappeared by the 1950s when Nevitt Sanford and his colleagues undertook their study of students who entered Vassar College in 1953 and 1954 and graduated in 1957 and 1958 (Brown & Pacini 1993a,b; Bushnell, 1962; Sanford, 1956). The researchers found that almost all the students anticipated that they would marry at graduation or a few years later.

Little change in marital plans among students at women's colleges seems to have occurred during the next 30 years. When Mirra Komarovsky (1985) studied a cohort of students who attended Barnard College from 1979 to 1983, she found that only 1% of them expected to be unmarried. The major difference Komarovsky found between the women she studied and earlier cohorts who attended women's colleges was the increased emphasis on occupational careers. More than 90% of the women who attended Barnard from 1979 to 1983 expected to be career women. Even though many expected to work only part time or intermittently, this finding contrasts sharply with those that resulted from Komarovsky's (1953) earlier study at Barnard College and the study of Vassar College in the 1950s, mentioned above. Komarovsky's survey of the women who attended Barnard in 1943 revealed that 61% of the students preferred *not* to work after marriage. Similarly, in the study at Vassar, Freedman (1956) found that only about one third of the Vassar women were interested in graduate schooling and in careers, and both he and Bushnell (1962) report that few Vassar students of that period planned to continue with a career if it should conflict with family needs.

The greater emphasis on careers that Komarovsky (1985) found at Barnard in the 1980s, coupled with the continuing heavy emphasis on marriage, raises questions about the extent to which the collegiate culture for women, with its emphases on friendships, dating, possible courtships, and eventual marriage, is compatible with the high level of academic performance that is often necessary for a successful career. Both Fass (1977) and Horowitz (1987) have documented ways in which peer pressures *against* academic seriousness and good grades were characteristic of collegiate cultures at men's colleges and coeducational universities, at least prior to World War II. Did the collegiate culture also undermine the academic performance and career plans of students at women's colleges?

The answer seems to be "no." Although weekending had become frequent enough in the 1920s to cause alarm among officials at single-sex colleges (see Edwards, Artman, & Fisher, 1928), it is doubtful that the "weekending habit" undermined the academic performance of women students to any greater extent than did earlier forms of student hedonism based on same-sex activities. Fass (1977) reports that college women in the 1920s made better grades than college men. In addition, studies investigating how college students of the 1920s were spending their time revealed that students at women's colleges spent about as much time (and in some cases more) on their academic work as students at co-educational universities (Goldsmith & Crawford, 1928; Hutchinson & Connard, 1926).

Even in the marriage-oriented 1950s, women attending Vassar were found to be "dutiful, hard-working, and generally accepting of the College status quo and of the demands made upon them" (Freedman, 1956, p. 15). They accepted the academic and intellectual aims of the college and took their studies seriously. Of course, some students had stronger interests in intellectual activities and academic work than other students in their class. Students called the most academically oriented students "the super-intellectuals" or "science-major types," a group they contrasted to their more socially oriented peers, the "good-time Charlies" or "Yale-weekend girls" (Bushnell, 1962). When asked to discuss academic endeavors, however, none of the Vassar study participants denigrated good grades, not even the "good-time Charlies."

Nor did these marriage-oriented students spend all their time looking for a husband. Freedman (1956) reports that Vassar's student culture seems to have encouraged dating and interest in men, especially during the first year, but also discouraged "too much" dating and interest in men. "Too much" seems to have been defined as an amount of heterosexual activity that would interfere with an acceptable level of academic performance and on-campus friendships.

Similar findings are reported by Komarovsky (1985). The high commitment to marriage she found among Barnard women from 1979 to 1983 did not produce high levels of dating activities or interest in men. In addition, Komarovsky reports that no differences in dating behaviors were found between "Traditionals," who planned to marry and not have continuous careers, "Career Steadfasts," who were committed to occupational careers throughout their years at Barnard, and "Shifters to Careers," who became more career-oriented during college. When she compared these three groups of students, she found that all groups contained about the same proportion of nondaters, occasional daters, and past or current "steady" relationships. These and other findings in her book are consistent with the conclusion that seriousness about careers was unaffected by involvement in the culture of romance.

Research concerned with women's colleges suggests that the student cultures of these colleges—with the possible exception of those in the antebellum South (Farnham, 1994)—were dominated neither by rebellion against the academic culture of the faculty nor by obsessive concerns about heterosexual relationships. Nor does the evidence suggest that there were sharp conflicts at the women's colleges between social life and academic success, between social life and career plans, or between same-sex friendships and heterosexual relationships. Instead, the student cultures of women's colleges seem to have fostered a mix of academic achievement, career orientation, same-sex friendships, heterosexual concerns, and enjoyable leisure activities. In the following sections of this chapter, I explore the form this mixture took at CWC in the 1990s.

COLLEGIATE CULTURE AT CWC

To learn more about faculty perceptions of the student culture, we presented them with a list of statements about activities and relationships that might or might not be important to CWC students (Appendix B, Figure B.10). To assess the extent to which faculty thought the student culture was focused on same-sex and heterosexual relationships, I analyzed the faculty's ratings of the importance students would assign to seven different relationships, four with same-sex peers (friends in high school, friends in college, all women at the college, and their roommate) and three with opposite-sex peers (potential dating partners, men at Canterbury College, and potential steady boyfriends). By a large and significant margin, the faculty thought that the friendships the students had formed in high school and at CWC were more important to them than any of the other relationships.

Interestingly, the two ratings of friendship were at the same level as the faculty ratings of the importance students would assign to "their future jobs and careers," "their grades," and "their college major." According to the faculty, friendships, careers, grades, and majors clustered together as the most important concerns of the students at CWC. Significantly below these concerns were relationships with men, as well as concerns about "how much they were learning in their classes." Although the faculty tended to see the students as "Friendly Careerists," this did not mean that they thought the students were uninterested in their relationships with men. On average, the faculty thought these relationships were "somewhat important" to the students.

What did the students think? Did they also evaluate the campus culture as one that was dominated by "Friendly Careerists" rather than concerns about men? To answer this question, I examined the answers CWC students gave in spring of 1991 to a page of statements describing their peers. Respondents were asked to indicate how true each of these statements was of the students at CWC on a scale ranging from "true of few or no students at my college" to "true of all or most students at my college" (Appendix B, Figure B.11). Using the factor analytic technique described in Appendix C produced five different clusters, each of which could be considered one type of CWC student (see Appendix C, Table C.4).

I labeled the first type the "Well-Rounded Students" because it included statements indicating that the students were warm and supportive friends; friendly and concerned about others; serious students who wanted to learn; serious about their future careers; worried about their grades; and put their future careers ahead of getting married and having children. This profile is similar to the Friendly Careerists identified by the faculty, the major difference being that Well-Rounded Students are more academically oriented ("a serious student who wants to learn") than the Friendly Careerists who, according to the faculty, did not consider "how much they were learning in their classes" to be very important.

The second type could be called the "Narcissistic Libertarians" because it included statements indicating that students are snobbish, spend too much time worrying about their looks, want to make themselves as attractive as possible, use illegal drugs, think men are more interesting than women, and drink alcohol. This profile is consistent with stereotypes about the "Coed" who participates in collegiate life by being rebellious, self-centered, and male-oriented. This cluster also echoes some of the findings about sorority women reported in Chapter 3.

I labeled the third type "Husband-Hunting Libertines." The husband-hunting part of this label is indicated by the high loading on this factor of the statement that students "are anxious to find a good husband" and, less directly, by *dis*agreement with the statement that "they put their future careers ahead of getting married and having children." The libertine part of this label was suggested by the high loading on this factor of the statements that these students "care more about dating than studying" and "are having sexual relations with members of the opposite sex on a regular basis." The description of the Husband-Hunting Libertines is similar to the profile of the good-time Charlies who were identified at Vassar in the 1950s and on many other campuses since the 1920s.

The fourth and fifth factors were narrower than the first three. The fourth consisted of only two statements, namely, that students are politically conservative and that they are prejudiced against members of other races. For obvious reasons, I called students of this type the "Reactionaries." The last type of students identified by the factor analysis was characterized by only one statement: "They are in favor of equal rights for women and men." Again, the reason for the label I chose—the "Egalitarians"—is obvious. The finding that egalitarianism was independent of all of the other student types is not very surprising given the findings reported in Chapters 2 and 3 that gender egalitarianism was embraced by almost all of the students at CWC and was deeply embedded in the campus culture.

How common were these five types of students at CWC in 1991? Not surprisingly, the type of student considered to be most common was the Egalitarian. Of the 292 students who rated this type, 231 (79.1%) thought that many, most, or all students at CWC were Egalitarians. The type of student considered to be least common was the Reactionary. Only 52 (17.8%) of the students thought that many students at CWC were Reactionaries, and only seven (2.4%) thought most or all of them belonged in this category.

Of more relevance to the question of whether CWC had a collegiate culture are the ratings of the Well-Rounded Students, the Narcissistic Libertarians, and the Husband-Hunting Libertines. These three types were all rated as significantly less common than Egalitarians and significantly more common than Reactionaries. Of the three, Narcissistic Libertarians were considered the most common, followed by Husband-Hunting Libertines, with Well-Rounded Students rated as a less common type than the other two. Although the differences in these ratings were significant, they were small. On average, the students who rated these three types thought more than some students but fewer than many fit into each category. Only one student thought there were no Narcissistic Libertarians on campus, and no one thought there weren't any Husband-Hunting Libertines or Well-Rounded Students.

The profile of CWC students that emerges from the students' ratings is somewhat at odds with the profile suggested by the faculty ratings. Although the questions asked were not the same, the faculty did assign a relatively lower importance to relationships with men and a relatively higher importance to friendships, careers, and grades than did the students. These differences in perceptions of the student culture probably reflect differences in the interactions that CWC students had with faculty and peers. Students were far more likely to discuss their majors, grades, and career goals with faculty than their sex life or family goals. And faculty were far more likely to see students interacting with same-sex friends on campus than with their dating partners or other college men. In contrast, the peer culture was far more likely to continue the tradition, described earlier in this chapter, of aiding and evaluating dating relationships and opposite-sex partner choice.

And, as noted in Chapter 3, students were very likely to learn of the alcohol and drug use of at least some of their peers.

Instead of a clear yes or no answer to the question of whether the student culture at CWC was a collegiate culture, the data suggest that the culture contained collegiate elements but was not overwhelmed by them. No single profile of the "typical" CWC student emerged, and the ratings given to the various types suggest that the students who would be matriculating at CWC in 1991 were likely to encounter students who had some of the characteristics of the Friendly Careerist and the Well-Rounded Student as well as some of the more collegiate characteristics of the Narcissistic Libertarian and the Husband-Hunting Libertine.

SOCIAL ORIENTATIONS AMONG ENTERING STUDENTS

Given the mixture of student types and characteristics that existed at CWC in spring of 1991, it seemed likely that the group who matriculated that year would also contain some students whose orientation was more collegiate than the orientations of their peers. To determine who those students were, I used the same page of the survey and the same factor analysis that had been used in Chapter 4 to assess students' academic and career orientations (Appendix B, Figure B.7, and Appendix C, Table C.3). Students were asked to indicate how important it was to them that going to college would provide them with opportunities to engage in five different social behaviors: to meet interesting members of the opposite sex; to be a sorority member or independent; to party and have a good time; to find a husband; and to make new friends. The factor analysis had revealed that these five items formed a cluster, and responses to all five items were significantly correlated with one another. I labeled this cluster the Social Orientation scale and calculated a scale score for each entering student who completed our questionnaire based on the average amount of importance she assigned to each of these five opportunities.

These calculations revealed surprisingly low levels of social orientation among the entering students. As indicated in Chapter 4, 69.2% of these students had rated the opportunities on the Career Orientation scale to be very important or most important to them, but only 14.7% of these same students gave such high ratings to the Social Orientation scale. The average scores on this scale of all the entering students who participated in our survey indicated that they considered social opportunities to be somewhat important to them personally, but significantly and substantially less important than both career opportunities and academic opportunities.

Were the entering students *less* social, on average, than their contemporaries at other colleges and universities? The answer seems to be "yes." When Astin and his colleagues (1991) asked first-year college students in 1991 to evaluate various reasons for selecting one particular college from among the many available in this country, they included one socially oriented reason on the list. The exact wording of that reason was "This college has a good reputation for its social activities" (p. 107), and 23.2% of the women who entered 4-year colleges and 30.4% of women entering universities gave a rating of "very important" to this reason. Although we cannot be certain, it seems likely that the reason entering women students were somewhat less likely to bring a collegiate orientation to CWC than their contemporaries brought to other colleges or universities was because CWC was a women's college.

But some first-year students did come to CWC in 1991 looking for the collegiate life. Who were they, and how did they differ from their less socially oriented peers? To answer these questions, I divided the entering students into two groups, those who scored above the average on the Social Orientation scale (46.8% of the respondents) and those who scored below (53.2%). Then I set out to determine four things about these students. First, I wanted to know whether the high and low scorers on the Social Orientation scale came from different social-class backgrounds. Second, I wanted to determine whether having a high social orientation lowered academic orientation, achievements, and educational plans. Third, I was interested in what relationship, if any, social orientation had with the career orientation and plans of the entering students. And, fourth, I was interested in determining whether heterosexual relationships and family plans were related to social orientation.

Social-Class Background

My interest in the relationship between social-class background and social orientation was stimulated by the work of historians suggesting that students from the upper middle class and the upper class have taken a less serious approach toward their higher education than students from the middle class or the working class. One evidence for this social-class effect is the difference between the students' goals at Southern and Northern women's colleges in the antebellum period (Farnham, 1994). The Southern women who came primarily from the plantation-owning and professional classes looked to higher education as a finishing school where they could polish their social graces and become interesting conversationalists. In contrast, Northern women came from more modest economic circumstances and took higher education more seriously as an avenue to gainful professional employment, particularly teaching.

This regional class distinction also became a distinction within regions and schools. Affluent Northern women, who had avoided college throughout most of the 19th century, arrived on campuses in larger numbers at the end of that century. It was they, according to Horowitz (1987), who were primarily responsible for the development of the sorority system and women's participation in the collegiate life in the following decades. Even today, it is generally the case that sorority members come from higher social-class backgrounds than nonmembers, and a significant tendency in this direction was found at CWC and reported in Chapter 3. So I was curious about whether social class would also predict how CWC students scored on the Social Orientation scale.

It did. More than half (58.3%) of those who labeled themselves upper middle class or upper class had above-average Social Orientation scores, but among those who identified as middle, working, or lower class, only 37.5% had Social Orientation scores that were above average. Not surprisingly, this finding was supported by others showing significantly higher levels of education and occupational prestige among fathers of students with higher Social Orientation scores. Only a quarter (25.7%) of high scorers had fathers who had *not* been to college, compared with 40.5% of the low scorers. Although the mothers of students with higher social orientations had slightly more education, but slightly less prestigious jobs, and were slightly more likely to be unemployed housewives than the mothers of students with lower social orientations, none of these differences was statistically significant.

Because the social class measures had about the same association with social orientation as they had with sorority membership, it was not surprising to discover that those who were above average on social orientation were significantly more likely than the less socially oriented to join one of the CWC sororities (68.2% and 40.3%, respectively). What is more surprising and interesting is that this difference remained significant even when social class was controlled. These findings mean that social orientation had a positive effect on joining a sorority that was independent of social class. Regardless of which class a woman belonged to, she was more likely to join a sorority if she had a higher, rather than lower, social orientation.

Another interesting finding about social-class background is that it seemed to have little effect on the ways in which scores on the Social Orientation scale were related to academic matters, career orientations and goals, or social relationships and family plans. Except where social class is specifically mentioned, none of the significant findings about Social Orientation effects reported in this chapter was due to social class, nor did controlling for social class reveal that seemingly nonsignificant findings were actually significant within certain classes. The best conclusion seems to be that, regardless of social class, being more socially oriented produced some significant effects that could not be explained by students' social-class background. Nevertheless, the long-standing historical tradition in which women from higher social classes approached college with a more social orientation was continued at CWC.

Academic Orientations, Achievements, and Plans

Analyses of the effects of social orientation on academic orientations, achievements, and plans produced two revelations. First, they revealed only minor relationships between social orientation and academic matters. Second, they produced almost no evidence in favor of the notion that a high social orientation undercuts academic aspirations or achievements. There was a significant, positive, but barely moderate relationship between scores on the Social Orientation scale and scores on the Academic Orientation scale, indicating that the incoming students who were socially oriented were slightly *more* academically oriented than the incoming students who were below the average on social orientation.

As far as academic achievements were concerned, there was a small, significant, and negative correlation between the grade point averages (GPAs) students had accumulated in high school and their Social Orientation scale scores. This finding gives some weak support to the proposition that having a social orientation might undermine academic achievement. Contrary to this proposition, however, there was no significant relationship between scores on the Social Orientation scale and the educational plans students announced in the summer of 1991. Although they had a slight tendency to do so, students with lower social orientations were not significantly more likely to pick liberal arts majors or to plan more years of schooling than the students who were more socially oriented.

Career Orientations and Plans

Scores on the Social Orientation scale were found to be moderately and positively correlated with the Career Orientation scale, as they had been with the Academic Orientation scale. Incoming students who were socially oriented were slightly *more* career oriented than incoming students who were below the average on social orientation. And the Strivers who were identified in Chapter 4 as students who gave "very important" ratings to both the Career and Academic Orientation scales also scored higher, on average, than other students on the Social Orientation scale. Sixty percent of the Strivers scored above average on social orientation compared with 42.9% of the Intellectuals, 41.7% of the Careerists, and 39.0% of the Unconnecteds.

Social orientation also had a significant relationship with career plans. One measure of career plans asked respondents to imagine themselves 20 years in the future and to indicate whether they planned to be full-time housewives or employed and, if the latter, whether they planned to be working full time or part time. Regardless of their social orientation, a majority of students expected to be working full time, but the proportion expecting to do so was significantly lower among those with a high social orientation. In that group, 76.1% planned to work full time, but among those with below average social orientations, an impressive 92.7% had the same plan. This finding suggests that, as a group, those with higher social orientations had somewhat weaker commitments to careers. Not much weaker, however, because only 4.2% of students in this group planned to be full-time housewives; the remaining 19.7% planned to work part time.

What kinds of careers did these students plan to have? Students who were more socially oriented were significantly more likely to choose sex-typed occupations than students who were below average on social orientation, and the latter were significantly more likely than their more socially oriented peers to choose untyped occupations. Sex-typed occupations included both those defined in Chapter 4 as predominantly male occupations and those defined as predominantly female occupations. Untyped occupations were those in which the gender composition was 40%–60% male and female. Among those whose social orientation was below average, 60.3% chose untyped jobs, but among those who were above average on social orientation, 59.1% chose sex-typed occupations, with 37.9% choosing those that were female-typed and 21.2% opting for male-typed occupations. Because many of the gender-typed jobs were either elite professions (e.g., lawyers) or traditional women's professions (e.g., teachers), this finding could be interpreted to mean that high scorers on the Social Orientation scale were more likely than low scorers to choose professional jobs.

Heterosexual Relationships and Family Plans

Social orientations also were significantly correlated with entering students' dating behaviors and intimate relationships with men. These were measured by presenting respondents with a list of statements and asking them to indicate which one best described their relationships with members of the opposite sex at the present time. Six different relationships were presented as options. The first two—"I am presently married" and "I am presently engaged"—were selected by only 2.0% of the respondents, and all of them had scored below average on the Social Orientation scale. The third option—"Although I am not engaged or married, I have a relationship with one person"—was chosen by about half of both the above-average and below-average scorers on the Social Orientation scale (48.6% and 54.3%, respectively). The fourth and fifth options yielded the significant difference between the more and less socially oriented students. Among the more socially oriented, 27.8% selected the statement that read, "I am dating more than one person at the present time," and 19.4% selected the next statement, "I am not dating anyone at the present time although I would be interested in doing so." Among the less socially oriented, only 11.1% said they were dating more than one person, and 28.4% said they weren't dating but would be interested in doing so. The last statement—"I am not dating anyone at the present time, and I have no interest in doing so"— was endorsed by only 4.2% of the high social orientation group and only 2.5% in the low group.

Despite significant differences in the dating patterns of those having higher and lower social orientations, the marital plans of the two groups were only slightly, and not significantly, different. The overwhelming majority in both groups—98.6% of the high scorers and 91.6% of the low scorers—believed that they would marry within the next 20 years, and most also expected to have children. Interestingly, in this era of rising rates at the national level of both cohabitation without marriage and single-parent families, not a single entering student at CWC selected the choice on the survey that read, "I will be unmarried with one child or more."

When asked about the number of children they planned to have, the more socially oriented opted for larger families than did their less socially oriented peers. Only 8.2% of the more socially oriented expected to be married without children compared with 13.3% of the less socially oriented. In both groups, the majority—65.7% of highs and 61.5% of lows—expected to have one or two children, but 24.7% of all those who scored high on the Social Orientation scale expected to have three or more children, whereas only 16.9% of the less socially oriented had this expectation.

Summary of Findings About Social Orientations of Entering Students

Taken together, the findings indicate that at the time they entered CWC, students who were above average on social orientation were somewhat— but not overwhelmingly—different from those who scored below average. Compared to their less socially oriented peers, the more socially

oriented were more likely to be dating, more interested in joining a sorority, and more interested in professional, rather than business or mana-
gerial, careers. They were also less committed to full-time careers but
more committed to marrying and having children. In contrast to the
Collegiate Coeds identified in the historical literature, they had not allowed their social orientation to interfere with their academic performance in any major way; their grades in high school were only slightly
lower, on average, than those of their less socially oriented peers, and
their scores on the scales measuring career orientation and academic
orientation were significantly higher.

What happened to the socially oriented (and less socially oriented)
women after they matriculated at CWC? Once they were no longer living
with their parents, did their social life begin to take on greater importance?
Did it interfere with their academic work and undermine careerism? Did
they become Husband-Hunting Libertines or Narcissistic Libertarians? Or
did they evolve into Well-Rounded Students? The next two sections of
this chapter provide some answers to these questions.

PARTICIPATING IN A YEAR OF THE COLLEGIATE CULTURE

The levels of social orientation that students brought with them to college
had significant effects on them during their first year at CWC. In this section of the chapter, I focus on three kinds of effects. First is the extent to
which more or less socially oriented students also became more or less
male-oriented. Second is the effect of social orientation on the kinds of
relationships with men CWC women formed or maintained during their
first year. Third is an assessment of the impact of social orientations on
students' academic performance.

In order to clearly understand these developments, it is necessary to
take account not only of the different level of social orientation students
brought with them to the college but also of whether or not they joined a
sorority. As noted above, first-year students who entered CWC in 1991
with higher levels of social orientation were more likely than those with
lower levels to join a sorority, but there were numerous exceptions. Almost
two fifths of the sorority pledges from the first-year class (39.2%) had
scored *below* average on the Social Orientation scale, and almost a third of
the first-year students who remained independent of the sororities (32.8%)
had scored *above* average on the Social Orientation scale. This section of
the chapter documents the fact that both sorority membership and social
orientation had partly overlapping, partly independent effects on the social
lives of first-year students at CWC.

Evaluating Peer Relationships

One set of findings that showed a difference between the effects of sorority membership and social orientation were the findings that resulted from
asking the first-year students in spring of 1992 to indicate the extent to
which seven different relationships were important to their own evaluations of themselves (Appendix B, Figure B.5). The relationships were the
same ones about which the faculty had been asked, and it turned out that
the faculty were correct in assuming that most of the students would give
higher importance ratings to the friendships they had formed at CWC than
to their relationships with the three kinds of male peers (dating partners,
all men at Canterbury College, or a steady boyfriend) about whom they
were asked.

Although this pattern of responses was true of both those who scored
above average and those who scored below average on the Social Orientation scale, there were significant differences between these two groups
in their ratings of men. Compared to the students who were less socially
oriented, those who were more socially oriented gave higher importance
ratings, on average, to being asked out on dates, to the men at Canterbury College, and to whether or not they had a steady boyfriend. These
differences remained significant when sorority membership was controlled,
and they were the only ratings of the seven relationships that were significantly affected by levels of social orientation. These findings support
two conclusions. First, social orientation had no effects on the importance
of relationships with same-sex peers, including high school friends, college friends, women at CWC, and roommates. Second, socially oriented
women exhibited significantly more "male orientation" than did less
socially oriented women.

Significant differences in the importance assigned to relationships also
appeared when the ratings of sorority members were compared to those
of independents, but the pattern of differences was not the same as the
one just described. Instead, sorority members assigned significantly more
importance than independents did to relationships with men at Canterbury College, a steady boyfriend, college friends, and women at CWC. All
of these differences remained significant when social orientation was controlled. Taken together, these findings support the conclusion that sorority members were somewhat more "peer oriented" than independents.
Regardless of their level of social orientation, sorority members assigned
greater importance not only to relationships with men but also to some
(but not all) of their relationships with same-sex peers.

One other difference between the way in which sorority members and
independents evaluated relationships *was* affected by the students' levels

of social orientation. This difference was the significantly higher importance sorority women, compared to independents, gave to dating. When
social orientation was controlled, this difference was no longer significant.
The reason for this change is that sorority members with low levels of social
orientation actually assigned slightly less importance to dating than did
independents who had high levels of social orientation. As noted above,
it was high social orientation more than sorority membership that promoted a "male orientation" among CWC students.

Forming Relationships With Men

Nevertheless, sororities played an important role in promoting dating behaviors among their members. When students were asked in spring of 1992
to respond to the same set of statements about their current relationship
with members of the opposite sex that they had responded to the previous summer, more than half of all sorority members said that they were
currently in a relationship with one person of the opposite sex, and the
proportion selecting this response was about the same for those with above-
average social orientations (57.8%) as for those whose social orientations
were below average (55.2%). If those who reported that they were currently dating more than one person and the two who had become engaged
are added, the proportion of all sorority women involved in relationships
with men rises to 75.6% for those with high social orientations and 79.3%
for those with low social orientations.

The contrast between these figures and those for the independent
women is striking. Among independents, 61.9% of more socially oriented
women and 44.2% of less socially oriented women were involved in relationships with one or more men. More than half (55.8%) of independents
who scored below average on the Social Orientation scale reported that
they were not dating anyone at the present time, although almost half
(48.8%) said they were interested in doing so.

Comparing these findings for the four groups of women with the responses they had given the summer before they matriculated reveals the
importance of joining a sorority and attending a women's college on students' relationships with men. For women who were highly socially oriented, joining a sorority allowed about the same proportion of them to
have relationships with men as had reported such relationships before
coming to CWC. For the group of women who were low on social orientation, joining a sorority enabled a higher proportion of them to date or
establish heterosexual relationships than had been able to do so before
coming to CWC. Among independents, the proportions of both those high
and those low on social orientation who were not dating, even though

they wanted to, was about twice as large as it had been the previous summer. Although more socially oriented independents were more likely to have heterosexual relationships in spring of 1992 than those less socially oriented, this difference had also been true (and of about the same size) the previous summer.

These findings suggest that sororities were able to compensate for the dampening effect that attending CWC had on the heterosexual activity of independent women. Sororities promoted the rating and dating complex by activating their linkages to fraternities at nearby colleges and universities, especially Canterbury College, by attending social events off campus, by sponsoring social events on campus, by encouraging new pledges to attend social events both on and off campus, and by helping new pledges to find suitable dates. A sorority member I've named Ronna informed us that meeting guys was the major reason first-year students joined sororities. The older members made certain that pledges met potential dating partners.

Ronna made her comment during an interview in which students were asked to talk about whether relations with the opposite sex and sex itself had been concerns of their classmates during their first year at CWC (Appendix D, Interview I). Over and over again, the women we interviewed stressed the importance of the men at Canterbury College to the social and sexual lives of CWC students. For example, what Ronna actually said was: "They [the older sorority members] take you over there [to Canterbury College], and they introduce you and everything."

Trudi was one of several students who mentioned one of the outcomes of these introductions: "At the beginning of the year there were an awful lot of girls staying at [Canterbury] all night long." Students referred to this practice as "shacking," and there seemed to be some confusion among the students about whether shacking always involved sexual intercourse. Mandi assumed that it did and contrasted shackers to other students who were more cautious sexually: "I'm sure there's people [CWC students] that are shacking over at [Canterbury] every night, but (laughs) for the most part, I think everyone is just kind of crossing her legs (laughs) and just kind of taking it just a little easier." Rose wasn't so sure what shacking meant: "Some [CWC students] go out and they can just shack with someone [but] not necessarily sleep with them or sleep next to them, you know." And Theresa was firmly convinced that all the AIDS posters in her dorm had produced one of their intended effects: "So many girls have, like, they've shacked over at [Canterbury] and things like that, but no [sexual intercourse] because they're too scared; so, it won't happen." Although Trudi, Mandi, Rose, and Theresa were all sorority members, independents were also aware of the importance of Canterbury College as a place to meet men, and they also talked about shacking.

One of the major differences between sorority women and independents to emerge from the interviews was the large number of complaints
by sorority members about the social scene and the men at Canterbury
College. Although complaints often focused on the difficulty in finding
men who would "treat them right," the fact that sorority women were
so much more concerned than independents about this problem suggests
that other factors were also at work. In particular, it became clear from
the interviews that those sorority women who did not already have relationships with men felt themselves to be under much more pressure
than the independents to establish such relationships. This pressure, in
turn, heightened their sense of competition and their resentment of the
Canterbury men.

In contrast to the noticeable effects of sorority membership on the
concerns expressed about opposite-sex relationships, it was difficult to
detect any systematic effects of social orientation levels in the interviews.
Although it is possible that this finding may have resulted from our decision to use an indirect method of probing into students' sex lives, it also
seems likely that the result may have reflected what was happening to
some of the less socially oriented students. Those who were sorority members spent the year "catching up" with the dating and mating rates of the
more socially oriented sorority women. To get this done, they probably
felt even more pressure than other sorority women to become concerned
with opposite-sex relationships and to link up with men at Canterbury
College and elsewhere. This must have been particularly difficult for them
because, as noted earlier, they assigned less personal importance to dating than did more socially oriented students, both sorority members and
independents.

Continuity and Change in Academic Achievements

To examine the effects on grades of both social orientation and sorority
membership, students were divided into four categories. Sorority members who scored low on social orientation were found to have the best first-
semester GPA (3.24), followed by independents who scored low on social
orientation (GPA = 3.07), followed by sorority members who had high
social orientations (GPA = 2.92), followed by independents with high social
orientations (GPA = 2.59). As these GPA rankings indicate, both social
orientation and sorority membership had significant, independent effects
on GPAs, with the effect of social orientation being greater than the effect
of sorority membership.

As most people would expect, high school GPAs also had significant
effects on GPAs earned during the first semester at CWC, indicating that

students who got better grades in high school also got better grades in college. Even with high school grades controlled, however, the effects of both social orientation and sorority membership on first-semester GPAs remained significant. In contrast to independents with low social orientations whose grades improved somewhat (but not significantly) between high school and their first college semester and sorority members whose grades changed hardly at all, independents with high social orientations saw their grades significantly worsen. Taken together, these findings about GPA support the conclusion that the higher social orientations some students brought with them to college worked against their higher academic orientations by either maintaining the significantly lower GPAs they brought with them (in the case of those who joined sororities) or lowering their grades even further (in the case of the independents).

The summer before the students matriculated, there had been only weak evidence that a high social orientation undercut their grades. After the students had left home and spent a few months at CWC, such evidence increased. The importance assigned to relationships with men, coupled with partying and shacking, was interfering with academic work. The students with higher social orientations had adopted the sexual behaviors, high interest in dating, and lower interest in studying that were included in the profile of the Husband-Hunting Libertines sketched by CWC students a year earlier. The first-year students may not have been interested in marriage, however, at least not immediately. Only one woman we interviewed said that the first-year students were looking for husbands and permanent relations, but almost all described behaviors of some students that would qualify them for the identity label of *Man-Hunting Libertines*.

PARTICIPATING IN 4 YEARS OF THE COLLEGIATE CULTURE

What happened to the Man-Hunting Libertines and the other first-year students in subsequent years at CWC? Did the importance of their relationships with men and their success in finding dating partners increase or decrease? Did their levels of social orientation and sorority memberships continue to affect their social lives and academic performance? Did career commitments and family plans undergo significant changes? To answer these and related questions, I examined the responses that *graduates* of CWC gave to the survey they participated in at the end of their college careers. I compared these responses to the responses that those same students had given in the summer of 1991 and in the spring of 1992.

Evaluating Peer Relationships

The final survey asked students about the importance of four relationships
with female and male peers they had been asked about in spring of 1992:
precollege friendships; friendships made while attending college; whether
men were asking them for dates; and whether they had an opposite sex
partner or not (see Appendix B, Figure B.6). To determine whether social
orientations or sorority membership had affected the importance of any
of these relationships *after* their first year, I controlled for the first rating
made by each student.

With both first ratings and sorority membership controlled, the findings for social orientation can be summarized by saying, first, that the effect
of social orientation on male orientation did not change from the first year
to graduation and, second, that during this same period, the effect of social
orientation on peer orientation increased. The first conclusion is based on
the findings that—with first ratings controlled—social orientation had no
significant effects on ratings of either being asked by men for dates or
having a male partner. Although women with high social orientations gave
significantly more importance to dating and male partners than did women
with lower social orientations, these differences were a continuation of
the differences that had already been present during the students' first year
at CWC. Continuing to attend CWC after the first year did not make socially
oriented women more male oriented.

The second conclusion is based on the finding that—even with first
ratings controlled—social orientation had significant effects on ratings of
friendships made while attending college. Women with above-average
social orientations rated these friendships significantly more important than
did women with below-average social orientations, something they had
not done at the end of their first year. This finding that women with higher
scores on the Social Orientation scale became significantly more peer oriented during their years at CWC than did women who were less socially
oriented was true of both sorority women and independents.

In contrast to the broader effects of social orientation at graduation than
during the first year of college, sorority membership actually had fewer significant effects on importance-ratings of relationships at graduation than it
had at the end of the first year when sorority members were found to be
more peer oriented than independents. At graduation, the only one of the
four relationships that sorority members rated significantly more important
than did independents was dating, and the difference in the ratings given
by the two groups was larger at graduation than it had been during the first
year. There were two reasons for this widened gap: Sorority members, especially those with low social orientations, increased the importance they

assigned to dating during their years at CWC, and independents decreased the importance they assigned to dating during this same period.

Heterosexual Relationships

To understand why some sorority women became more concerned about dating, it is useful to look at how graduating CWC students responded to the same set of statements about relationships with members of the opposite sex that we had presented them with in the two previous surveys. As we had done before, we asked them to pick the one statement that best described their own relationship at the present time. At the end of their first year, more than 70% of sorority members who eventually graduated from CWC had been actively involved with men—either by partnering with one or by dating more than one—and this was true of members with both high and low social orientations. By graduation, this figure had risen to 82.1% for the sorority members who had high levels of social orientation, and only two members of this group were still dating multiple partners; the rest had established a relationship with one man, including one marriage and seven engagements. Only 17.9% of the socially oriented sorority women were not dating or in a partnership, but all of them said they were interested in doing so.

In contrast, the proportion of sorority members with below-average social orientations who had established a relationship with one man had dropped to 57.1%, and all the rest (42.9%) indicated that they were not currently dating although they were interested in doing so. The proportion of sorority women with low social orientations looking for dates was about 40% more than the proportion of graduating independents, regardless of levels of social orientation, who were also looking (30.3%). The dating that sororities had been able to facilitate among first-year members with low social orientations had declined considerably by the time those members became seniors.

Although help in finding dates had declined, pressure to find them had not. Because this pressure to be involved in the rating and dating complex was specifically focused on having male partners for dances, parties, and other social events in which the sorority was involved, members, in comparison to independents, became more concerned about dating— but not more peer oriented—during their years at CWC.

Reconciling the Collegiate and Academic Cultures

Despite the increase in the importance sorority women assigned to dating, their GPAs did not decline during their years at CWC. Graduating sorority women who were more socially oriented had first-semester GPAs of 2.96, and those who were less socially oriented had GPAs of 3.27. At graduation, these same two groups of women had GPAs of 3.24 and 3.29, respectively. As these figures indicate, the grades of the less socially oriented sorority members were consistent throughout their undergraduate years, but the grades of the more socially oriented sorority members increased significantly from their first semester to graduation. An examination of grades on a year-by-year basis shows that this was a gradual increase, with the GPA gap between these two groups of sorority women getting smaller with each year of undergraduate school. Obviously, by graduation there was no longer any significant effect of social orientation on GPAs of sorority members.

Among independents who graduated from CWC, those who had scored above average on the Social Orientation scale were also able to close the gap between their average GPA and the average GPA of their less socially oriented counterparts. By graduation, the GPAs of the more and less socially oriented independents were 3.22 and 3.28, respectively, compared with 3.02 and 3.30 for these same women at the end of the first semester. This finding coupled with those just reported for sorority members gives clear evidence that the significant effect of social orientation on GPA that had occurred during the first year at CWC was a temporary phenomenon. By graduation, the sizable effect of social orientation on first-semester grades had been eliminated.

As had been true at matriculation, social orientation continued to have no significant effects on educational choices students made at CWC. Among both those who scored above average and those who scored below on social orientation, 82% of the students had vocational majors at graduation. Although there seemed to be some difference between the educational plans of the two groups, with 61.9% of the socially oriented planning to complete educational programs beyond the baccalaureate degree versus only 37.5% of the less socially oriented, this difference proved to be due to social class. Within social-class categories, social orientation had no sizable or significant effects on educational plans. The findings for sorority membership were identical to those for social orientation. Sorority membership had no effect on whether a student chose a vocational or liberal arts major, and its seeming effect on educational plans was due to the higher social-class background of sorority members. Although social class had no effects on the educational plans of matriculating CWC students, it had strong, significant effects on those plans at graduation.

The significant effects that social orientation had on career choices and family plans prior to matriculation had disappeared by graduation. Compared to the less socially oriented graduates, socially oriented graduates

were no longer significantly more likely to choose gender-typed or professional careers, to say that they would marry and have more children,
or to plan on working less than full time in the future.

Regardless of social orientation, sorority membership, or social class,
almost three quarters of graduating CWC students (73.0%) who told us
their career and family plans at both the beginning and end of their college careers expected to be employed full time 20 years after they completed each of our questionnaires. This proportion is more than twice as
large as the proportion of Career Steadfast students found by Komarovsky
(1985) at Barnard College only 12 years earlier. Of the Career Steadfast
graduates at CWC, only one expected to be unmarried and without children 20 years after graduation; only one other expected to be unmarried,
but cohabiting, with children at that same time; and five expected to be
married without children. All the rest expected to marry and have children. Of all the Career Steadfast students, more than one fourth (26.7%)
said that they would continue working full time even when their children
were infants or preschoolers, with another quarter (26.7%) saying they
would cut back to part-time work during this period. Almost all of the
Career Steadfast graduates from CWC (98.3%) expected to be back to work,
most of them (86.7%) full time, by the time their children entered elemen-
tary school.

Only two CWC students (2.7%) met the criteria necessary to fit into
Komarovsky's (1985) Traditional category. One of these expected at both
matriculation and graduation to be a full-time married homemaker with
children, and the other reported at both points in time that she expected
to be married, have children, and work only part time. The remaining
quarter (24.3%) of the students were Shifters, with exactly one third of
them being Shifters to Careers and the remaining two thirds being Shifters
to Non-Careers. All of these figures contrast sharply with those reported
by Komarovsky, who classified one quarter of the students she studied in
the Traditional category, another quarter in the Shifters to Careers category, and only 9% in the Shifters to Non-Careers category.

Despite the somewhat higher proportion of Shifters to Non-Careers
among the CWC students (16.2%), there can be no doubt that many more
of the CWC students were committed to careers than were members of
the class of 1983 at Barnard. Even among the Shifters to Non-Careers, not
a single graduate of CWC shifted to full-time homemaking. All Shifters to
Non-Careers expected to work part time, and more than half of them
expected to be working full time when their children were in high school
and college.

Although the Shifters to Non-Careers had certainly not abandoned
their entire commitment to occupations and careers, they are similar to

Southern University women described by Holland and Eisenhart (1990) as having scaled down their career ambitions between the time they entered college and the time they graduated. Early in their book, Holland and Eisenhart indicate that the scaling-down process, characteristic of two thirds of the women they interviewed, was due to these women's involvement in the culture of romance, but later they describe a more complex process:

> The women's experience in the world of romantic relationships both affected and were affected by their experiences with schoolwork. . . . As their career identities eroded, their focus on romantic relationships increased. Next their efforts at schoolwork decreased, then their rewards from it decreased, and their focus on romantic relationships further increased. (p. 213)

The scaling-down process at CWC seems to have operated somewhat differently. Social orientation, sorority membership, success in finding dates or in establishing a male-female partnership were all reasonable indicators of involvement in the collegiate culture of romance at CWC, but *none* of these indicators differentiated the Shifters to Non-Careers, who scaled down their career ambitions, from the Shifters to Careers, who scaled up. Nor were these two groups different from each other or from their peers in the kinds of marital and child-bearing plans they had for the future. Particularly surprising were the results of an analysis of the students who *changed* their family plans while at college. These students constituted 15.8% of CWC graduates who let us know both sets of plans, and half of them switched from planning to have children to planning not to have them, whereas the other half made the opposite switch. Every single one of these students, regardless of the direction of her switch in child-bearing plans, was a Career Steadfast student. The reasons for switching their family planning were unrelated to the amount of their career commitments.

What did differentiate the Shifters to Careers from the Shifters to Non-Careers were their grades. As a group, Shifters to Careers had higher GPAs from their first semester to their last than did Shifters to Non-Careers. By graduation, the median GPA for those who had scaled down their career ambitions was 3.2, but the median GPA for Shifters to Careers was 3.7, and only one student in this group (compared with 33.3% of the Shifters to Non-Careers) had a GPA below 3.1. The grades of the Shifters to Non-Careers were not low enough to put their graduation in jeopardy, but they seem to have been weak enough by CWC standards to have caused students to lower their career ambitions. In contrast, the significantly higher grades of the Shifters to Careers seem to have encouraged them to get more seriously committed to full-time careers.

Possibly, the difference between findings at CWC and at Southern University is due to a weaker culture of romance at women's colleges compared to that at coeducational universities. Although a single-case study cannot disprove this explanation, it gains little support from the interviews we conducted with CWC students. They indicated a fairly high level of commitment to the culture of romance, including frequent desperation to find dates and male partners.

Another reason for the difference might be higher academic standards at Southern University than at CWC. As Dahlia told me in her senior year at CWC:

> I've done a substantial amount of partying, and I've enjoyed my classes. The curriculum here is up to par, but it's not so hard that it doesn't allow for free time. As far as on the whole, yeah, it's been a great experience. Heck of a trip.

Had Dahlia faced the kind of rigorous science and mathematics curriculum in which half of the students interviewed at Southern University were enrolled, it is likely that she either would have had less time for partying or would have had to scale down her career. Consider, for example, the plight of Linda, a student described by Holland and Eisenhart (1990):

> Once in college, Linda had difficulty maintaining the high grade point average she had come to expect of herself in high school. She spent long hours laboring over schoolwork. "I'm worrying all the time," she told us. "I even feel guilty if I'm not studying." After barely a semester at college, she decided that despite her hard work she could not make the grade-point average required to get into the specialized therapy program she was interested in. She was very much disappointed. (p. 4)

Linda's story is a familiar one to all faculty who have watched valedictorians from academically weak high schools be amazed and overwhelmed by the competition of university classmates who have been better educated at stronger high schools.

Given the frequency with which poor grades are cited as reasons for down-scaling careers at Southern University (see, e.g., Holland & Eisenhart, 1990, pp. 181–201), one cannot help but wonder if at Southern, as at CWC, it was grades more than involvement in the collegiate culture of romance that prompted women to lower their career aspirations. Even if this was not the case at Southern, it is clear that at CWC the negative effects of the collegiate culture on students' grades was a temporary phenomenon largely confined to the first year. Although some man-hunting, libertine, and libertarian behaviors continued, the students who remained to graduate became more similar to the Friendly Careerists and Well-Rounded Students previously described by their faculty and peers. Apparently, they learned how to deal with both the collegiate culture and the academic and careerist demands of the faculty. Some did so by dropping out of the rating and dating game, a few others by down-scaling their career ambitions, but many were able to combine an active social life, good grades, and a high level of family and career aspirations. The opportunity to do this may been one of the major advantages offered to students by a nonelite women's college where neither the academic demands nor the social pressures were overwhelming.

HOMOSOCIALITY AND HETEROSEXUALITY IN THE COLLEGIATE CULTURE

Throughout this chapter I have referred to relationships between women as homosocial and those between women and men as heterosexual. I have done so because I believe that these two terms capture the assumptions that are made in almost all writings about collegiate cultures and sororities. To describe a relationship as heterosexual is to make two assumptions. The first rests on the literal meaning of heterosexual relationship, namely, that the relationship is between members of different sexes, and despite a growing literature revealing the arbitrariness of sexual categories (e.g., Connell, 1999; Kessler, 2000), "different sexes" is assumed to refer to males and females. The other assumption is that the male-female relationship either includes sexual and romantic activities or has the potential for doing so. To describe a relationship as homosocial is also to make two assumptions. The first is that the relationship is between persons of the same sex, and the second is that the relationship does *not* include sexual and romantic activities and should *not* include such activities in the future.

At CWC, as in many other venues, relationships among women were assumed to be homosocial, and relationships between women and men were assumed to be heterosexual. Because these two kinds of relationships were taken for granted as normal relationships, they were never explained. Interviewers were expected to know—and they did—that when a student talked about her or another woman's "boyfriend," she was talking about a heterosexual relationship. But when that student talked about her or another woman's "girlfriend," she meant a homosocial relationship lacking in sexual activity and romantic potential.

The normalizing assumptions about heterosexuality and homosociality served to marginalize or erase two other kinds of relationships: heterosocial and homosexual relationships. Strictly speaking, one could define hetero-social relationships as comparable to homosocial relationships in their focus on friendship that lacks sexual activity and romantic potential. In practice, however, the line between heterosocial and heterosexual relationships is rarely seen as rigid and impenetrable. Instead, male-female friendships are often seen—by others if not by the participants—as having sexual and ro-mantic potential. In contrast, much social effort goes into maintaining the line between homosocial and homosexual relationships and into denying the sexual and romantic potential of same-sex friendships.

Evidence for the permeability of the heterosocial and heterosexual distinction came from the students we interviewed. Although a few of them talked about male-female relationships that may have been heterosocial, they never ruled out the possibility that these relationships could become romantic or sexually active. The comments by Ella are typical of this mix-ing together of the heterosocial and the heterosexual:

> A lot of the girls want a boyfriend and want to get close to a guy or whatever and they go out and get fixed up . . . and a lot of [other] girls just want guys for friends which is good, too, but I mean guys are a real important issue. . . . We're always talking about guys . . . I think we're at the age where that's an important factor of our life and high on the priority list.

Another example of the mixing of (presumably) heterosocial relation-ships and heterosexual activities was offered by Francie, whose comment suggests that men friends, like acceptable dating partners, could improve women's standing in the rating and dating complex:

> Seems like a lot of girls really don't have boyfriends; they just kind of date around. But they have a lot of friends. . . . Some of them are kind of promiscuous, but that's going to be true everywhere. . . . I think they're more concerned about having male friends than they are about female friends, to an extent. . . . Because I think that they think that if they have so many guy friends that they'll be more accepted and, like, when [they] go to parties [they] can talk to him and him and him.

Not a single student we interviewed in the spring of 1992 focused her attention primarily on relationships with men that were *not* based on heterosexual assumptions. Nor did any of them compare and con-trast heterosexual relationships to other kinds of male-female relation-ships based on other kinds of assumptions.

Although the question in our interview about whether CWC women were concerned about relationships with men presented students the opportunity to talk in detail about women who weren't and why they weren't, not a single woman did so. Only three of the students we interviewed alluded to homosexuality, and Ardyth was the only one of them to indicate that homosexual activities might be going on at CWC when she said, "There might be some people here [at CWC] that are interested in turning on other girls but I'm not into that." Then, brushing this topic aside, she immediately returned to her earlier commentary on CWC women's relationships with men: "I think that it's like, it's kind of like a hobby, you know, chasing after a guy, you know, it's something to do."

Although not as directly, the other two first-year students who alluded to homosexual relationships echoed Ardyth's blunt "I'm not into that" by distancing not themselves but other CWC students from the possibility of being in violation of heterosexual assumptions. Of the two, Doris was the more direct in her reference to homosexuality: "I know a lot of girls who'd rather be with their, you know, girlfriends. Not with, I'm not saying they're kind of strange or anything." Dara's comments were more ambiguous: "They worry about not having a boyfriend, not having somebody steady. . . . And they almost seem willing to just latch on to whoever comes along just so that they can have somebody and people won't think they're strange or they're not fitting in or something, you know?" Whether or not Dara thought that "strange" and "not fitting in" meant having or wanting homosexual relationships, as I suspect she did, it is clear that she thought the way to be normal and acceptable at CWC was to have relationships that were heterosexual.

The marginalizations and erasures of homosexuality at CWC contrast sharply with the report by Bromley and Britten (1938) that in the 1920s campus leaders in several of the larger women's colleges made "out and out homosexuality" something of a fad (p. 118). The fad seems to have died out by 1938 when Bromley and Britten published the results of their recently completed study of 1,364 undergraduates attending 46 different colleges and universities in the United States. Although homosexuality was not as prominent as it had been a decade earlier, Bromley and Britten identified "the homosexually inclined" as one of their six main groups of undergraduate women, and they devoted a chapter of their book to this group.

The study led by Sanford (1956) that was conducted at Vassar in the more repressive 1950s seems to have ignored the topic of homosexuality entirely, but Komarovsky (1985) reports that two of the Barnard students she interviewed in 1979, 1980, and 1983 identified themselves as lesbians, that the college had a lesbian club, that the college newspaper had published lengthy articles based on discussions with members of the lesbian club, and that a course on the topic of the lesbian in literature had been offered at the college.

Why were self-identifications and activities of this type absent from CWC, and why were even the words *homosexuality* and *lesbianism* never used by the students we interviewed? A convincing answer was provided by Jolene, who had been a member of the entering class at CWC in 1991 but had left the college at the end of her sophomore year. A year later, she enrolled in another women's college in the region that I will call Roberts College for Women, a college Jolene found more to her liking than CWC. In my lengthy interview with her, she discussed many differences between the two colleges. One theme that ran through her commentary was the greater diversity and respect for diversity that she found at Roberts and the greater pressures to conform to the more monolithic student culture, centered on attracting men at Canterbury College, that she had experienced at CWC.

At the end of the interview, Jolene used this theme to talk about lesbianism. Her first comment was that she suspected that there was a secret group of lesbians at CWC, and it was secret because it would not have been accepted by other students. Apparently, it was also so secret—if it existed—that Jolene herself was unable to seek help or support from this group for a new student who arrived at CWC when Jolene was a sophomore and a resident assistant in one of the dormitories. This new student let Jolene know that she was a lesbian, and Jolene felt that this woman had come to CWC because she assumed that a women's college would be a supportive environment for her. But Jolene said that all she could say to this new student was "you'd better leave," because she sincerely believed that CWC would be an inhospitable place for a lesbian.

Support for Jolene's belief appeared in the campus newspaper the year after she left CWC. Despite the headline "Homosexuals at [CWC] Feel Ignored by Programming," the article was primarily a report of the opinions of *one* unnamed "third semester junior." It began with a statement by CWC's president about school policy: "We consider the sexual preferences of our students, faculty, and staff to be a private and personal matter. [CWC] respects the choices of all individuals relating to political, religious, ethnic, and other personal matters." Contrary to this official policy of tolerance, "the junior" is quoted as saying that homosexual women are not willing to come forward at CWC because they fear "not wanting to be seen with, being blown off, and treated as a leper." Evidence to support this fear is provided in the article by an unnamed "straight senior" who defends the rights of gay women to attend CWC but is also quoted as saying that she "would be highly uncomfortable living on the same floor or sharing a community bathroom with a lesbian."

   Jolene contrasted her own belief that lesbians would be rejected at CWC with the greater acceptance they received at Roberts College where the then-current student body president was an "out lesbian." "Of course," said Jolene, "this is a bit of a shock for the freshmen" at Roberts, but to Jolene, the lesbian president was emblematic of the diversity and tolerance for diversity she enjoyed at her new college. If the freshmen were shocked to encounter a student leader who was proud of her lesbian identity, that was OK with Jolene because, according to her, learning to understand and respect diverse sexual orientations "[is] part of what a college education is all about." Maybe at Roberts College, but definitely not at CWC.

CHAPTER 6

Community: Connections and Defections at CWC

To describe a college as a community is to call attention to the similarities and ties among its participants. Because of this focus, community is sometimes seen as an antonym of both diversity and individual autonomy. Perhaps to counter this perspective, recent calls for community-building in colleges (e.g., Boyer, 1987; Carnegie Commission, 1990) have stressed purposefulness, openness, justice, discipline, caring, and the desirability of clear links between college goals and the needs of the persons seeking education. However praiseworthy, this ideal continues a long tradition of focusing on the unifying aspects of community while minimizing the constraints and ignoring the dissension that are inevitable parts of community life.

In contrast, this chapter is guided by the assumption that communities provide both constraints and opportunities simultaneously and sometimes by means of the same characteristic. At the campus level, the interplay of constraints and opportunities can promote both cohesion *and* dissension. Similarly, at the more individual level, there are characteristics of the college that tie some students to the institution while encouraging others to leave it. The next section of this chapter presents information about college-wide characteristics of CWC that affected community among students and their retention.

The forces fostering and undermining community are not limited to the campus-wide level. Intermediate structures can often be the means by which students are tied to their college. Four of these structures were prominent at CWC and are analyzed in this chapter: sororities, intercollegiate athletics, extra-curricular organizations, and friendship networks. Finally, I close the chapter by highlighting three contradictions embedded in college communities and summarize findings concerning their effects on students at CWC.

THE CAMPUS COMMUNITY

Of the 185 first-year students who entered baccalaureate programs at CWC in 1991, only 90 (48.6%) eventually received their bachelor's degrees from CWC. Of these 90, 78 graduated in 4 years or less; 10 more graduated in either December of 1995 or May of 1996; one graduated in December of 1996; and the last one received her degree in May of 1997. Astin (1997) has recently provided formulae based upon national data for calculating expected retention-to-graduation rates. The more complex formulae require information that was not available for most of the CWC students, but the simplest formula predicts graduation rates based only on high school GPAs that were available for all of them. Using this formula, the expected 4-year rate of bachelor's degree completion for students entering CWC in 1991 was 44.4% and the expected 6-year completion rate for this group was 49.1%. Since Astin (1997, p. 564) suggests that only 10% differences between expected and actual retention-to-graduation rates should be considered significant from both a practical and statistical perspective, these findings support the conclusion that the CWC retention rates were consistent with national retention-to-graduation rates for students with comparable grades in high school.

There are some reasons to argue that CWC should have had higher retention rates than it achieved. Astin's (1997) analyses of national data from 365 baccalaureate-granting colleges and universities in the United States show that retention-to-graduation rates for women are significantly higher than those for men; that retention-to-graduation rates for minority students are significantly lower than rates for the White majority; and that both small size and residential facilities on campus tend to increase an institution's retention rates. Given that CWC was a small, residential women's college with few minority students, a case could be made that CWC's retention rates should have exceeded the national average for institutions enrolling students with similar academic backgrounds. Nevertheless, Astin (1997) cautions: "Small size and residential facilities do not *necessarily* create actual retention rates that are higher than expected. . . . Rather there are *tendencies* for size and residence to [increase] retention" (p. 654).

At CWC, evidence emerged to support the proposition that small size and residential facilities—especially the rules governing those facilities— were institutional characteristics that fostered both the retention of some students and the departure of others. When a sample of graduating students were asked to talk about their positive undergraduate experiences, the reasons they had chosen CWC, and the reasons why they would recommend CWC to high school graduates (Appendix D, Interview III), almost all of them mentioned the small size of the college. Most of them, like Kinsey, linked college size to personal attention from the faculty:

> Oh, I think that I like the fact that it's a small school because you get more attention. It's easier to get hold of a professor, and they know you by name, and they're, I don't know, I just like the fact that it's small, a small campus. I don't know, I just feel like I'd just be lost anywhere else.

Other students took the small size of the campus for granted and focused their remarks more on the benefits of small classes. Georgia reported that what stood out as most positive for her was:

> Oh, mainly just the small classes, being able to interact with the teacher. Getting to know them on a one-to-one basis and to the point that if you have a question you can go to the teacher and ask them. It's not a class of, like, 100 people. You know people that are in there. That's what I like! (laughs)

Georgia's remarks were echoed by those of several other students, including Donna:

> And you know, the teachers working here are really great. I like the smaller classes, the more one-on-one. I wouldn't want to be number 110. I like it when they call me by my name. You know, it's just a very friendly atmosphere.

Clearly, small size of the campus and the classes helped to build a sense of CWC as a caring community among most of the students who remained at the college until graduation. For some students, however, small size was aversive. Among students who left and were interviewed about their reasons for leaving, 16.4% mentioned small size as a reason for their departure from CWC. This fact was not lost on some of the students who remained. Kinsey, who liked the smallness of CWC, said that she would be reluctant to recommend the school to others because:

> At [CWC] everybody either hates it or they like it a lot. There doesn't seem to be a whole lot of in between. . . . People come here and they immediately hate it and they don't like the small school atmosphere or they enjoy it, they like it, you know, it takes someone that wants . . . a smaller town, smaller campus, smaller group

of people to know and maybe not as many social things to run out and do like you would on a major campus and stuff.

And Bernice flatly stated that "if you're coming from a big town, the small town [and small campus] is just gonna kill ya. And I think that's why a lot of people transfer out of here."

Even for those who valued the personal attention and care they found at CWC, smallness could be a disadvantage as well as a pleasure. Peer-group surveillance, gossip, and pettiness were mentioned by several students as drawbacks of attending a small college. To Dahlia these disadvantages were serious enough that she wished she had attended a large university: "This place is very small and, you know, gossip here is just—runs rampant. I mean, one person knows, everybody knows; and of course it wouldn't slow down on a big campus, but it would stay within your circles, not the entire campus."

If surveillance by peers was considered a disadvantage of being at a small college, surveillance by faculty was not. Without exception, those students who commented on faculty surveillance interpreted it as a sign of concern and helpfulness. Instead of resenting faculty concerns about class attendance, the students who mentioned them, like Laurel, thought faculty concerns were generally helpful to students:

> The professors, you know, if you are, if you've missed class they're not gonna just say, oh, she's just missing class, let's just forget about it. They'll, you know, they'll call you or they'll see you in the dining hall and say, "Hey," you know, "You're here eating lunch. Why weren't you at my 10 o'clock [class]?" or whatever, you know, and they keep track of you. Which for some people, that's good; they need that.

One student who benefited personally from faculty concerns about atten-dance was Francie:

> Instructors, they like you to go to class where if, like, in a big univer-sity, usually the attendance policy is not that important whereas here it is. And I knew that would motivate me just sort of like individual attention. . . . Faculty are very, they treat you, it's kind of like, kind of like one of their children, a lot of them that I knew. [I've] gotten really close to a lot of them, and they're really helpful.

Although Francie seemed oblivious of the fact that some people might find a "parentlike" faculty overly protective, Ginger was aware that some of the faculty's helpfulness could be considered "hand-holding." Never-theless, she found it a positive experience:

> Oh, I really like the fact that this school kind of holds your hand when you come here and says, "Okay, this is what you do, this is your [faculty] advisor and you go to him, and this is the date of registration, and this is the day you go to your advisor for registra-tion, and this is that." I have an older brother who goes to a big—went to a big, big university [where they] didn't have a clue who he was. [He] always missed registration days, never got any of his classes, never went to his advisor, never had a clue what classes he needed. . . . But I've been pretty fortunate to have a real competent advisor who's helped me out, gotten the classes I've needed when I needed them. . . . I think counseling is, when you're coming in as a freshman, really important. I really got a lot out of that.

If faculty rules and advising procedures were considered helpful signs of caring, residence-hall rules were not. As noted in Chapter 2, during the period of our study, residence halls at CWC, including those occu-pied by sororities, were locked at 10 p.m., after which time no visitors were allowed. Although the rules governing deportment in the residence halls at CWC were far less strict than those that existed at women's col-leges in the 19th century (see Woody, 1929), they were stricter than those found on most American college campuses in the 1990s. Of particular an-noyance to the students were the rules against alcohol possession on cam-pus, even if students in a given room or at a given party were of legal age, and rules against male visitation. Kinsey described the alcohol policy as "kind of stupid and outdated." And Carol was one of those who voiced similar sentiments about the strict limits on male visitation: "I feel if I have a boyfriend I should be able to see him whenever I want in *my* room or *my* house—not even in my room, just in our parlor or something. Not sitting in a car."

Although it is clear that students' complaints at CWC did not lead to the kinds of collective resistance to college authority that have occurred in the past on coeducational campuses (see Fass, 1977; Horowitz, 1987), it is less clear whether residence-hall restrictions undermined community and fostered withdrawals from CWC. Only five of the students who left prior to graduation mentioned restrictiveness or one of its synonyms ("too confining," "provincial") as a reason for leaving. Probably the most accu-rate analysis of the impact of residence-hall rules came from a student I call Melody, who had the wisdom to understand that the same rules that offended some students could meet the needs of others:

As far as the rules go in the dorm, that's a hard issue. A lot of girls
come in here as freshmen thinking they're away from home, no
more mommy, no more daddy, they can do whatever they want.
And [they] soon find out that there's also a "big hold" of the
college. The college is mommy, basically. And, that could be [in] a
good way, too, because there's people who need that. But there are
people who don't want that. And it's, what I've noticed about this
college in particular is they don't have the happy median. It's
"hold" or nothing. So it would be nicer if they would just find a
median, maybe a dorm or so that would [accommodate] those who
want more freedom or wanted to be more free and [other dorms]
for those who would rather be held onto.

Melody's language of "holding" and "being held onto" calls attention to
the possibility that even residence-hall rules and their enforcement can
be seen by some as integral to a caring and secure community.

In contrast to the very few students who mentioned restrictiveness as
a reason for leaving CWC, almost half (46.2%) of those interviewed mentioned at least one academic reason. The most common of these reasons
had to do with either curricular limitations at CWC or curricular opportunities offered by other institutions of higher education. A few students left
CWC because they wanted a more practical, "useful" education with fewer
liberal arts requirements. Those identified in Chapter 4 as Intellectuals were
more likely to leave than Strivers, Careerists, or the Uninvolved; and students who sought sex-typed careers that were predominantly male were
more likely to leave than those seeking predominantly female careers or
careers that are no longer sex-typed. In addition, 62.2% of those who entered CWC with liberal arts majors left before graduating compared to 47.8%
of those entering with vocational majors. Although none of these tendencies was statistically significant, each of them is consistent with the proposition that the students most likely to leave CWC were those whose choices
and goals deviated from the dominant academic culture at CWC, which
stressed careerism—leading primarily to female-typed professions or untyped
occupations—over the liberal arts and the male-dominated professions.
These findings are consistent with the stress that organizational theorists have
given to "person-environment fit" as a predictor of satisfaction and retention (Burnett, Vaughan, & Moody, 1997; Chatman, 1991).

Another way to think about the fit between the person and her college environment is to measure the extent to which she subjectively iden-
tifies with the college. This was done in the survey administered to first-year
students at CWC in spring 1992. They were asked to indicate how important "being a student at CWC" was to their evaluation of themselves

(Appendix B, Figure B.5). On average, the identification with CWC of the students who eventually graduated was significantly higher than the identification with CWC of the students who subsequently left. Whereas eventual graduates considered "being a student at CWC" to be very important, on average, eventual dropouts rated their identification with CWC as only somewhat important to their self-evaluations.

The decision to stay at or leave a college is not entirely in the hands of the students, however. They may regard their college as a caring community, be willing to tolerate seemingly outdated restrictions, find that their career plans are strongly supported, and self-identify with the college, but they may still be forced to leave. Although CWC, like all colleges, had the right to expel students for egregious or persistent rule violations, no such cases involving the students we studied came to our attention. Instead, when the college forced students in our study to leave, it was for the far more common reason of academic failure. Of the 95 students who did not graduate from CWC, two left before receiving any grades, and 18 left with GPAs below the 2.0 average required for graduation. Even when these 18 were omitted from the analysis, the average GPA of students who left CWC (2.86) was significantly lower than the average GPA of CWC graduates (3.23).

Given this finding, it is surprising that only six of the students who left CWC mentioned low grades or bad study habits as one of their major reasons for leaving. Although some may have been too embarrassed about their grades to mention them, the more likely reason for not doing so was that GPA at the time of leaving CWC was not a permanent barrier to returning at some time in the future. As noted above, most students left with GPAs higher than the 2.0 average required to graduate. Among those with lower GPAs, most could have returned to CWC on academic probation and worked with faculty to improve their performance. Even those who had already exhausted their probationary status could have attended a community college or some other institution of higher education and reentered CWC once their GPA had reached a satisfactory level. These latter two paths were taken by a few of the students who eventually graduated, and the availability of such options may have diminished the importance assigned to grades by those who left but did not return to CWC.

Among the many researchers who have found that grades are a significant predictor of persistence at colleges and universities, two ways of interpreting grades have emerged. On the one hand, some of these researchers (reviewed by Pantages & Creedon, 1978) treat grades as an individual achievement, based on a student's abilities and effort. On the other hand, some researchers (reviewed by Pascarella & Terenzini, 1991) view grades as an indicator of students' involvement in the academic community, which, in turn, affects the likelihood that they will remain at their college or university. The data we collected at CWC provided support for both of these perspectives, but more for the second. In support of an individualistic interpretation of grades, high school GPAs were found to have a strong, significant effect on the GPAs students earned at CWC. When high school GPAs were controlled, however, other individual characteristics that might have affected college grades—such as scores on national tests or social-class background—had no significant effect on the GPAs students earned at CWC. Taken together, these findings suggest that students who came to college with good academic records continued to perform better in college than students who had academic difficulties in high school.

Beyond individualism, however, the effects of community can be seen by comparing the GPAs of three groups of students who represent three different levels of involvement in the CWC community. The first group, those who left CWC prior to graduation, had the lowest average GPAs, 2.64 for the entire group and, as noted above, 2.86 for those who left CWC in good academic standing. The second group consists of those who remained at CWC to graduate but whose choice of a liberal arts major made them somewhat marginal to the careerist community of students at CWC described in Chapter 4, with the results that they became less certain than other students of their career plans and less likely to interact with faculty about academic and career-related matters. These students graduated with an average GPA of 3.06. Finally, the most involved group consisted of those students with vocational majors who were described in Chapter 4 as "knowing what they were doing" and were characterized earlier in this chapter as having achieved a good person–environment fit at CWC. Although most students, regardless of major, appreciated the friendliness of CWC faculty, vocational majors were more likely to seek out faculty regarding academic matters which, as noted in Chapter 4, improved their grades. This group of students graduated from CWC with an average GPA of 3.28, even though their high school GPAs were almost identical (3.05 vs. 3.01) to those of the less career-focused and less academically involved liberal arts majors.

Although grades earned at CWC seem to have been a strong enough sign of academic involvement to differentiate between students who left and those who graduated, the correlation between grades and persistence was far from perfect. Some students with "failing" grades early in their college careers eventually graduated from CWC, and some students with excellent grades—like 10 of those with GPAs over 3.5—left CWC. Like small size, good grades could bind some students to CWC while suggesting to others that this might not be the kind of college at which they belonged.

Interestingly, however, more than one third (35.5%) of the reasons for leaving that were given by the students who had GPAs higher than 3.5 were reasons that had nothing to do with the academic attractions of other institutions or with any characteristics of CWC, academic or otherwise. In contrast, fewer than one quarter (23.5%) of the reasons given by the students who left CWC with GPAs below 3.5 fell in this same category. This difference suggests that some students who were doing very well at CWC, but left anyway, might have stayed at CWC had they not been pulled away for personal and familial reasons, such as a parental divorce, a job opportunity, health reasons, or a marriage.

Among all the students who left, most of the reasons for leaving that were nonacademic or unrelated to CWC were reasons having to do with the "pulls" of other communities to which the students were committed. The strongest pull came from the family and local community that the student had left to attend CWC. One quarter of all students who left CWC (25.6%) felt that the college was too far away from their home and from opportunities in or near their home community, and another 5.1% mentioned the fact that their parents had recently moved "too far away" as their reason for leaving CWC. To check whether the pull of a distant family and hometown really did reduce student persistence, I compared the persistence rates of students who had graduated from a high school in the state in which CWC was located and students who graduated from high schools in other states. This comparison revealed that the pull of a more distant home community did have a significant negative effect on student persistence. More than half of all in-state students (56%) stayed at CWC to graduation, but only two fifths (40%) of the entering students who came from other states eventually graduated from CWC.

But distance from home could also create community at CWC. Some of the students from other states whom we interviewed revealed that their best friends were other out-of-state students, friendships they attributed to shared understandings of the feelings created by being so far from family and being unable to return home on weekends as many in-state students did. Billye, an in-state student, thought that the first-year friendships among out-of-state students were superior to those formed at CWC by students whose families and precollege friends lived closer to the college. Billye explained the reasons for her opinion as follows:

Yeah, most [CWC students] like to—they want to keep a good relationship with their close friends [at CWC]. They want to keep that, they don't want to do something to jeopardize [their relationships with other CWC students] because a lot of people have come here from far away and don't know anyone else; so, they've gotten

really close to some [other CWC students], and they want to keep
[those relationships]. So they're concerned with being close with
other [CWC students].

On a related note, Marilyn said that the in-state students who went
home frequently were "not getting the full college experience." Although
Marilyn, who was interviewed in her first year at CWC, stressed the development of independence and problem-solving abilities as central to this "full
college experience," Fawn, who was interviewed in her senior year, thought
the full college experience meant participating in campus organizations and
attending on-campus events. When asked why some students did not take
part, she also suggested that out-of-state students were more involved in
the campus community and more closely tied to one another:

I think a lot of [those who don't participate in campus events are]
people who don't live very far away. They go home on weekends so
they never really make a tie to school. It's really funny because most
of the people that hang out together are—they're grouped by, a lot
of times, by how far away they live because a lot of people that have
to stay on weekends, I mean, they'll get to know each other; so,
people from really far away, they're all kind of one group . . .

Like other characteristics of the CWC community examined in this
chapter, a substantial distance between the college and students' home
communities fostered cohesion among students and their participation in
campus activities while at the same time encouraging defections from the
college. No characteristic of the college emerged that promoted only ties
to the college or fostered only anger, disunity, and departures. Characteristics of the college in which most students found pleasure—such as its
small size and high level of faculty concern—drove some away. Characteristics of the college that offended many students—such as strict rules in
residence halls—gave other students necessary guidance and a sense of
security. The extent to which a student's academic and career interests
were *unlike* those of most other students, one way to conceptualize a lack
of person–environment fit, seemed to drive some students out of the college, but the effect was not a significant one, and some students who didn't
seem to "fit" remained to graduate. Even strong subjective identification
with the college, a high GPA, and close proximity to home—all significant
predictors of student retention at CWC—did not prevent some students
from leaving CWC prior to graduation. Taken together, these findings
suggest how difficult it would be to create a college community that would
foster complete cohesion and prevent students from responding to the

"pulls" of the familial, occupational, and romantic relationships that are embedded in the noncollege communities to which they also belong.

THE SORORAL COMMUNITY

In their review of 25 years of research on the effects of sororities and fraternities, Winston and Saunders (1987) conclude that "there is evidence to support the contention that membership in a Greek-letter social organization is positively related to remaining in college" (p. 10). Similarly, in their extensive review of college effects on students, Pascarella and Terenzini (1991) conclude:

> Within residential institutions generally, it is likely that certain specific residential contexts are particularly potent in enhancing persistence [of students in college]. Some evidence suggests that fraternities and sororities can assume this role, particularly during the freshman or sophomore years. (p. 419)

Can these general conclusions about the effects of sororities on student persistence at college be generalized to CWC? To answer this question, I compared persistence rates of CWC students who joined sororities with those of independent students. This comparison showed that at CWC, as at other institutions of higher education, sorority membership had a significant, positive effect on students' persistence at college. Among the students who entered CWC in fall of 1991 and joined sororities during their first year, more than three fifths (61.5%) eventually graduated from CWC. Among those students who entered that same fall but did *not* join sororities their first year, only one third (34.8%) eventually graduated from CWC.

Despite its strong effect, sorority membership was no guarantee that a student would remain at CWC until graduation. Almost two fifths (38.5%) of sorority members left CWC prior to graduation. A small number of students who dropped out of CWC prior to graduation ($n = 5$) mentioned sororities as one of their major reasons for leaving the college. All five indicated that they thought sororities were too dominant at CWC. Surprisingly, three of the five were sorority members at the time they left the college. Two of them indicated that they wanted to drop out of their sorority, but felt they couldn't do so and remain at CWC. Like high GPAs, relatively short distances from home, small college size, and other campus-wide determinants of persistence at CWC, sororities helped to integrate some students into the college community while repelling others.

Among those who stayed and were interviewed in their senior year, most of the sorority women mentioned membership and involvement in their sorority as a very positive experience. One of the more exuberant of these respondents was Bonny, who extolled her sorority because of "just the bond that you get from it. It's incredible. My best friends are there. They are my sisters. I mean, we eat together, live together, sleep together. I mean, we're everything together."

Neither Bonny nor the others who praised their experiences as sorority members clearly said that their membership was the major, or only, reason they stayed at CWC. The only student who explicitly made this linkage was Jewell, who had transferred to a state college but then returned to CWC. Jewell described her sorority sisters as very supportive of her and told me that "the only reason I came back [to CWC] was because of my sorority."

The failure of the other sorority members to attribute their persistence at CWC directly to their sororities leaves open the possibility that it was not their sorority membership *per se* but rather something associated with it that accounted for the greater likelihood of sorority women than independents to graduate from CWC. The three significant predictors of students' persistence at CWC already identified in this chapter are subjective identification with CWC, proximity to home (in-state vs. out-of-state high school), and GPA. If any or all of these predictors were highly correlated with sorority membership, then there would be a possibility that one or more of these predictors might explain why sorority members were more likely than independents to graduate from CWC. Did this possibility exist? The simple, direct answer to this question is "no." Only small, nonsignificant differences were found between sorority members and independents in average identification with CWC, proximity to home, and first-semester GPAs at CWC. The positive effect of sorority membership on graduation rates was independent of the effects of the other significant predictors of graduation.

Another possible explanation for the significant effects of sorority membership on student persistence has been suggested by Astin (1985), whose review of research on college dropouts led him to conclude that many forms of student involvement on campus will have significant, positive effects on graduation rates and other student outcomes. The implications of Astin's review and subsequent research findings have been clearly identified by Winston and Saunders (1987), who have noted:

> If Astin (1985) is correct in saying that involvement of almost any kind will promote retention [of college students], then the fact that a student joins a sorority or fraternity may not be as significant as whether the student becomes involved in some student organization. (p. 10)

If this argument is correct, then it is possible that students' persistence at CWC was as much affected by their involvements in athletic teams, extracurricular organizations, or even friendship networks as by their membership in a sorority. The following sections of this chapter investigate these possibilities.

ATHLETIC TEAMS AS COMMUNITIES

Like many small colleges, CWC was a member of the National Association of Intercollegiate Athletics (NAIA). Under NAIA auspices, CWC women participated in six intercollegiate sports competitions: basketball, soccer, softball, swimming and diving, tennis, and volleyball. These sports competitions received considerable publicity. On campus, about one third to one half of each issue of the school newspaper was devoted to reports of NAIA athletic events. In addition, competitions in which CWC was involved were also covered in all of the weekly and daily newspapers that were published in the towns in which CWC and its (mostly in-state) rival teams were located.

Only a minority of CWC students participated in intercollegiate athletics. Of the 185 who entered in 1991, the number was only 33. Thirty of these participated during their first year, 25 during 1992–1993, 20 the following academic year, and only 14 during 1994–1995. A few participated in more than one sport during their first or second year, but by their third year all of those who continued to play focused their energies on only one sport.

For those few who did participate, intercollegiate sports did seem to tie them to their teammates and to the college. Of those who played NAIA sports during at least one year, more than three fifths (63.6%) eventually graduated from CWC. In contrast, among those who never participated on an NAIA athletic team while at CWC, fewer than half (45.4%) eventually received a CWC baccalaureate degree. This simple finding became more complex, however, when the effect of sports participation was considered in conjunction with the other ties that bound CWC students to the college, particularly the tie of geography.

As noted above, students who graduated from high schools located in the same state as CWC were more likely to remain at CWC than were students who came from other states. So, when I discovered that student athletes were also significantly more likely to come from in-state than out-of-state high schools, alarm bells went off. Perhaps athletics had nothing to do with creating community for (some) CWC students; maybe athletic participation was just another way of measuring geographic distance between CWC and the students' home towns. A careful check of the data revealed that this possibility was *not* supported. Athletic participation *did* have a positive effect on eventual graduation from CWC, but this effect was strong and significant only for in-state students.

An easy way to think about this finding is to compare the graduation rates for four groups of students. The first group consists of students who had graduated from high schools in the same state as CWC and who had played NAIA sports for CWC. Almost three quarters of these students (73.9%) eventually graduated from CWC. The second group consists of students who also graduated from high schools in the same state as CWC but who never played NAIA sports for CWC. About one half (49.4%) eventually graduated from CWC. Next come the students who graduated from out-of-state high schools. Among these students, the proportion graduating from CWC was about the same for those who played NAIA sports for CWC (40.0%) as among those who never played NAIA sports for CWC (41.3%). Thus the data showed a significant interaction between sports participation and geography in their effects on CWC graduation rates.

What accounted for this effect? We found nothing in our surveys or interviews that would allow us to test answers to this question systematically. What we suspect, however, is that in-state students got extra benefits—in the form of hometown publicity—from participating on CWC teams. Not only newspapers, but regional TV and radio broadcasts often reported news about NAIA games in which CWC or her opposing teams were involved. Such events would not have been reported routinely in the states from which many of the out-of-state athletes came. In addition to publicity, it seems likely that family and friends of in-state athletes were more likely to attend sporting events in which those athletes participated than were family and friends of out-of-state students.

Although publicity and fan support may have tied in-state student athletes more closely to their team and athletic participation, it's not at all clear that these factors tied them more closely to other aspects of the college. No significant relationship was found between participation in sports and self-identification with the college. Nor were athletes different from nonathletes in either sorority membership or their involvement in the academic life of the college, as indicated by their grades. For athletes, as for nonathletes, those who identified with the college, joined a sorority, and did well academically were more likely to graduate from CWC than their counterparts who failed to do each of these things.

EXTRACURRICULAR COMMUNITIES

Despite its small size, CWC offered its students a broad array of clubs, offices, and organizations in which they could participate. These included positions in student government or residence-hall government; memberships or offices in honorary societies or in clubs associated with a particular major field; involvement in the school newspaper, yearbook staff, or dramatic events; and membership in various charitable, political, self-help, religious, or cultural groups. The survey we conducted in 1992 (Appendix B, Figure B.13) revealed that about two thirds of the students (65.3%) had participated in at least one extracurricular activity—not counting NAIA athletics or sorority-sponsored activities—during their first year at CWC, and about one third of the first-year students (33.5%) were active in more than one of these extracurricular activities.

In contrast to sorority and athletic-team memberships, involvement in other kinds of extracurricular activities seemed to do little to tie students to one another or to CWC. The proportion of students who eventually graduated was just as high among the students reporting no extracurricular involvements during their first year as among those reporting involvement in one or more extracurricular activities. Whereas sorority and athletic team members almost always mentioned those memberships as highlights of their college careers, few of the graduating students interviewed in their last year at CWC mentioned other extracurricular activities as important, positive experiences. Also in contrast to their sorority and athletic-team memberships about which no graduating students complained, extracurricular opportunities and involvements were mentioned by some students as negative or disappointing experiences at CWC. Francie, for example, complained about the lack of opportunities to play intramural sports, and Fawn complained that the administration of CWC "had let go the choir director" and was about to eliminate the position of the only remaining musician on the faculty. As a result, she said, "I wasn't able to pursue my music as much as I wanted to. It was kind of hard to believe there's no music on campus, and I think that's something I miss out a lot on because I was really into it in high school."

In addition to complaining about missing opportunities, a few students, like Barbie, lamented the lack of student activism on campus:

> I guess there's a lot of apathy here, which I don't know if it's just this college or if a lot of people have to deal with that at college, but I guess it's just like I came to college thinking, "Oh, boy, I'm going to change the world" and then I got here and realized the world wasn't happy about being changed. (laughs) So that was kind of a negative thing.

When asked to elaborate her comment about apathy, Barbie gave the example of the environmental club:

I mean, it was a positive thing. I was a leader in the club, but it was
a negative thing in that it was really hard to do because, you know,
whenever the club was started it was like during that whole 20-
year anniversary of Earth Day and all that, so it was like it was just
a fad and now the fad has passed and no one cares. So that was
disappointing.

Though she was not someone who wanted to change the world,
Bernice also complained that: "Nobody gets involved on this campus,
which is a major problem." When asked why she thought this was the
case, she replied:

You know, I've tried to figure that out for 4 years now. And I don't
know. . . . But they do offer a lot of things on this campus. I mean,
they go out of their way to bring in speakers, to bring in musicians,
to do things for the kids on this campus and they cannot get people
to go. I don't know what it is. People aren't that busy, but they just
don't participate.

Bernice's bewilderment contrasts with the comments by Fawn, quoted
earlier in this chapter, to the effect that on-campus participation was particularly low among local students because they tended to go home frequently. Fawn's ability as a social analyst was vindicated by the information
we obtained from surveys and college records. These sources revealed that
students who had graduated from high schools located in the same state
as CWC were significantly *less* likely to be involved in extracurricular activities (other than NAIA athletics) during their first year of college than
students who came to CWC from other states. Despite this negative correlation, involvement in extracurricular activities—unlike involvement in
NAIA athletics—did not interact with geography to affect commitment to
CWC. Neither among in-state students nor among those who came from
elsewhere did extracurricular involvements have significant effects upon
the likelihood of graduating from CWC.
     These findings lend no support to the suggestions by Astin (1985) and
Winston and Saunders (1987) that involvement in other kinds of student
organizations and activities will have the same positive effect upon graduation rates as has been found for sorority memberships. Perhaps this is true
at some colleges and universities, but it certainly was not true at CWC. To
be effective in tying students to any institution of higher education, extracurricular memberships and activities have to create communities that are
supportive and rewarding. Although sororities were found to do this at
CWC, and NAIA teams seemed to do this for in-state students, other extra-

curricular activities at CWC were largely unsuccessful in this regard. Most students did not consider them to be central to their college experience, nor were extracurricular involvements significantly related to self-identification with the college.

Unlike sorority and athletic-team memberships, however, other extracurricular involvements were significantly correlated with students' grades. Aside from the fact that some organizations, especially honorary societies, had academic requirements for membership, this finding suggests the possibility that better students involved themselves more in extracurricular activities as a way of enhancing their credentials on future applications for jobs and for graduate and professional schools. If so, then extracurricular participation would have been seen by these students as more of an indicator of individual effort or achievement than as an opportunity for collective activity or community involvement.

This possibility seems credible when one considers the fact that memberships in sororities or NAIA teams are unlikely to impress employers or admissions committees for graduate and professional schools as much as would an applicant's involvements in service organizations, clubs associated with her major, or election to an important office on campus. Thus it seems likely that there are two kinds of intermediate structures on campus: those that constitute student communities and strengthen ties to the college and those that are useful as venues for individual achievement and for enhancing credentials useful in future careers. At CWC, athletic-team memberships (for in-state students) and sororities fit into the first category, and other extracurricular involvements fit into the more individualistic category.

COMMUNITIES OF FRIENDS

The high value that undergraduate women place on close friendships has been widely documented in the research literature (Bank, 1995; Bank & Hansford, 2000; Fehr, 1996), and both the surveys and the interviews that we conducted at CWC provided ample evidence that friendships were an enjoyable part of the lives of the students we studied. Almost all of the graduating seniors we interviewed mentioned friendships as an important, positive experience at CWC—frequently their most valued experience— and many expected that they would still be in touch with their CWC friends a decade or more after graduation. But some students who left CWC also reported that they had formed close friendships at the college, reports that raised questions about the extent to which friendship ties at CWC also tied students to the college.

To answer this question we investigated the extent to which responses that CWC women gave at the end of their first year to questions about friendships could be used to predict whether they subsequently graduated from CWC. The questions that produced these responses were designed to determine whether students considered themselves to be members of an identifiable friendship circle (clique, crowd, group, gang) at CWC and whether they had formed a best friendship at CWC. The answers to these questions revealed that the overwhelming majority of the CWC students (97.6%) had either a best friend or a friendship circle or both at the college by the end of their first year.

Given the findings already reported in this chapter, it is not surprising that the first-year students who considered themselves to be part of an identifiable friendship circle at CWC were significantly more likely to be sorority members than independents. Nor is it surprising that out-of-state students were significantly more likely than in-state students to participate in a college-based friendship circle. Despite these relationships, there was no significant effect of being in a friendship circle on graduation rates. With or without controls for sorority membership and geographic background, students in friendship circles at the end of their first year were no more likely to graduate from CWC than students who did not participate in a friendship circle.

The proportion of students who said that their best friend attended CWC (32.3%) was far less than the proportion who reported being part of a circle of friends at the college (74.4%). This smaller proportion of students with their best friend at CWC was largely due to having their best friend elsewhere rather than to an unwillingness to name one friend as "best." Only 11% of the first-year students reported that they had no single best friend, but more than half of the students (56.7%) reported that they had a best friend who did not attend CWC. Among those who had a best friend at the end of their first year of college, the likelihood of their graduating from CWC could not be predicted from knowing whether the best friend also attended CWC. Graduation rates were similar among those with a best friend at the college and among those with a best friend elsewhere (52.8% and 57.0%, respectively).

Although selecting as a best friend someone who attended CWC did not, by itself, tie students to the college, *evaluations* of college friendships proved to have significant effects. These evaluations were measured by asking students to compare the best friend they had at CWC with their best female friend prior to coming to CWC. Of those who rated their best on-campus friendship more important than the best same-sex friendship they had prior to attending CWC, more than three fifths (63.1%) eventually graduated from CWC. In contrast, among those who rated their best on-campus friendship less important than the best same-sex friendship they had prior to attending CWC, fewer than half (47.1%) eventually graduated from CWC.

Further evidence that forming an important friendship on campus tied students to the college came from the finding that there was a significant relationship between the ratings students gave to on-campus friendships and their self-identifications with the college. Among those who rated their best CWC friend as more important than their pre-CWC friend, being a student at CWC was rated, on average, as a very important component of their self-evaluation. Among those who rated their CWC friend as less important than their pre-CWC friend, being a student at CWC was rated only somewhat important, on average. Despite this significant difference, self-identification with CWC did not explain away the effect of important friendships at CWC on graduation rates. Nor could this effect be explained away by grades, geographic background, sorority membership, or participation on an NAIA team, none of which was significantly related to friendship ratings.

Taken together, the findings reported in this section of the chapter suggest that friendship formation at CWC was not enough to tie students to the college. Almost all of the students made friends, and the formation of a best-friend relationship or a friendship circle was just as likely among those who left CWC as among those who eventually graduated. What did matter was forming an *important* friendship, a friendship that was better than those one had formed prior to attending CWC. When this happened, students' ties to the college were strengthened, and they were more likely to graduate from CWC.

THE CONTRADICTIONS OF COMMUNITY LIFE

The findings reported in this chapter reveal that the process of creating college communities is more complicated and contradictory than has been fully recognized by either models of student retention or idealizations of community life. The most obvious contradiction results from the findings that the very same characteristics of CWC that created community for some students and tied them to the college repelled others and motivated them to leave. None of the characteristics of the college or its intermediate structures that were examined in this chapter was found to promote only unity or to foster only disaffection. These findings suggest how difficult it is to create a college that is a purposeful, open, just, disciplined, caring community with clear links between college goals and the needs of the persons seeking education (Boyer, 1987; Carnegie Commission, 1990). What some will consider to be legitimate purposes, others will question. What some will call justice and necessary discipline, others will perceive as unfair constraints. What some will regard as caring, other will feel to be intrusiveness.

Such disagreements are certainly not unique to CWC, but they were undoubtedly exacerbated by the ambiguities surrounding the ways in which the college regarded undergraduate women. Although in loco parentis may have been replaced nationally by a legal code that regards college students as adults (Hoekema, 1994), it was obviously true that administrators and faculty at CWC treated their students in a protective manner. This protective stance could be seen not only in the rules and regulations governing hours, alcohol use, and male visitation but also in the quasi-parental manner of interaction that so often occurred between faculty and students. On the other hand, as shown in previous chapters, the college fostered individual achievement and personal autonomy. So, in contrast to the idealized communities advocated by communitarian educators, the very purposes of CWC—like those of other colleges and universities—were somewhat conflicted. One goal was to turn students into autonomous career women, but another was to protect them from their desires to engage in risk-taking behaviors. Small wonder that students were also conflicted in their responses to the opportunities, constraints, and supports that the college provided.

A second major contradiction characteristic of community life at CWC was not so much a contradiction within the college as it was a conflict between loyalties to the college or its intermediate structures and loyalties to the hometown. This contradiction between communities has largely been ignored in models used to predict student persistence at college (e.g., Pascarella & Terenzini, 1983; Tinto, 1975). Because such models are often developed and used by educators who are interested in increasing student retention rates, they tend to focus on characteristics of the college that could be improved to achieve this goal. Although some of the background that incoming students bring with them is usually taken into account in retention models, little attention is paid to the ongoing relationships that students have with hometown friends and family members after they arrive at college. Yet our findings suggest that the pull of the hometown has important effects not only on student retention but also on the kinds of communities in which students participate while they are at college.

The contradiction students experience between their college or its intermediate structures and their hometown is not a simple tug-of-war between two opposing forces that yields one clear winner. By all accounts, students who came to CWC from other states were very likely to be actively involved with other students on the campus. Although no more (or less) likely than in-state students to join sororities, they were significantly more likely than their in-state counterparts to form friendship circles and to participate in extracurricular activities (with the exception of NAIA athletics). Despite their more active involvements with other young women on campus, they were also more likely than in-state students to drop out of CWC, and there is little doubt that "the pulls" of events and relationships in their hometowns were the major reasons for their departures.

These findings suggest an interesting dilemma for administrators and faculty at small colleges with declining enrollments. If all they want to do is to retain students, then it might be best to recruit those who live close enough that they can continue to participate in hometown relationships and activities while attending college. On the other hand, if they also want to create a vital campus community of shared experiences in which students form friendship circles, attend campus events, and participate in extracurricular activities, then it might be best to recruit those from hometowns too far away for frequent visits. Obviously, geographically based recruitment is not the only or best way to deal with problems of retention or lack of involvement in the college community, but our findings suggest that the retention of students who are heavily invested in their hometown relationships contributes very little to creating a vital, communal life on the campus.

Finally, our findings shed some new light on a contradiction that, unlike the two already discussed, has received considerable attention in the literature concerned with women's higher education (e.g., Horowitz, 1987; Newcomer, 1959; Solomon, 1985). This is the contradiction between the demands of the formal or official structures of the college, on the one hand, and the less formal, student-run, and student-created social structures, on the other. Historically, this was a conflict between the demands of the faculty-run curriculum and the student-organized extracurriculum that originally included athletics and sororities as well as many clubs, offices, and campus events. Eventually, the extracurriculum, including intercollegiate athletics, became part of the official structure of colleges and universities, with sororities becoming quasi-official structures that managed to retain some autonomy from the institutions of higher education in which they were located.

Our study yielded no support for Newcomer's (1959) fear that students' participation in what she regarded as an overly elaborated extracurriculum would interfere with their academic studies. At CWC, membership in a sorority or NAIA athletic team had no significant effect on students' grades, and participation in the rest of the extracurriculum was positively, rather than negatively, correlated with students' academic achievements. Although it is possible that this finding might be different at a more elite college or university where academic demands are more rigorous than they were at CWC, we suspect that most extracurricular involvements are not demanding enough to undermine students' grades. Instead, it seems likely that students at elite colleges would tend, even more than did the higher achieving students at CWC, to use extracurricular involvements as ways to enhance their credentials and, thereby, their future career opportunities.

Although Newcomer's (1959) concern about the extracurriculum undermining academic achievement seems unwarranted, her recognition of the importance to women students of their friendships was amply supported by our study. Over and over again, students told us how much they valued the friendships they formed at CWC, and there was no question that those who valued their sorority membership did so because of the friendships that membership produced. When students were asked at the end of their first year and, again, at the end of their 4 years at CWC to evaluate the importance of various kinds of college experiences and relationships (see Appendix B, Figures B.5 & B.6), the ratings they gave to the friendships they had formed since coming to college were substantially and significantly higher than the ratings they gave to their relationships with the CWC faculty or to the clubs and activities in which they were involved. On the campus of CWC, students assigned the most value to the kind of voluntary friendship that some feminists (e.g., Esterberg, 1997; Friedman, 1995) have identified as the best and most egalitarian community for women.

CHAPTER 7

Lessons From Central Women's College

In July 1996, the governing board of CWC announced that the under-graduate college would become a coeducational institution with full implementation to take place in fall of the following year. The president of CWC made public comments indicating that the board members were firmly committed to the decision, and her options were either to accept the decision, and make it a positive experience, or to oppose it and "have it happen anyway." She embraced the first option and, over the next year in speeches and campus publications, she offered cheery assessments of why the change was both inevitable and good for the college and its students.

These assessments were characterized by three major themes. The first could be called the "not really a change" argument in that it asserted that the shift to coeducational status would not make much difference because men had always been part of CWC. The reference was partly to the small number of male undergraduates enrolled at Canterbury College who had taken courses at CWC since 1962 and partly to men enrolled in graduate programs who, in 1996, accounted for approximately 25% of all student enrollments. Because men had always been part of CWC, the president claimed, the decision to become a fully coeducational institution would not produce a real change in the undergraduate experiences of CWC's women students.

Not surprisingly, this rationale was challenged by students when they returned to campus for the 1996–1997 academic year. The lead article in the first issue of the student newspaper to appear that year was headlined "[CWC] To Go Coed in 1997," a decision that was described as "drastic and seemingly sudden" and one that would forever change the college. In both the lead article and an editorial, students complained that they would lose the special benefits they received from attending an all-women's college. In response, the president declared that "[CWC] would remain a women-centered university." Although this pledge was consistent with the position that the decision to admit men to the undergraduate college was "not really a change," what it meant to be "women-centered" was never clarified, leading one student to remark that the president's pledge was only "an appeasement to angry students."

Whatever her intent, the president's assurances about remaining "women-centered" clearly implied that this is what CWC was as long as its undergraduate college enrolled only women. And, although some of the students were skeptical about her promise that a coeducational CWC could be "women-centered," they accepted this phrase as an accurate description of their women's college. But how accurate was it? The following section of this chapter addresses the question of whether and in what ways CWC was a women-centered college in the 5 years prior to the decision to become a coeducational institution. Against the background of national arguments about women's colleges and women-centered education, relevant findings already presented in this book are summarized, and new findings about the benefits and limitations of women's education at CWC are presented.

The third theme to emerge from the president's defense of the decision to "go coed" seemed to contradict the themes of "not really a change" and "continuing to be women-centered." In the president's own words, this third theme was "campus diversification," which she described as one of her major goals throughout her presidency. Charging that "our community is not reflective of the real world," she argued that the lack of opportunity to interact with men of their own generation detracted from the quality of the education women received at CWC. Her argument echoed the major claim that had been made by advocates of coeducation throughout the history of women's higher education, but especially since the rise of second-wave feminism. The third section of this chapter examines this argument in light of research findings from CWC concerning the meanings that diversity had for the students.

Not mentioned in the public statements about the decision to "go coed" were concerns about recruitment and retention of enough students to make the on-campus, residential undergraduate program an economically viable endeavor. Many faculty assumed that the desire to increase the size of and income from the on-campus student body was the major reason for the decision to admit men. This assumption is consistent with the finding nationally that declining enrollments and fiscal shortfalls have caused several women's colleges either to become coeducational or to close (Bonvillian & Murphy, 1996; Harwarth et al., 1997; Miller-Bernal, 2000). Whether the assumption made by the CWC faculty was correct, whether coeducation led to enrollment and financial gains, and whether CWC somehow remained women centered are questions that can only be resolved by a new research project focused on CWC as a coeducational institution. Instead, the goal of this chapter is to complete the story of CWC as it was before men were enrolled on campus. The rest of that story focuses not only on what it meant to talk about women-centered education and campus diversification but also on the lost opportunities that were produced by CWC's responses to the historical and contemporary contradictions in women's higher education.

WOMEN-CENTERED EDUCATION

In recent years, a substantial literature has appeared that compares women's colleges with coeducational institutions (e.g., Miller-Bernal, 2000; Riordan, 1992, 1994; Smith, Wolf, & Morrison, 1995; Tidball, 1989). Although some of these studies have been criticized for making unsubstantiated claims concerning specific benefits of women's colleges, these studies have been largely successful in convincing readers that women's colleges are places that "take women seriously" (Tidball, Smith, Tidball, & Wolf-Wendel, 1999) and provide them with the kind of women-centered education that other educators and researchers (e.g., McCoy & DiGeorgio-Lutz, 1999; Sadker & Sadker, 1994) have found to be lacking at coeducational institutions. These studies also provide some explicit and implicit definitions of what a women-centered education is and what it means to take women seriously. In the rest of this section, findings from our research at CWC are used to examine four of these definitions.

Faculty Attention

At the most fundamental and consensual level, being women-centered is a matter of focus, and it would be foolish to deny that women students are the focus of attention for faculty and administrators at women's colleges. To ignore women students would be to ignore *all* of the students, without whom there would be no college. So it is hardly surprising to read claims that women receive more attention in classes at women's colleges than at coeducational institutions where they must compete with men for faculty recognition. These claims were also common among the graduating seniors from CWC whom I interviewed in 1995 (Appendix D, Interview III), several of whom compared their experiences in all-women classes with those in coeducational classes.

"Teachers here pay attention to you," said Lotus, who found this not to be the case at Canterbury College where "teachers call on males first before they call on females." A different comparison, but the same conclusion, was expressed by Georgia. Comparing CWC with the coeducational high school she had attended, she remarked:

> Having all women in a class just makes a difference; there's no bias, and you just feel more comfortable. . . . Having men in your class distracts a lot of people. . . . [In all-women classes], I think sometimes the teachers are more fair, you know.

Jewell, who attended a coeducational university in the middle of her career at CWC, gave a particularly good description of what Bernice Sandler and her colleagues (Hall & Sandler, 1982; Sandler, Silverberg, & Hall, 1996) have called the "chilly climate for women" in many coeducational classrooms:

> When I compare what I'm like in the classroom here [at CWC] to when I was at [the University], I don't think I said "boo" in one of my classes at [the University]. I just sat there and took notes. I mean, it's stereotypical, but the men ran the classes.

The possibility that this chilly climate for women might also spread across a coeducational CWC was suggested by Melody, who opined that one of the good things about attending a women's college was that

> Women seem to tend to have more, get more attention in classrooms. They tend to be more aggressive when there's just plain women, only women in the classrooms. . . . [In] male and female, coed [classrooms], the males tend to be more aggressive and the females more passive.

When I asked Melody how she had arrived at these opinions, she did not cite her high school or some other college or university but rather CWC itself where, as she put it, "I've attended a coed class, a few coed classes, here at [CWC] and have noticed." If class attendance at CWC by a few men enrolled at Canterbury College could stifle women's class participation, it seems reasonable to hypothesize that this effect would increase when a larger number of undergraduate men actually enrolled at CWC.

How important it is that women receive a lot of attention in college classrooms depends, in large part, on the correlates and consequences of attention, but these relationships are hard to test and confirm both at CWC and in the existing research literature. To students like Lotus and Georgia, it seemed clear that getting attention in class was a matter of gender fairness. Their perception suggests one of the mechanisms by means of which the advocacy of gender-egalitarianism was sustained and increased at CWC. As reported in Chapter 2, the major change in norms and values that occurred among the students who entered CWC in 1991 and eventually graduated was a shift toward the higher levels of gender egalitarianism shared by faculty and existing students at CWC. It seems entirely reasonable to suggest that faculty attention in the classroom and the support from faculty documented in Chapters 4 and 6 contributed to this shift.

Faculty support also had positive effects on the average academic performance of CWC students, at least as measured by their grades. And the following statement by Kinsey suggests that self-confidence might have been the link between faculty attention and support, on the one hand, and academic performance, on the other:

> I think the thing that I got most from this school is confidence. I don't know if that sounds kind of corny, but I think I got a lot of confidence from here because . . . you never had to be apprehensive to ask a question or whatever. If you were wrong . . . a teacher wouldn't go, "No!" or something like that. They'd say something like, "You're on the right track, but," then tell you the right answer—that type deal. I think that probably has helped me the most or will help me the most because I used to be quiet and shy and was too scared to ask a question.

Kinsey's comments make clear both the need that some students have for encouragement and the fact that it's not just faculty attention but *supportive* attention of the kind described more fully in Chapters 4 and 6 that is likely to have positive effects on students.

Leadership Opportunities

Like claims about women receiving more faculty attention at women's colleges, claims about more leadership opportunities for women at those college are largely consensual and unlikely to be challenged by research or argumentation. If women don't fill the student leadership positions at women's colleges, who will? In contrast to women's colleges where all of the student leaders are women, it would be difficult, if not impossible, to find a coeducational institution where the proportion of student leaders who were women was even close to 100%. Thus the question is not whether women's colleges provide women with more leadership opportunities, but rather what the correlates and consequences of holding leadership positions might be.

One correlate was suggested in Chapter 6 where a positive, significant relationship was reported between GPA and participation in extracurricular activities (but not sororities or athletic teams). Since most students who participated in these activities did hold some kind of leadership position during their college careers, this finding could be taken to mean that campus leadership and grades went hand-in-hand at CWC. A correlation is not a cause, however, and it seems likely that energetic, ambitious women at CWC tended to seek out both leadership opportunities and the academic opportunities (such as help from the faculty) that led to higher grades. Nevertheless, it is important to note that CWC was a place that offered women both kinds of opportunities.

Indeed, the college not only offered leadership opportunities but also encouraged students to take them, as the following comment by Opal suggests:

> I think [CWC] has offered me a lot of leadership opportunities because it's all women, and you're kind of pushed. (Pause.) They don't push you, but there's so many more opportunities and you don't feel outnumbered [by men]; you don't feel self-conscious. You can kind of "go get 'em" a little bit more.

Pushy or not, such encouragement was probably necessary if nonelite students were going to fill all of the available positions of leadership on the campus. In addition, Opal's comment suggests that leadership opportunities, like faculty attention, may have raised the self-confidence of CWC students.

Self-Esteem

Unlike attention and leadership opportunities, which are obviously more available to women at women's colleges than at coeducational institutions, the effects of women's colleges on students' self-esteem are less obvious and more controversial. Although it seems reasonable to argue that a women-centered education ought to increase the positive feelings women have about themselves, not all studies have found a significant effect of women's colleges on those feelings. Using national data collected by the Cooperative Institutional Research Program, Daryl Smith and her colleagues (1995) found no *direct* effects of women's colleges on the outcome measure they called "sense of competence." This outcome was a complex measure, however, including such things as self-ratings of leadership ability and popularity with the opposite sex.

Using a less complicated and more widely accepted measure, Riordan (1992) studied the self-esteem of women who participated in the National Longitudinal Study of the High School Class of 1972. He found that women who attended women's colleges for at least 2 years, between 1972 and 1979, had significantly higher self-esteem in 1986 than women who attended coeducational institutions of higher education for the same length of time. When he controlled for the self-esteem levels that the women had in their last year of high school, however, Riordan found that the relationship between type of college (women-only vs. coeducational) and self-esteem became smaller and nonsignificant. These findings suggest that the women in this study who went to women's colleges had higher self-esteem when they entered college than did women who went to coeducational institutions. Although attending women's colleges did not raise these women's self-esteem, the experience of attending a women's college for 2 years helped students maintain the higher self-esteem they brought with them from high school.

In contrast to Riordan's findings, research by Miller-Bernal (2000) suggests that at least some women's colleges may have a positive effect on the self-esteem of their students. Miller-Bernal studied women students at four colleges: a women's college, a women's college coordinate with a men's college, a long-time coeducational college, and a former men's college that had recently become coeducational. Miller-Bernal measured self-esteem by asking students the extent to which they agreed with the statement: "On the whole, I am satisfied with myself," a statement that was also part of the self-esteem measure used by Riordan (1992). Women students were asked to answer this questions during their first year of college and, again, during their sophomore year. Miller-Bernal (2000) reports that the students at the women's college were the only one of the four groups of women she studied whose self-esteem increased during this period. Whereas 30% of the women had strongly agreed with the statement measuring self-esteem when they entered college, 47% strongly agreed with the statement in their sophomore year. In contrast, the self-esteem scores of women at the coordinate college remained the same during this period, and those at the two coeducational colleges declined.

Findings from the three studies just reviewed support three different conclusions about the effects of women's colleges on self-esteem. The study by Smith and her colleagues (1995) suggests little, if any, direct effect of women's colleges on self-esteem; Riordan's (1992) findings indicate that students at women's colleges have higher self-esteem than women at coeducational institutions because of selective recruitment; and Miller-Bernal (2000) found that self-esteem among women increased if they

attended a women's college. Which of these three conclusions best described the effects of CWC on the self-esteem of the students we studied?

To answer this question, we measured the self-esteem of students prior
to their matriculation, at the end of their first year, and during their last
year at CWC. The measure used (see Appendix B, Figure B.4) asked students to indicate the extent to which they agreed with 10 statements, including all of those used as self-esteem measures by Riordan (1992) and
Miller-Bernal (2000). Although our study does not permit us to compare
the self-esteem scores of CWC students with those of students who never
attended a women's college, it does permit us to compare the scores of
students who graduated from CWC with those of students who did not.

These comparisons support that conclusion that spending all or most
of one's undergraduate career at CWC significantly increased students' self-
esteem. This conclusion is supported by four specific findings. First, there
was no significant difference in the average self-esteem scores of matriculating students who eventually graduated from CWC and matriculating
students who did not subsequently graduate from CWC. Second, for the
students who left CWC, there were no significant changes in their average
self-esteem scores across the three different surveys. Third, for the students
who graduated from CWC, average self-esteem scores at graduation were
significantly higher than they had been prior to matriculation and also
significantly higher than they were at the end of their first year at CWC.
Fourth, average self-esteem scores of graduating CWC students were significantly higher on the third survey (but not the other two) than average
self-esteem scores of students who had left CWC.

To check whether these findings about average differences could have
resulted from the scores of only a few students, I calculated the number of
students whose self-esteem scores had increased, decreased, or remained
the same across the three surveys. These calculations also revealed substantial differences between CWC graduates and those who left the college.
Among those who graduated from CWC, almost three fifths (58.7%) showed
increases in self-esteem between matriculation and graduation, with slightly
more than a third (36.0%) showing decreases. Among those who left CWC,
only a third (34.4%) showed increases in self-esteem during this same period, and more than half (54.7%) showed decreases. As these figures indicate, leavers were also twice as likely as CWC graduates to have the same
level of self-esteem across time (10.9% and 5.3%, respectively).

To check whether college graduation or nearing college graduation
was the cause of the higher self-esteem of CWC students, I compared self-
esteem scores of eventual CWC graduates with scores of students who left
CWC and had either graduated from another institution of higher education or were enrolled and definitely planning to earn a bachelor's degree

from another institution. This comparison did not reduce the significant difference in self-esteem scores between the two groups. Regardless of their progress toward a college degree at the time of the third survey, students who had left CWC scored significantly lower than eventual CWC graduates on the measure of self-esteem.

Our findings are consistent with the conclusion that continuing one's college career at CWC through graduation had positive effects on the self-esteem of the majority who did so. Although these findings are more similar to those reported by Miller-Bernal (2000) than to those reported by Riordan (1992) or Smith and her colleagues (1995), the effect of CWC on self-esteem seems to have taken longer to become positive and significant than the effect of the women's college studied by Miller-Bernal (2000). As indicated above, we found no significant changes in the self-esteem scores of CWC students during their first year of college, and this was true of both those who eventually graduated and those who left. The fact that Miller-Bernal's second measure of self-esteem was administered during the sophomore year, rather than at the end of the first year, may be one reason for the seeming difference in findings. Another may be the findings reported in Chapter 5 showing that many CWC students spent much of their first year involved in social activities away from campus and uninvolved in studies or career-related opportunities at CWC.

This latter set of findings suggested the possibility that CWC had its positive effect on students' self-esteem after their first year because it was in those later years that students also began to focus on their studies and to improve their grades. Contrary to this line of reasoning, however, among those who eventually graduated from CWC, there were no significant associations between GPA and self-esteem scores and no significant associations between changes in GPAs and in self-esteem scores. The final GPAs of graduates whose self-esteem improved while they were at CWC was almost identical to the GPAs of graduates whose self-esteem had declined (3.26 and 3.34, respectively). This finding is similar to the report by Miller-Bernal (2000) that "students' doing poorly or well academically was not related to their self-esteem" (pp. 273–274).

Although there probably were a few students whose grades affected their self-esteem, CWC seems to have offered students multiple routes to improvement of their feelings about themselves. I arrived at this conclusion after examining a large number of undergraduate experiences that might have improved students' self-esteem and finding no significant, positive effects. I began this examination process with the assumption that the supportive attention from faculty and staff at CWC and the leadership opportunities the college offered must surely have fostered increased self-esteem in CWC students. However, when I examined the effects of students' opinions about how caring the CWC faculty and administration were (Appendix B, Figure B.8) and their involvements in sororities, athletic teams, and other extracurricular activities (Appendix B, Figure B.12), I found no support for my assumption. The only significant relationship that emerged was a moderate, *negative* effect of participation in extracurricular activities (but not sororities or athletic teams) during the first year at CWC on subsequent changes in self-esteem. Although the actual self-esteem scores of graduating students were not significantly related to their involvement in the extracurriculum, significantly more of the students who were *un*involved increased their self-esteem while at CWC than did the students who were moderately or highly involved in extracurricular activities and leadership positions. Again, the findings at CWC are similar to those reported by Miller-Bernal (2000), who concluded that "it was not the most active students who as seniors said that their self-confidence had increased the most during their college years" (p. 272), and "students who perceived their colleges as supportive of women did not, in general, have higher levels of self-esteem" (p. 273).

Where the findings about self-esteem at CWC differ most from those at the colleges studied by Miller-Bernal (2000) is in the effects of students' social life on their self-esteem. Miller-Bernal reports that students who said they had an active social life—although not necessarily one that involved dating—also had higher self-esteem, and she concludes that "informal activities, even more than participation in college-sponsored ones, appear to reinforce young women's positive feelings about themselves" (p. 275). This proved not to be true at CWC. Answers to *none* of the questions graduating seniors were asked about their own social life or about the social climate at CWC were significantly correlated with their self-esteem or improvements in their self-esteem.

The failure to identify experiences or perceptions of CWC students that could predict self-esteem suggests two possibilities. One, already mentioned, is that there were many different experiences that raised the self-esteem of students who eventually graduated from CWC, and no single experience affected the self-esteem of a large enough number of these students to produce a statistically significant effect. For some students, it was academic involvements and achievement that made them feel better about themselves, whereas for others, it was faculty support, or a particular extracurricular activity, or some aspect of their social life at CWC that had this same effect. A second possibility is that the self-esteem of the majority of the students who remained at CWC was positively affected by characteristics of the college that we failed to measure adequately. If I were to nominate such characteristics, they would include the day-to-day interactions in classes and on campus between faculty and students and among the students themselves. All of these interactions offer participants the opportunity to take women, including themselves, more or less seriously, and the usual assumption is that the more seriously they are taken, the higher their self-esteem will be. It is the absence of information about the daily interactions of women students, not only at CWC but nationally, that is so frustrating to those who want to make the case for women's colleges and for women-centered education. Even though many people who attend, teach at, or study these colleges have the feeling that they are beneficial places for women, it is beyond the abilities and resources of participants or researchers to conclusively demonstrate all of the complex, ongoing interaction processes by means of which these benefits—such as the improved self-esteem of CWC students—are accomplished.

Opportunities to Achieve

Perhaps the most controversial claim about the benefits of women's colleges is the assertion that their graduates have higher aspirations and are more successful than the women graduates of coeducational institutions. Influential advocates of this position have been M. Elizabeth Tidball and her collaborators who have produced several studies that Tidball (1980) has interpreted as showing that women who graduate from women's colleges are about twice as likely as women graduates of coeducational colleges to earn doctorates in the physical sciences and to be cited in national publications, such as *Who's Who Among American Women*, as leading, high achievers in their fields of endeavor. These studies have been criticized for overemphasizing elite women's colleges (Oates & Williamson, 1978) and for their failure to separate the ambitions that women brought with them to college from the effects of the colleges themselves (Baker, 1976; Stoecker & Pascarella, 1991).

The importance of distinguishing between elite and nonelite colleges can be seen in findings that resulted from a study sponsored by the U.S. Department of Education (Harwarth et al., 1997). Using the Carnegie classification system, this study divided private 4-year institutions into two categories called Baccalaureate I and II. The categories are based on the proportion of bachelor's degrees given in the liberal arts, 40% or more for Baccalaureate I colleges and less than 40% for Baccalaureate II colleges, but the categories also correspond to the selectivity of the colleges with the older, more elite colleges such as the Seven Sisters falling into the first category, and the less elite colleges such as CWC falling into the second. Among other issues, the study examined the college majors of all women who received degrees from these two categories of colleges during the 1992–1993 academic year.

Consistent with claims by Tidball and Kistiakowsky (1976), women who graduated from women's colleges in the Baccalaureate I category were more likely than those from all 4-year Baccalaureate I institutions to major in traditionally male-dominated fields such as the physical sciences. When they looked at nonelite Baccalaureate II institutions, however, the researchers found that graduates from women's colleges were no more likely to major in traditionally male-dominated fields. In addition, the findings show that women from the elite women's colleges were more than four times as likely as women from the nonelite women's colleges to major in the physical sciences (3.0% vs. 0.7% of graduates, respectively), a finding that is not too surprising in light of the fact that *none* of the students in the cohort we studied at CWC graduated with a major in the physical sciences and very few planned careers in male-dominated fields.

Since Tidball began her effort to make the case for the higher achievements of graduates from women's colleges, research has appeared suggesting that even nonelite women's colleges offer their students some advantages when compared with the advantages women receive from attending nonelite coeducational institutions. The beneficial outcomes that have been reported for nonelite women's colleges or for all women's colleges, nonelite as well as elite, include increased educational aspirations and attainment (Brown, 1982; Smith, 1990), greater recognition for achievements and leadership (Tidball, 1980), more doctorates in all fields (Tidball, 1980; Tidball et al., 1999), and higher status occupations and higher income (Riordan, 1994). What actually causes these outcomes remains in doubt, however. In a study using national, longitudinal data, Stoecker and Pascarella (1991) were able to control not only for the selectivity of the colleges students attended but also for college size and for the educational and occupational aspirations students brought with them to those colleges. When these latter controls were used, the impact of women's colleges on women's career achievements became small and nonsignificant. The debate may not be over, however, because Stoecker and Pascarella (1991) studied only the *early* achievements of women during the 10-year period from when they began higher education. As they admit, the kinds of career prominence that lead to citations in *Who's Who in American Women* take longer to establish and might be affected more by attending a women's college.

The controversies concerning the achievements of graduates from women's colleges have been lively and interesting, but they have also been quite limited. They have focused on a relatively narrow range of individual accomplishments. Although it is true that *Who's Who in American Women* does recognize success in traditional women's fields, there is little doubt that the model of success employed by that publication and by most of the research reviewed above is the same model that would be used for assessing the success of men. The emphasis is on the number of years of education and number of degrees attained, as well as on vocational achievement as measured by reputational prestige and conventional status rankings. As a result, even if a definitive study were to appear showing that women's colleges are places that produce proportionately more high-achieving women than do comparable coeducational colleges, the results would tell us little about how "women-centered" those colleges were. Indeed, it might be the women's colleges that most strongly endorse "male standards" of success that produce the greatest number of high-achieving graduates.

To suggest a rejection of male standards of achievement does not mean that a women-centered education should prevent women from achieving successes as good as any man's, but it does suggest that a women-centered education should also be an emancipatory education. As noted in Chapter 4, this means challenging traditional, male-oriented notions of the liberal arts, as well as challenging gender-typed versions of careerism. An emancipatory education should also enable women to conceptualize and strive for success on their own terms, and this often means broadening notions of high achievement to include successful marriages, parenting, citizenship, and friendships. The key phrases are *broad* opportunities and *high* achievement. A women-centered education that can become a model, rather than a follower of men's education, is one that offers students the broadest opportunities for high achievement in a context that recognizes that being a successful person requires more than attaining lots of education and a high-status occupation.

Looking back on the findings reported in this book, one can find examples of ways in which CWC did offer its students broad opportunities and higher standards for success than they might otherwise have achieved. On average, the academic performance of the students improved, especially after their first year of college. Those who entered with a career orientation found considerable support for careerism but also found themselves expected to complete coursework in the liberal arts. Over time, most students who remained to graduate learned to pursue a social life that did not interfere with their ability to meet the academic demands of the faculty. Curricular and extracurricular success were found to go hand-in-hand. Gender egalitarianism, personal autonomy, and traditional family life were valued by faculty and students, and the overwhelming majority of graduating students planned to combine successful occupational careers with successful marriages and motherhood.

Looking back, one can also find examples of ways in which CWC failed to offer its students broad opportunities or to impose high standards on them. Neither citizenship training nor feminist analysis were effective parts of the curriculum or extracurriculum at CWC, as evidenced by the high

levels of ignorance and inconsistency graduating seniors revealed concerning political labels, public policies, and the meanings of feminism. And the
finding, reported in Chapter 5, that students were able to survive and
improve academically even if they were very active in the culture of
romance and heterosexuality suggested that academic standards may not
have been very demanding. This was borne out by the responses students
and faculty gave to the measure of academic rigor discussed in Chapter 4
(see also Appendix B, Figures B.8 and B.9). Although only two faculty gave
CWC the lowest possible rating for academic rigor, only two others gave it
the highest possible rating. On average, both the faculty and the students
considered the college to have neither very low nor very high standards.

Undoubtedly, there were some students who would have benefited
from being held to a higher standard. Paulette was probably one of them.
When asked during her senior year to describe important, negative experiences at CWC (Appendix D, Interview III), she responded:

> I think the thing that I've been most disappointed in is not being
> challenged enough. Being able to get very good grades, I know I
> can do well anyway, but being able to just kind of fool around and
> kind of survive. It didn't live up to my expectations. So I'd have to
> count that as a negative.

Later in the same interview, Paulette indicated that she would not recommend CWC to high school graduates who were looking for an academic
challenge, and she closed the interview by saying:

> I'm kind of disappointed in the fact that I didn't grow much. I wasn't
> challenged at all academically in this school and, as a matter of fact,
> there are probably some places I probably slid back on. Probably
> that's my own fault. If I had wanted a better school I could have
> gone somewhere else, and I'm just realizing that now. I was happy
> to slide along.

Paulette's comments make clear that the kinds of supportive attention from faculty that students (including Paulette) found so praiseworthy at CWC were not always consistent with high standards. Many students
might have benefited from the same kind of "push" toward stronger academic efforts that Opal found useful for getting herself involved in the
extracurriculum. And once students like Kinsey had received enough
supportive encouragement to overcome their shyness and reticence to
speak up in class, they might have developed even more self-confidence
if they had been challenged to correct their own wrong answers and to

elaborate their partial answers rather than relying on the faculty to do it for them.

On the other hand, one must acknowledge that pushing students too hard or setting standards that few can meet will probably result in high stress, lowered satisfaction, and higher attrition. At the same time that Harriet and I were studying students at CWC, Arthur Levine and Janet Cureton (1998) were surveying and interviewing undergraduates and student leaders across the United States. The result of their research was a portrayal of contemporary American college students as hopeful, but fearful, workaholics who were "often too busy or too tired to have a social life" (p. 96). Surely, there can and should be a compromise between the unpleasant student lives they portray and the willingness to "slide along" at CWC that made Paulette so critical of herself.

MEANINGS OF DIVERSITY

Implicit in many arguments about women-centered education is the assumption that it requires not only a supportive focus on women but also separation from men. In this view, men in coeducational situations will demand or receive more than their fair share of attention with the result that women students become more passive, less self-confident, and less likely to assume leadership roles or to take advantage of educational opportunities. Most of the seniors whom I interviewed at CWC shared this view, although several claimed that it was something they had learned while attending college. Very few indicated that they had selected CWC because it was a women's college, but almost all said they were happy they had done so and that they considered the fact that it was a women's college to be an extra bonus. Typical was the remark of Jewell, who said that the fact that CWC was a women's college "was a negative in the beginning, but now I consider it a strong plus."

Very few students expressed reservations about the benefits of an all-women college. Of those who dropped out of CWC and were interviewed about their three major reasons for doing so (Appendix D, Interview II), only five mentioned the fact that CWC was a women's college as one of those reasons. Of those who were interviewed in their senior year and eventually graduated from CWC (Appendix D, Interview III), only two thought that the lack of gender diversity in their classes might have been a·disadvantage. Fawn was one of them, but her concerns turned out to be rather mild. She began by saying that because she was at a women's college, "I feel like I miss out on some things. I know I do. So I feel funny. I mean, I felt funny going home and being around guys. I feel funny because

I'm not used to it, and that's probably something I'm going to have to work at because it's been a while." When asked if she thought that not having been "around guys" would hurt her on the job market or in her career, she replied: "I don't think so. . . . Since I recognize it, then I can work on it."

Carol's statements echoed Fawn's both in the concerns she expressed and in the mildness of her complaints. Because she took no classes at Canterbury College and none of the Canterbury men were in her CWC classes, Carol saw college men only on weekends, but she opined, "It would be nice to interact with boys on a daily basis. Not that they're everything, but . . . I would have liked to have had classes with boys just because I think it would be more challenging."

Surprisingly, the most vociferous complaint about the lack of diversity at CWC concerned race, rather than gender. Although the CWC graduates who were interviewed in their senior year were explicitly asked about their reactions to the fact that CWC was a women's college, they were not asked about the racial composition of the student body. Nevertheless, Melody felt strongly enough to say the following:

> I didn't like the fact that this school in general doesn't have very many racially different people in it. Like, there's about, I would say, five Black women on this campus which I think is kind of really rare, and it would have been a lot better if there were more [because] when I go out in the world . . . it's like a culture shock. . . . Like last summer there was, I had to work with five different Black people, and I hadn't had that contact before. . . . And learning how to deal with that outside of college, it was different. I figured I'd have to deal with it as a college student. . . . It went fine; it was just a shock. I just, it just shocked me to think that [CWC] as a college did not recruit the racial balance that other colleges would have done.

Melody's estimate of only five African-American students on campus was accurate for at least part of her college career. Of the four African Americans who had matriculated with her in 1991, only two remained to graduate. One of these two worked in the admissions office and participated in their minority recruitment effort. When asked about the small number of African Americans at CWC, she responded:

> It really hasn't bothered me, but a lot of [African Americans] that do look at the college, they do look at the ratio of diversity, and they don't feel comfortable; so, they don't come here . . . I've given a lot of tours with minority students and stuff and they're like, "So, how many are here?" And at one point I was like, "Five." You

know, you could count them on one hand, and I wanted [the number of African Americans] to go up in double digits, and we're almost there. We're nine now; so, I'm very happy. Nine, ten, something like that.

This increase raised the proportion of African Americans in the CWC on-campus student body to less than 2%, a figure far below those reported at that time for private women's colleges nationally (Harwarth et al., 1997). Those figures indicate that traditionally White women's colleges in the Baccalaureate I or elite category enrolled an average of 14.1% Black students in 1993, whereas women's colleges in the same Baccalaureate II category as CWC had student bodies that were 10.9% Black. The proportions of CWC students from other U.S. minority groups were also tiny, but the college probably matched or exceeded most other nonelite women's colleges in its enrollments of international students, especially from Asia. During the period of our study, most of these students were in special programs that did not lead to baccalaureate degrees. Only one international student entered the baccalaureate program as a first-year student in 1991, and she left after one year. Yet, judging from the president's public statements in the mid-1990s, it was undoubtedly the expanding international programs that she had in mind when she talked about the "campus diversification" that had been accomplished at CWC.

Programs for international students were not much in the minds of the CWC seniors who spoke to me about campus diversity, although Melody did say that she thought it was "different" to find more "Asian kids" on campus than African Americans. Unlike Melody or Fawn and Carol, few students mentioned either race or gender. Nor were the other social categories usually used to define social diversity, such as social class, ethnicity, religion, or sexual orientation, used by the seniors when they talked about CWC as a place where they had met and learned to get along with a lot of people who were different from themselves. In the absence of salient social categories, the students tended to volunteer other criteria for defining these differences, including individual differences in personalities and opinions, and the campus-based distinction between sorority members and independents.

With regard to sororities, many of the seniors, like the first-year students quoted in Chapter 3, considered them to be an important component of campus life at CWC. In contrast to the earlier interview, the senior-year interview did not ask students directly about sororities. Nevertheless, sorority membership (or nonmembership) was the most salient characteristic used by the seniors to define themselves and to differentiate among CWC students. Some remarked that they personally tried to be friendly

with everyone, but others perceived barriers and continuing tension between the two groups. Although no one said so, the interviews gave the
impression that the separation between sorority members and independents had become greater, though not more hostile, since the first year, a
likely possibility given the segregated housing arrangements in which most
CWC students lived during their sophomore, junior, and senior years.

The findings reported in this book suggest that sororities provided no
great benefits to the college as a whole. Membership did not increase the
academic involvements and achievements of students, at least as measured
by grades. Nor were sorority women more likely than independents to
involve themselves in extracurricular activities or NAIA athletics. Those
members who considered their sorority affiliation to be the highlight of
their years at CWC usually cited the friendships they had formed with their
sorority sisters, but evidence presented in Chapter 6 shows that sorority
members were no more likely than independents to form friendships at
CWC that were more important than their previous friendships. And the
positive effects of sororities on student retention are partly offset by our
findings that a few students left the college because of the sorority system
and that the important friendships both independents and sorority members formed at CWC significantly increased their retention rates. Perhaps
if there had been no sororities creating friendship boundaries, students
would have felt free and been able to form more of these important and
rewarding relationships.

If sororities seemed to provide CWC with no major benefits, they also
seemed to do no great harm. Undoubtedly, the small size of the campus and
the college-controlled housing and eating arrangements muted antagonisms
between the two groups. Also, as noted repeatedly throughout this book,
many of the significant differences between sorority members and independents were due to selective recruitment rather than to the experience of
sorority membership. Nevertheless, sororities did institutionalize social-class
differences on campus, and they reinforced—and in some cases promoted—
gender propriety, concerns about physical appearance, status striving, alcohol use, and the dating and rating game. These were not components of the
core mission of the college, and they improved neither students' self-esteem
nor their curricular or extracurricular achievements.

LOST OPPORTUNITIES AT CWC

As this book has tried to show, the major historical contradictions that
have characterized women's colleges, and all of higher education for
women, continued to evidence themselves at CWC in the last decade of

the 20th century. Readers who wish to resolve those contradictions by recognizing that women's colleges offer women supportive attention and leadership opportunities and by hoping or proclaiming that these collegiate virtues emancipate women and turn them into gender-egalitarian, confident, career-oriented achievers will find evidence to support their claims in this book. But support can also be found in this book for those who assert that women's colleges can be too protective, too traditional, too focused on caring and community, and not focused enough on challenging students or on fostering the highest levels of nontraditional achievements. As this book has also shown, both of these resolutions of the contradictions facing women's colleges fail to do justice to the ways in which traditionalism and emancipation, careerism and social life, and community and individual achievement work together to shape the college careers of American women.

In its years as a women's college, the greatest shortcoming of CWC was not that it was too protective and controlling of its students or that it failed to hold them to the highest academic standards or that, by supporting sororities, it divided them and sent them messages about the overriding importance of active heterosexuality. The major shortcoming was that it never asked its students to take themselves seriously *as women*. Never were they required to learn about the history and legacy of women's colleges. Never were they taught to analyze feminist theories and ideologies, many of which are centrally concerned with social divisions produced by race-ethnicity, social class, and sexual orientation. Never were they asked to consider what it meant to call CWC a women-centered college or what it might mean if the college became coeducational.

Few students realized what they had missed. Most expressed satisfaction with the college and its faculty, a finding consistent with the high levels of student satisfaction at women's colleges (vs. coeducational institutions) that have been reported by Astin (1977, 1993) and Smith (1990). But Laurel was one student who understood what was missing. Although generally satisfied with her undergraduate career at CWC, Laurel had a vision of what the college could have been and what it might have become if it had remained a college for women. From her come the final words of this book and the valedictory to Central *Women's* College:

> I didn't realize the advantages of an all-women's school until I was here [at CWC]. . . . Social life is important . . . but I feel like here at [CWC] too much emphasis is placed on that . . . and [on having] a boyfriend. . . . I think, umm, [CWC] being an all-women's institution needs to, and I think they're starting to change and they're starting to do this, but I think they need to

promote being all-women and how being a woman is a good
thing. And, you know, that you can do anything you want to do.
You don't need a man. I mean, you can be independent and do
your own thing and just to feel, you know, feel positive about
yourself and that you don't . . . need someone else to be somebody. That, you know, you're your own individual plus you're a
woman; so, you know, I think they need to promote that and
show how that does have benefits.

APPENDIX A

Description of Instruments and Samples

Five surveys and three interviews provided the data analyzed in this book. They are described here in chronological order.

Survey I: Spring 1991

Self-administered questionnaire distributed to all students attending a representative sample of CWC classes during a 1-week period. Questionnaires returned by students enrolled in a class but not in the college itself were discarded. No student refused to participate.
Total number of usable questionnaires collected = 293

Survey II: Summer 1991

Self-administered questionnaire mailed to students who had been admitted to the first-year class at CWC and who had indicated that they would attend CWC. Questionnaires returned by those who never attended were discarded as were those returned by students enrolling in a 2-year vocational program.
Total enrolled in fall 1991 = 185
Total who completed Survey II = 157

Survey III: Spring 1992

Self-administered questionnaire distributed to all first-year students who matriculated in fall 1991 and were still enrolled during the second semester.
Total eligible to receive Survey III = 165
Total who completed Survey III = 164

Interview I: Spring 1992

Interviews were conducted by two CWC staff women who did not know most of the first-year students and who were hired and trained for the task. Of the 165 first-year students matriculating in fall 1991 and still enrolled in spring 1992, a random sample of 50 were selected to be interviewed. Of these, only one refused to be interviewed but scheduling problems prevented eight other interviews from being completed by the deadline. Appendix D contains those questions on the interview schedule that are relevant to the book. Total who completed Interview I = 41

Interview II: Spring 1994–Summer 1995

The primary purpose of the interview was to obtain agreement to complete Survey IV, but respondents were also asked why they had left [CWC] and whether they had continued their higher education. Interviews were conducted on the telephone by a research assistant employed by the Center for Research in Social Behavior, University of Missouri-Columbia, who did not know any of the students at CWC. Of the 185 first-year students matriculating in fall 1991, 95 left the college without obtaining a baccalaureate degree. Three of these were eliminated from the study because they left during their first semester, and they had *not* completed Survey II. Efforts were made to contact the remaining 92, but in nine cases, no current telephone number could be found for either the former student or her parents/guardians. Of the remaining 83 cases, only one former student refused to cooperate. It was not always possible to speak directly with the former student, however, and in eight cases the student's address was obtained from a relative or roommate. Total who completed Interview II = 74

Survey IV: Spring 1994–Fall 1995

Slightly different versions of this survey were sent to (a) 90 students who had entered the first-year class in fall 1991 and graduated from CWC and (b) 83 students who had dropped out of CWC and did not return to graduate, who were eligible for Interview II, and whose current address could be determined.
Total who completed Survey IV = 159 (82 graduates and 77 dropouts)

Interview III: Late Spring and Late Fall 1995

I conducted all of these interviews in a private office on the CWC campus. The spring sample was a random sample of all students from the original

first-year class of 185 who were (a) enrolled at CWC that semester and (b) scheduled to graduate in May or December 1995. Only one member of the sample declined to be interviewed, but two could not be reached, and scheduling problems prevented interviews with four.
Sample drawn in spring 1995 = 27
Sample interviewed in late spring 1995 = 20

In the fall, one afternoon and evening was set aside to interview as many students as possible from the original first-year class of 185 who (a) were enrolled at CWC that semester and (b) had not been interviewed the previous spring. Six students agreed to be interviewed on the date set for that purpose.
Sample interviewed on November 1, 1995 = 6
Total sample who completed Interview III = 26

Faculty Survey: Summer 1997

A list was compiled of all faculty who had been at CWC during the entire period from 1991 to 1995. Of the 46 faculty identified, 43 had been employed full time, and three had been employed on a part-time basis. At the time of the survey, 32 were still employed at CWC (two part time), and 14 had retired or left CWC (one part time).
Total who were sent the Faculty Survey = 46
Total whose completed Faculty Survey was received = 34

APPENDIX B

Survey Measures

The survey measures used in the study appear in this appendix in the order in which they are introduced in the text. For each measure, questions taken from other sources are designated as such. Questions for which no such attribution is made were devised by Bank and/or Yelon.

Figure B.1. Measure of Gender-Related Norms

This measure appeared on Surveys I, II, and IV, and on the Faculty Survey.

Items c, d, and j were taken from the "Attitudes Toward Sex Roles" questionnaire developed by Komarovsky (1985), and the rest were developed after reviewing the large number of sex-role attitude statements presented by Mason (1975) and Beere (1979).

The statements listed on this page describe opinions about the roles of women in society. There are no right or wrong opinions, and you may or may not agree with these statements. Please read each statement carefully, then circle the number that indicates the extent of your agreement.

I disagree strongly					I agree strongly	
1	2	3	4	5	6	7

Please circle a number

a.	Men and women should always be given equal pay for equal work	1	2	3	4	5	6	7
b.	Women who have children ought to put their children ahead of their careers	1	2	3	4	5	6	7
c.	A woman should be as free as a man to propose marriage	1	2	3	4	5	6	7
d.	Swearing and obscenity are more repulsive in the speech of a woman than a man	1	2	3	4	5	6	7
e.	If a husband and wife are both working full time outside the home, they should each do half of the housework in the home	1	2	3	4	5	6	7
f.	A college woman has the right to expect her professors to treat her as seriously as they treat their male students	1	2	3	4	5	6	7
g.	It is more important for a man than for a woman to have a successful, well-paying career	1	2	3	4	5	6	7
h.	If a woman wants to attend a dance or party, she should feel free to invite a man to be her date	1	2	3	4	5	6	7
i.	If two women are friends, they should never date each other's current boyfriends	1	2	3	4	5	6	7
j.	Women should worry less about their rights and more about becoming good wives and mothers	1	2	3	4	5	6	7
k.	Women who are married ought to put their husbands ahead of their own careers	1	2	3	4	5	6	7
l.	College women should concentrate more on their studies and less on their social lives	1	2	3	4	5	6	7
m.	Women should feel free to compete with each other for the attractive and interesting men	1	2	3	4	5	6	7

Figure B.2. Measure of Values

This measure appeared on Surveys I, II, and IV, and on the Faculty Survey.

Six of these values were taken from the list of terminal values developed by Rokeach (1973) and applied to educational settings by Feather (1975). The other four values—a happy marriage, loving children, a successful career, and sexual fulfillment—were added because of their relevance to the themes of gender traditionalism and emancipation for young, American women.

I. Listed in alphabetical order below are ten values or goals that people might have for their lives. For each goal please circle the number that best indicates how important that goal is to you personally.

Not at all important to me	Slightly important to me	Somewhat important to me	Very important to me
1	2	3	4

Please circle a number

___ A happy marriage	1	2	3	4
___ A prosperous life (financial security)	1	2	3	4
___ A successful career	1	2	3	4
___ Freedom (independence, free choice)	1	2	3	4
___ Loving children	1	2	3	4
___ Salvation (being saved, heaven)	1	2	3	4
___ Sexual fulfillment	1	2	3	4
___ Self-respect (self-esteem)	1	2	3	4
___ Social approval (admiration)	1	2	3	4
___ True friendships	1	2	3	4

II. Your next task is to *RANK ORDER THE TEN GOALS LISTED ABOVE* in order of their importance to YOU as goals for YOUR life. Look over the list carefully, decide which goal is most important for you, place the number 1 on the line in front of that goal. Then, decide which goal is second most important to you, and place the number 2 on the line in front of that goal. Continue until you have ranked all ten goals in order of their importance to you. The number ten should appear on the line in front of the goal that is least important to you.

Figure B.3. Measure of Opinions About Political and Social Policies

This measure appeared on Surveys II and IV and on the Faculty Survey.

Next, a set of statements about some current political and social issues. How much do you agree or disagree with these statements?

I disagree strongly					I agree strongly	
1	2	3	4	5	6	7

Please circle a number

a. The possession and use of marijuana should be legalized — 1 2 3 4 5 6 7

b. Military spending should be the top budget priority of the U.S. government — 1 2 3 4 5 6 7

c. Some sort of religious education should be given in public schools — 1 2 3 4 5 6 7

d. Companies that employ an all white labor force should be required to hire a reasonable number of Afro-Americans and Hispanics — 1 2 3 4 5 6 7

e. It should be illegal to burn the American flag — 1 2 3 4 5 6 7

f. Pornography should be regarded as a form of free speech and protected under law — 1 2 3 4 5 6 7

g. Drug dealers should be given harsh, mandatory prison sentences — 1 2 3 4 5 6 7

h. Homosexuals should be given the same legal rights as heterosexuals — 1 2 3 4 5 6 7

i. Prayer should not be allowed in the public schools — 1 2 3 4 5 6 7

j. Good health care should be available to all Americans regardless of their ability to pay — 1 2 3 4 5 6 7

k. A couple should have sexual intercourse only if they care deeply about each other — 1 2 3 4 5 6 7

l. The richer a person is, the higher rate of taxes that person should pay — 1 2 3 4 5 6 7

m. The legal drinking age should be 21 throughout the United States — 1 2 3 4 5 6 7

n. Legal abortions should be available to all American women — 1 2 3 4 5 6 7

o. There is nothing more important for the U.S. government to spend money on than cleaning up and protecting the environment — 1 2 3 4 5 6 7

Figure B.4. Multiple Measures of Self-Orientations

The set of statements appearing on this and the following page appeared on Surveys I, II, III, and IV, and contained the following measures discussed in the book:

   (1) Need-for-Social-Approval scale: Items d, m, s, t, and z (t and z were reverse-scored)

   (2) Concern-for-Appearance scale: Items g, p, dd, hh, and ll (dd and hh were reverse-scored)

   (3) Self-Esteem scale: Items a, b, f, i, o, u, y, cc, ee, and kk (f, o, cc, ee, and kk were reverse-scored)

Items on this scale were taken from the Self-Esteem measure developed by Rosenberg (1979).

On this page and the following one is a set of statements that may or may not be characteristic of you. Please read each statement carefully, then circle the number that indicates your opinion of how true the statement is of you.

Never true of me	Seldom true of me	Sometimes true of me	Often true of me	Almost always true of me
1	2	3	4	5

Please circle a number

a.	I feel that I am a person of worth, at least on an equal basis with others	1	2	3	4	5
b.	I feel that I have a number of good qualities	1	2	3	4	5
c.	I feel that no one really knows me well	1	2	3	4	5
d.	I worry about what other people think of me	1	2	3	4	5
e.	I am terrified of gaining weight	1	2	3	4	5
f.	All in all, I am inclined to feel that I am a failure	1	2	3	4	5
g.	Looking good is very important to me	1	2	3	4	5
h.	I give too much time and thought to food	1	2	3	4	5
i.	I am able to do things as well as most other people	1	2	3	4	5
j.	I feel that people are around me but not with me	1	2	3	4	5
k.	I am preoccupied with the desire to be thinner	1	2	3	4	5
l.	I feel more comfortable with people of my own sex than with people of the opposite sex	1	2	3	4	5
m.	I want people to like me	1	2	3	4	5
n.	I feel that food controls my life	1	2	3	4	5

(continued)

Figure B.4 (continued)

		Please circle a number				
o.	I feel I do not have much to be proud of	1	2	3	4	5
p.	I try to look as attractive as I possibly can	1	2	3	4	5
q.	I feel extremely guilty after overeating	1	2	3	4	5
r.	I feel there are people who really understand me	1	2	3	4	5
s.	I want other people to approve of me	1	2	3	4	5
t.	What I think of myself is more important than what other people think of me	1	2	3	4	5
u.	I take a positive attitude toward myself	1	2	3	4	5
v.	I think about dieting	1	2	3	4	5
w.	I feel "in tune" with the people around me	1	2	3	4	5
x.	I can eat carbohydrates and sweets without feeling guilty	1	2	3	4	5
y.	On the whole, I am satisfied with myself	1	2	3	4	5
z.	I don't care if other people think I am attractive	1	2	3	4	5
aa.	I exaggerate or magnify the importance of weight	1	2	3	4	5
bb.	In general, I find people of the opposite sex more interesting than people of my own sex	1	2	3	4	5
cc.	I wish I could have more respect for myself	1	2	3	4	5
dd.	When I am in a social situation, I don't give much thought to my appearance	1	2	3	4	5
ee.	I certainly feel useless at times	1	2	3	4	5
ff.	I find myself preoccupied with food	1	2	3	4	5
gg.	I can find companionship when I want it	1	2	3	4	5
hh.	How I feel matters more to me than how I look	1	2	3	4	5
ii.	I feel that my interests and ideas are not shared by those around me	1	2	3	4	5
jj.	If I gain a pound, I worry that I will keep gaining	1	2	3	4	5
kk.	At times I think I am no good at all	1	2	3	4	5
ll.	I worry about my appearance	1	2	3	4	5
mm.	I care more about other people than I care about myself	1	2	3	4	5

Figure B.5. First Measure of Components of Self-Evaluation

This measure appeared on Survey III.

Finally, on this last page of the questionnaire, we are interested in learning more about the ways that you think about yourself: *How important to your evaluation of yourself are each of the following characteristics?*

Not at all important to me	Slightly important to me	Somewhat important to me	Very important to me	Most important to me
1	2	3	4	5

Please circle a number

a.	Being a student at (CWC)	1	2	3	4	5
b.	The shape of your body	1	2	3	4	5
c.	Being a sorority member or an independent	1	2	3	4	5
d.	The friendships you made before coming to college	1	2	3	4	5
e.	Friendships you've made since coming to college	1	2	3	4	5
f.	Being a freshman in college	1	2	3	4	5
g.	Whether men are asking you for dates or not	1	2	3	4	5
h.	Your relationship with your mother	1	2	3	4	5
i.	The grades you received last semester	1	2	3	4	5
j.	Your relationships with women at (CWC)	1	2	3	4	5
k.	Your relationships with men at (Canterbury)	1	2	3	4	5
l.	The grades you received so far this semester	1	2	3	4	5
m.	Your weight	1	2	3	4	5
n.	Your relationships with faculty at (CWC)	1	2	3	4	5
o.	The college-sponsored clubs and activities you are involved in (if none, skip to p. below)	1	2	3	4	5
p.	Whether you have a steady boyfriend or not	1	2	3	4	5
q.	How physically attractive you are	1	2	3	4	5
r.	Your relationship with your roommate	1	2	3	4	5
s.	Your relationship with your father	1	2	3	4	5
t.	Your college major	1	2	3	4	5

Figure B.6. Second Measure of Components of Self-Evaluation

This measure appeared on Survey IV.

Next, we are interested in learning more about the ways that you think about yourself. *How important to your evaluation of yourself is each of the following characteristics?*

Not at all important to me	Slightly important to me	Somewhat important to me	Very important to me	Most important to me
1	2	3	4	5

Please circle a number

a.	Being (or having been) a college student	1	2	3	4	5
b.	The shape of your body	1	2	3	4	5
c.	Being or not being a sorority/fraternity member	1	2	3	4	5
d.	The friendships you made before going to college	1	2	3	4	5
e.	The friendships you made while attending college	1	2	3	4	5
f.	Being the sex (male or female) that you are	1	2	3	4	5
g.	Whether members of the opposite sex are asking you for dates or not	1	2	3	4	5
h.	Your relationship with your mother	1	2	3	4	5
i.	The grades you received in college	1	2	3	4	5
j.	Your relationships with women	1	2	3	4	5
k.	Your relationships with men	1	2	3	4	5
l.	Being from your social class	1	2	3	4	5
m.	Your weight	1	2	3	4	5
n.	Your relationships with college faculty	1	2	3	4	5
o.	The clubs and organizations you belong to (if none, skip to p. below)	1	2	3	4	5
p.	Whether you have an opposite-sex partner or not	1	2	3	4	5
q.	How physically attractive you are	1	2	3	4	5
r.	Being the race-ethnicity that you are	1	2	3	4	5
s.	Your relationship with your father	1	2	3	4	5
t.	Your relationships with family members (other than your mother and father)	1	2	3	4	5

Figure B.7. Measure of Students' Orientations Toward College

This measure appeared on Survey II.

Going to college offers hundreds of different opportunities, a few of which are listed on this page. How important is each of the following opportunities to you personally?

Not at all important to me	Slightly important to me	Somewhat important to me	Very important to me	Most important to me
1	2	3	4	5

Please circle a number

a.	Opportunity to get qualified for an interesting career	1	2	3	4	5
b.	Opportunity to make new friends	1	2	3	4	5
c.	Opportunity to join a sorority/fraternity	1	2	3	4	5
d.	Opportunity to do what my parents want me to do	1	2	3	4	5
e.	Opportunity to gain a better understanding of the world	1	2	3	4	5
f.	Opportunity to develop my leadership skills	1	2	3	4	5
g.	Opportunity to be with people like myself	1	2	3	4	5
h.	Opportunity to study and learn new things	1	2	3	4	5
i.	Opportunity to be more independent from my parents	1	2	3	4	5
j.	Opportunity to meet interesting members of the opposite sex	1	2	3	4	5
k.	Opportunity to take interesting classes	1	2	3	4	5
l.	Opportunity to party and have a good time	1	2	3	4	5
m.	Opportunity to develop my reading and writing skills	1	2	3	4	5
n.	Opportunity to meet people of different races and backgrounds than my own	1	2	3	4	5
o.	Opportunity to get ahead in the world	1	2	3	4	5
p.	Opportunity to find a husband/wife	1	2	3	4	5
q.	Opportunity to learn more about the great art, music, and literature of the world	1	2	3	4	5
r.	Opportunity to train for a higher paying job	1	2	3	4	5
s.	Opportunity to do what most of my friends are doing	1	2	3	4	5

Figure B.8. Measure of Students' Evaluation of CWC

This measure appeared on Survey IV and contained the following scales discussed in the book:

    (1) Liberal Arts Emphasis scale: Items e, m, and q

    (2) Academic Rigor scale: Items h and s (s was reverse-scored)

    (3) Career Emphasis scale: Items a, f, o, and r

Please give us your *current opinions* about (CWC).

Definitely false	More false than true	More true than false	Definitely true
1	2	3	4

		Please circle a number			
In general, I now think that CWC :					
a.	provides good opportunities to get qualified for interesting careers	1	2	3	4
b.	is a place where I was able to make good friends	1	2	3	4
c.	has an administration that does not care about students	1	2	3	4
d.	offers courses that are too difficult for me	1	2	3	4
e.	gives students a better understanding of the world	1	2	3	4
f.	is a good place to develop leadership skills	1	2	3	4
g.	enrolls students who have a lot in common with me	1	2	3	4
h.	provides good opportunities to study and learn new things	1	2	3	4
i.	is a place where I became a more independent person	1	2	3	4
j.	is a good place to meet interesting members of the opposite sex	1	2	3	4
k.	offers interesting classes	1	2	3	4
l.	is a good place to party and have fun	1	2	3	4
m.	provides good opportunities to develop your reading and writing skills	1	2	3	4
n.	enrolls students from a variety of interesting backgrounds	1	2	3	4
o.	helps students get ahead in the world	1	2	3	4
p.	has a faculty that cares about students	1	2	3	4
q.	encourages students to learn more about the great art, music, and literature of the world	1	2	3	4
r.	is a good place to train for high-paying jobs	1	2	3	4
s.	has low academic standards	1	2	3	4

Figure B.9. Measure of Faculty Members' Evaluation of CWC

This measure produced the following scales discussed in the book:
- (1) Liberal Arts Emphasis scale: Items e, m, and q
- (2) Academic Rigor scale: Items h and s (s was reverse-scored)
- (3) Career Emphasis scale: Items a, f, o, and r

Colleges have many different characteristics, a few of which are listed on this page. If you had to describe (CWC) from 1991–1995, how true of the undergraduate college would you find each of these statements to be?

Definitely false	More false than true	More true than false	Definitely true
1	2	3	4

Please circle a number

From 1991–1995, I think that (CWC) . . .

a.	provided good opportunities to get qualified for interesting careers	1	2	3	4
b.	was a place where students and faculty became friends	1	2	3	4
c.	had an administration that did not care about students	1	2	3	4
d.	offered courses that were too difficult for many students	1	2	3	4
e.	improved students' understanding of the world	1	2	3	4
f.	was a good place to develop leadership skills	1	2	3	4
g.	had a top-quality administration	1	2	3	4
h.	put a strong emphasis on studying and learning	1	2	3	4
i.	encouraged students to become independent from parents	1	2	3	4
j.	put a strong emphasis on traditional family values	1	2	3	4
k.	offered interesting classes	1	2	3	4
l.	had too many students who would rather party than study	1	2	3	4
m.	provided good opportunities for students to develop their reading and writing skills	1	2	3	4
n.	enrolled students from a variety of interesting backgrounds	1	2	3	4
o.	encouraged students to become work and career oriented	1	2	3	4
p.	had a faculty that cared about students	1	2	3	4
q.	encouraged students to learn more about the great art, music, and literature of the world	1	2	3	4
r.	was a good place to train for high-paying jobs	1	2	3	4
s.	had low academic standards	1	2	3	4

Figure B.10. Measure of Faculty Opinions About Student Culture

On this page of the questionnaire, we are interested in learning more about what you think of the undergraduates at (CWC) from 1991–1995. *How important to most of those students do you think each of the following was?*

Not at all important to them	Slightly important to them	Somewhat important to them	Very important to them	Most important to them
1	2	3	4	5

Please circle a number

a.	Being a student at (CWC)		1 2 3 4 5
b.	The shape of their body		1 2 3 4 5
c.	Being a sorority member or an independent		1 2 3 4 5
d.	The friendships they formed in high school		1 2 3 4 5
e.	The friendships they formed in college		1 2 3 4 5
f.	Their future jobs and careers		1 2 3 4 5
g.	Whether men were asking them for dates or not		1 2 3 4 5
h.	Their relationships with their mother		1 2 3 4 5
i.	How much they were learning in their classes		1 2 3 4 5
j.	Their relationships with women at (CWC)		1 2 3 4 5
k.	Their relationships with men at (Canterbury)		1 2 3 4 5
l.	Their grades		1 2 3 4 5
m.	Their weight		1 2 3 4 5
n.	Their relationships with faculty at (CWC)		1 2 3 4 5
o.	The college-sponsored clubs and activities they were involved in		1 2 3 4 5
p.	Whether they had a steady boyfriend or not		1 2 3 4 5
q.	How physically attractive they were		1 2 3 4 5
r.	Their relationships with their roommate		1 2 3 4 5
s.	Their relationships with their father		1 2 3 4 5
t.	Their college major		1 2 3 4 5

Figure B.11. Measure of Students' Opinions About Student Culture

This measure appeared on Survey I.

Below is a set of statements that may or may not be characteristic of students at *your* college. Please read each statement carefully, then circle the number that indicates your opinion of how true the statement is of students at your college.

True of few or no students at my college	True of some students at my college	True of many students at my college	True of all or most students at my college
1	2	3	4

Please circle a number

a.	They are serious about their future careers	1	2	3	4
b.	They care more about dating than studying	1	2	3	4
c.	They are in favor of equal rights for women and men	1	2	3	4
d.	They are having sexual relations with members of the opposite sex on a regular basis	1	2	3	4
e.	They are prejudiced against members of other races	1	2	3	4
f.	They are anxious to find a good husband/wife	1	2	3	4
g.	They want to make themselves as attractive as possible	1	2	3	4
h.	They are serious students who want to learn	1	2	3	4
i.	They are friendly and concerned about other people	1	2	3	4
j.	They are worried about their grades	1	2	3	4
k.	They drink alcohol	1	2	3	4
l.	They are politically conservative	1	2	3	4
m.	They use illegal drugs	1	2	3	4
n.	They're snobbish and think they're better than they are	1	2	3	4
o.	They spend too much time worrying about their looks	1	2	3	4
p.	They are warm and supportive friends	1	2	3	4
q.	They think men are more interesting than women	1	2	3	4
r.	They put their future careers ahead of getting married and having children	1	2	3	4

Figure B.12. Measure of Student Involvement in Extracurricular Activities

This measure appeared on Survey III. Names of organizations unique to CWC have been replaced by descriptive labels in parentheses.

Below is a list of ways to get involved at (CWC). Please read each activity carefully, then circle the number that indicates your interest and involvement in this activity.

I am *not* interested or involved in this activity	I am interested but not involved in this activity	I am both interested and involved in this activity
1	2	3

Please circle a number

1.	Running for an office in your residence hall	1	2	3
2.	Applying to be a class representative for Student Alumnae Council	1	2	3
3.	Trying to get nominated for one of the national or international honorary societies (e.g., Alpha Psi Omega in drama; Beta Beta Beta in biology, etc.)	1	2	3
4.	Joining International Studies Club	1	2	3
5.	Joining American Society of Interior Design	1	2	3
6.	Running for an office on the College Government Association Executive Cabinet	1	2	3
7.	Joining Disciplae Legis (legal organization)	1	2	3
8.	Joining Phi Beta Lambda (business)	1	2	3
9.	Joining Students for Social Work	1	2	3
10.	Joining (student service organization)	1	2	3
11.	Joining (clubs associated with a particular major)	1	2	3
12.	Joining Big Brother/Big Sister Program	1	2	3
13.	Working on the (school newspaper)	1	2	3
14.	Working on (yearbook or other campus publication)	1	2	3
15.	Trying to get nominated for President's (honorary)	1	2	3
16.	Joining (service and leadership organization)	1	2	3
17.	Joining (college booster organization)	1	2	3

On the following page were questions about sorority membership followed by:

Are there any organizations or activities at (CWC) *that are not listed on this or the previous page* in which you have been active this year?

No.............1
Yes.............2

If yes, what organizations or activities? _____

_____

_____

APPENDIX C

Statistical Conventions and Manipulations of Survey Responses

All correlations reported in this book were calculated using the formula for Pearson's product–moment correlation. Throughout the book, correlations are described as weak if the Pearson product–moment coefficient is .22 or less. Coefficients greater than .22 but less than .39 are described as moderate, and those at .39 or above are called strong. This means that a weak correlation explains less than 5% of the variance in its correlates, a moderate correlation explains 5% to 15% of the variance, and a strong correlations explains more than 15% of the variance.

All differences between scale scores reported in this book were calculated using the *t*-test formula for independent samples, when comparing different groups, and for matched samples, when comparing the same group over time. Following recommendations by Cohen (1988), effect sizes for differences between groups were calculated using the Effect Size Index: *d*, and they are described as small if the difference is about one quarter of a standard deviation in the combined distributions of the relevant measure, moderate if the difference is equal to half a standard deviation, and large if the difference exceeds three-quarters of a standard deviation.

All results reported in this book that are based on correlation coefficients, *t*s, regression analyses, or other statistical tests are described as significant if they are large enough to have occurred by chance only 5% of the time or less ($p \leq .05$; two-tailed).

Factor Analysis of Gender-Related Norms

Responses to the measure shown in Figure B.1 that were given by students on Survey I were factor analyzed using the principal-components method of factor extraction followed by rotation using a varimax criterion (Wilkinson, 1990). These procedures yielded four factors with eigenvalues greater than 1.00. Loadings on these four factors are presented in Table C.1. I named

174

Table C.1. Rotated Factor Loadings for Questions About Gender Norms[a]

Questions	Factor 1	Factor 2	Factor 3	Factor 4
TRADITIONAL FAMILY NORMS				
Women who have children ought to put their children ahead of their careers (2)	.745	.140	−.063	−.185
Women should worry less about their rights and more about becoming good wives and mothers (10)	.691	−.290	−.106	.054
Women who are married ought to put their husbands ahead of their own careers (11)	.667	−.137	.117	.168
It is more important for a man than for a woman to have a successful, well paying career (7)	.455	−.348	.321	.052
GENDER EQUALITY NORMS				
A college woman has the right to expect her professors to treat her as seriously as they treat their male students (6)	.029	.798	−.062	.097
If a woman wants to attend a dance or party, she should feel free to invite a man to be her date (8)	−.080	.643	−.044	.189
Men and women should always be given equal pay for equal work (1)	−.152	.594	.120	−.221
If a husband and wife are both working full time outside the home, they should each do half of the housework in the home (5)	−.139	.452	−.144	.387
PROPRIETY NORMS				
A woman should be as free as a man to propose marriage (3)	−.050	.198	−.710	.243
Swearing and obscenity are more repulsive in the speech of a woman than a man (4)	.425	.158	.600	.074
If two women are friends, they should never date each other's current boyfriends (9)	−.246	.029	.495	.199
SELF-ORIENTED NORMS				
College women should concentrate more on their studies and less on their social lives (12)	.056	−.010	−.088	.713
Women should feel free to compete with each other for the attractive and interesting men (13)	.031	.094	.135	.588
PERCENT OF VARIANCE EXPLAINED	15.244	14.843	10.060	9.766

[a]Numbers in parentheses after each norm indicate the order in which items appeared on the questionnaire.

the first factor *Traditional Family Norms* because items with the highest loadings on this factor measured the extent to which women and their careers should take second place to husbands and children. I named the second factor *Gender Equality Norms* because all four items with the highest loadings measured the extent to which men and women should either perform the same behaviors or be treated equally.

Although the statement that "a woman should be as free as a man to propose marriage" would seem to be another measure of gender equality, the factor analysis revealed that this item produced a high loading on Factor 3 but not on Factor 2. Respondents who disagreed with this norm were also likely to think that women shouldn't swear and that they should respect the dating relationships of their friends. Because the commonality among these items seems to be their emphasis on women's proper or conventional behaviors, I named this factor *Propriety Norms*.

Although the two items with high loadings on Factor 4 focus on somewhat different domains of student experience, they both seem to stress the extent to which people should pursue their own personal goals instead of being oriented to their friends or to sociability more generally. On the basis of this reasoning, I decided to call this factor *Self-Oriented Norms*.

Respondents to all four surveys on which this measure appeared were assigned scores on the four scales identified by the factor analysis reported in Table C.1. These scores consisted of the total of responses given to each item with a factor loading of .450 or above divided by the number of such items. As suggested by the factor analysis, item 3 among the propriety norms ("A woman should be as free as a man to propose marriage.") was reverse-scored to make it consistent with the other two norms on that scale. Using these procedures resulted in four scales with a possible range from 1 to 7 and with higher scores indicating more traditionalism, gender egalitarianism, propriety, and self-orientation.

Factor Analysis of Values

Factor analysis of the 10 value ratings made by CWC students in the spring of 1991 (see Appendix B, Figure B.2) was conducted using the principal-components method of factor extraction followed by rotation using a varimax criterion (Wilkinson, 1990). These procedures yielded four factors with eigenvalues greater than 1.00, and loadings on these four factors are presented in Table C.2.

I called the first factor *Achievement Values* because the values with the highest loadings on this factor represented achievements in four domains: economic, social, sexual, and occupational. In contrast to the stress on children, marriage, and religious salvation of the second factor, which I

Table C.2. Rotated Factor Loadings for Ratings of Values[a]

Values	Factor 1	Factor 2	Factor 3	Factor 4
ACHIEVEMENT VALUES				
A prosperous life (financial security) (2)	.844	.011	−.178	−.034
Social approval (admiration) (9)	.587	.196	.169	.323
Sexual fulfillment (7)	.582	.216	.191	.178
A successful career (3)	.546	−.090	.316	−.357
TRADITIONAL FAMILY VALUES				
Loving children (5)	.153	.796	−.028	.037
A happy marriage (1)	.057	.766	−.119	.200
Salvation (being saved, heaven) (6)	.032	.688	.202	−.131
AUTONOMY VALUES				
Freedom (independence, free choice) (4)	.058	.048	.777	−.122
Self-respect (self-esteem) (8)	.094	−.007	.699	.298
TRUE FRIENDSHIP				
True friendship (10)	.105	.024	.075	.824
PERCENT OF VARIANCE EXPLAINED	17.447	17.890	14.504	11.059

[a] Numbers in parentheses after each value indicate the order in which items appeared on the questionnaire.

named *Traditional Family Values*, the third factor is more self-oriented. I decided to call it *Autonomy*. Only one value, *True Friendship*, received a high loading on the fourth factor, but this factor is not analyzed in the text.

Respondents to all four surveys on which this measure appeared were assigned scores on the first three value scales identified by the factor analysis reported in Table C.2. These scores consisted of the total of ratings given to each value with a factor loading of .500 or above divided by the number of such items. Using these procedures resulted in scales with a possible range from 1 to 4 with higher scores indicating higher values placed on achievement, traditionalism, and autonomy.

Factor Analysis of Students' Orientations Toward College

Factor analysis of the opportunities offered by college (see Appendix B, Figure B.7) made by CWC students in summer of 1991 was conducted using the principal-components method of factor extraction followed by rotation using a varimax criterion (Wilkinson, 1990). These procedures yielded five factors with eigenvalues greater than 1.00, and loadings on these five factors are presented in Table C.3.

Table C.3. Rotated Factor Loadings >.450 for Ratings of College
Opportunities[a]

Opportunities	Factor 1	Factor 2	Factor 3	Factor 4	Factor 5
ACADEMIC ORIENTATION					
To meet people of different races and backgrounds than my own (n)	.751				
To develop my reading and writing skills (m)	.748				
To gain a better understanding of the world (e)	.736				
To learn more about the great art, music, and literature of the world (q)	.648				
To study and learn new things (h)	.623				
To take interesting classes (k)	.516				
SOCIAL ORIENTATION					
To meet interesting members of the opposite sex (j)		.782			
To join a sorority/fraternity (c)		.714			
To party and have a good time (l)		.695			
To find a husband/wife (p)		.611			
To make new friends (b)		.610			
CAREER ORIENTATION					
To get qualified for an interesting career (a)			.797		
To train for a higher paying job (r)			.593		
To develop my leadership skills (f)			.518		
To get ahead in the world (o)			.489		
PARENTAL ORIENTATION					
To do what my parents want me to do (d)				.806	
PEER ORIENTATION					
To do what most of my friends are doing (s)					.725
To be with people like myself (g)					.580
To be more independent from my parents (i)					.576
PERCENT OF VARIANCE EXPLAINED	17.873	14.134	12.206	7.518	8.532

[a] Letters in parentheses after each opportunity indicate the order in which items appeared on the questionnaire.

I called the first factor *Academic Orientation* because the opportunities with the highest loadings on this factor represented opportunities for students to broaden themselves and to involve themselves in academic matters. For obvious reasons, I named the second and third factors *Social Orientation* and *Career Orientation*. Although I labeled the fourth and fifth factors *Parental Orientation* and *Peer Orientation*, they are not analyzed in the text.

Respondents were assigned scores on the first three orientation scales identified by the factor analysis reported in Table C.3. These scores consisted of the total of ratings given to each value with a factor loading of .450 or above divided by the number of such items. Using these procedures resulted in scales with a possible range from 1 to 5 and with higher scores indicating more academic, social, and career orientation.

Factor Analysis of Students' Opinions About Student Culture

Factor analysis of the evaluation of CWC students (see Appendix B, Figure B.11) was conducted using the principal-components method of factor extraction followed by rotation using a varimax criterion (Wilkinson, 1990). These procedures yielded five factors with eigenvalues greater than 1.00, and loadings on these five factors are listed in Table C.4.

I called the first factor the *Well-Rounded Students* because of the combination of being a serious student, career-oriented, and also warm and people-oriented. I used the label *Narcissistic Libertarians* for the second factor because it describes someone who is self-centered and willing to go beyond legal restraints. *Husband-Hunting Libertines* is the label chosen for the third factor because it is a profile of students who are both sexually permissive and anxious to marry. The names for the last two factors, the *Reactionaries* and the *Egalitarians*, are obvious from the items that load on each factor.

To compare these profiles in the text, each respondent was assigned a score on the five factors. These scores consisted of the total of ratings for the statements loading >.450 on each factor divided by the number of statements. Using these procedures resulted in five scales with a possible range from 1 to 4 and with higher scores indicating more endorsement of the statements in each profile.

Table C.4. Rotated Factor Loadings >.450 for Opinions About Student Culture[a]

Types of Students	Factor 1	Factor 2	Factor 3	Factor 4	Factor 5
THE WELL-ROUNDED STUDENTS					
They are warm and supportive friends (p)	.772				
They are friendly and concerned about other people (i)	.733				
They are serious students who want to learn (h)	.729				
They are serious about their future careers (a)	.680				
They are worried about their grades (j)	.628				
They put their future careers ahead of getting married and having children (r)	.477				
THE NARCISSISTIC LIBERTARIANS					
They are snobbish and think that they are better than they are (n)		.777			
They spend too much time worrying about their looks (o)		.734			
They want to make themselves as attractive as possible (g)		.533			
They use illegal drugs (m)		.511			
They think men more interesting than women (q)		.497			
They drink alcohol (k)		.489			
THE HUSBAND-HUNTING LIBERTINES					
They are anxious to find a good husband (f)			.678		
They care more about dating than studying (b)			.613		
They are having sexual relations with members of the opposite sex on a regular basis (d)			.547		
They put their future careers ahead of getting married and having children (r)			−.497		
THE REACTIONARIES					
They are politically conservative (l)				.804	
They are prejudiced against members of other races (e)				.557	
THE EGALITARIANS					
They are in favor of equal rights for women and men (c)					.821
PERCENT OF VARIANCE EXPLAINED	18.622	14.883	10.123	7.267	6.965

[a] Letters in parentheses after each opportunity indicate the order in which items appeared on the questionnaire.

APPENDIX D

Interview Schedules

This appendix contains only those sections of the interview schedules that are referred to in the text.

Interview I

Q-6. Let's talk next about your undergraduate experiences. If you think back over your freshman year at [CWC], are there experiences that stand out as important and positive, experiences that made you happy, that you are pleased about?

General Probe: Are there other experiences since coming to CWC that have been important and positive for you?

Q-7. After respondent has no more information to give about positive experiences: If you think back over your freshman year at [CWC], are there experiences that stand out as important and negative, experiences that made you sad or angry, that you are disappointed about?

General Probe: Are there other experiences since coming to [CWC] that have been important and negative for you?

Q-8. All things considered, has your freshman year been a positive or negative experience for you? Why?

Q-9. If you could start your freshman year over again, is there anything that you would do differently? What? Why?

So far we've been talking about *your* relationships and *your* experiences. Now we'd like to ask you some questions about the other young women who are freshmen at [CWC]. We're interested in what you have learned this year about the concerns and problems of these women.

Q-10. What kinds of things have freshmen women at [CWC] been thinking and talking about this year?

Probes: What's on their minds? What's important to them? What do you hear them talking about?

Q-11. Do you think freshmen at [CWC] are concerned about their courses? If yes, why? If no, why not?

Q-12. Do you think freshmen at [CWC] are concerned about their weight and their bodies? If yes, why? If no, why not?

Q-13. Do you think freshmen at [CWC] are concerned about their relationships with their parents? If yes, why? If no, why not?

Q-14. Do you think freshmen at [CWC] are concerned about their use of alcohol? If yes, why? If no, why not?

Q-15. Do you think freshmen at [CWC] are concerned about their relationships with one another? If yes, why? If no, why not?

Q-16. Do you think freshmen at [CWC] are concerned about their relationships with members of the opposite sex? If yes, why? If no, why not?

Q-17. If not covered in response to Q-16, do you think freshmen at [CWC] are concerned about sex? If yes, why? If no, why not?

Q-18. Do you think freshmen at [CWC] are concerned about their use of drugs? If yes, why? If no, why not?

Q-19. Do you think freshmen at [CWC] are concerned about grooming and attire, such things as clothes, cosmetics, hairdo, etc.? If yes, why? If no, why not?

Q-20. Do you think freshmen at [CWC] are concerned about their relationships with the faculty? If yes, why? If no, why not?

Q-21. Do you think freshmen at [CWC] are concerned about the differences between being a Greek and an independent? If yes, why? If no, why not?

Q-22. Do you think freshmen at [CWC] are concerned about what they will do after they graduate from college? If yes, why? If no, why not?

Q-23. And, the very last question I have to ask you is whether there is anything else you want to tell us about your undergraduate experiences or about the concerns and experiences of other freshmen at [CWC]?

Interview II

Since leaving [CWC], did you enroll at any other universities or colleges? If yes, which ones, and when did you attend there?

One last question. If you had to name the three most important reasons why you left [CWC], what would they be? (If respondent hesitates, repeat that all responses are confidential and her name will never be used in any reports based on the study.)

Of the reasons you've given, is there one that stands out as most important? If yes, which reason is that? (Place a star by the response.)

Interview III

Q-1. Let's begin by talking about your positive undergraduate experiences. If you think back over your years at [CWC], what are the experiences that stand out as important and positive, experiences that made you happy, that you are pleased about?

General Probe: Are there other experiences since coming to CWC that have been important and positive for you?

Q-2. After respondent has no more information to give about positive experiences: If you think back over your years at [CWC], are there experiences that stand out as important and negative, experiences that made you sad or angry, that you are disappointed about?

General Probe: Are there other experiences since coming to [CWC] that have been important and negative for you?

Q-3. All things considered, have your years at [CWC] been a positive or negative experience for you? Why?

Q-4. If you could start your undergraduate career all over again, is there anything that you would do differently? What? Why?

Q-5. Why did you decide to enroll at [CWC] in the first place? (If no mention is made about its being a women's college, ask: Did the fact that [CWC] is a women's college influence your decision to come here?)

Q-6. Would you advise young women who are graduating from high school this year to enroll at [CWC]? Why or why not? (If no mention is made about its being a women's college, ask: Would the fact that [CWC] is a women's college affect the kind of advice you would give about enrolling here?)

Next, I'm going to ask you two questions about labels that you may or may not want to put on yourself. I'm really most interested in why you would or wouldn't use these labels.

Q-7. Would you describe yourself as a feminist? Why or why not?

Q-8. Would you describe yourself as a political liberal or a political conservative, or would you use some other political label? Why?

The next three questions ask about concerns that you may have. I'm interested in learning whether your concerns have changed during the years you've been at [CWC].

Q-9. During your years at [CWC] do you think you have become more or less concerned about your grades? Why?

Q-10. During your years at [CWC] do you think you have become more or less concerned about your appearance? Why?

Q-11. During your years at [CWC] do you think you have become more or less concerned about your relationships with the other students enrolled at [CWC]? Why?

Now, I want to ask you some questions about your future.

Q-12. If you imagine yourself 10 years from now, do you think you will still be in touch with any of the other students that you met at [CWC]? (Probe to determine how many students she expects to be in contact with and how frequent and close she expects these contacts to be.)

Q-13. If you imagine yourself 10 years from now, do you think you will still be in touch with any of the faculty, staff, or administrators that you met at [CWC]? (Probe to determine how many faculty/staff/administrators she expects to be in contact with and how frequent and close she expects these contacts to be.)

Q-14. Of all the things you've learned and experienced during your undergraduate years, what do you think will have the most effect on your life in the years to come?

Q-15. And the very last question I have to ask you is whether there is anything else you want to tell me about your undergraduate experiences.

References

Adams, E. K. (1912). The vocational opportunities of the college of liberal arts. *Journal of the Association of Collegiate Alumnae, 5*(3), 256–266.

Alva, S. A. (1998). Self-reported alcohol use of college fraternity and sorority members. *Journal of College Student Development, 39*(1), 3–10.

Arthur, L. B. (1998). Dress and the social construction of gender in two sororities. *Clothing and Textiles Research Journal, 17*(2), 84–93.

Astin, A. W. (1977). *Four critical years.* San Francisco: Jossey-Bass.

Astin, A. W. (1985, July/August). Involvement: The cornerstone of excellence. *Change,* 35–39.

Astin, A. W. (1993). *What matters in college? Four critical years revisited.* San Francisco: Jossey-Bass.

Astin, A. W. (1997). How "good" is your institution's retention rate? *Research in Higher Education, 38*(6), 647–658.

Astin, A. W., Dey, E. L., Korn, W. S., & Riggs, E. R. (1991). *The American freshman: National norms for fall 1991.* Los Angeles: UCLA, Higher Education Research Institute.

Astin, A. W., & Lee, C. B. T. (1972). *The invisible colleges.* New York: McGraw-Hill.

Astin, A. W., Parrott, S. A., Korn, W. S., & Sax, L. J. (1997). *The American freshman: Thirty year trends.* Los Angeles: UCLA, Higher Education Research Institute.

Atlas, G., & Morier, D. (1994). The sorority rush process: Self-selection, acceptance criteria, and the effect of rejection. *Journal of College Student Development, 35*(5), 346–353.

Baier, J. L., & Whipple, E. G. (1990). Greek values and attitudes: A comparison with independents. *NASPA Journal, 28*(1), 43–53.

Baker, L. (1976). *I'm Radcliffe! Fly me! The Seven Sisters and the failure of women's education.* New York: Macmillan.

Bank, B. J. (1995). Friendships in Australia and the United States: From feminization to a more heroic image. *Gender & Society, 9,* 79–98.

Bank, B. J., & Hansford, S. (2000). Gender and friendship: Why are men's best same-sex friendships less intimate and supportive? *Personal Relationships, 7,* 63–78.

Beard, P. (1994, November). The fall and rise of the Seven Sisters. *Town & Country, 148,* 159–174.

Beck, D. B. (1998). The "F" word: How the media frame feminism. *NWSA Journal, 10*(1), 139–153.

185

Beere, C. A. (1979). *Women and women's issues: A handbook of tests and measures.* San Francisco: Jossey-Bass.

Bellafante, G. (1998). Feminism: It's all about me! *Time, 151*(25), 54–60.

Bonvillian, G., & Murphy, R. (1996). *The liberal arts college adapting to change: The survival of small schools.* New York: Garland.

Boyer, E. L. (1987). *College: The undergraduate experience in America.* New York: Harper & Row.

Bromley, D., & Britten, F. (1938). *Youth & sex: A study of 1300 college students.* New York: Harper & Brothers.

Brown, D. R., & Pacini, R. (1993a). The Vassar classes of 1929–1935: Personality patterns in college and adult life. In K. D. Hulbert & D. T. Schuster (Eds.), *Women's lives through time: Educated American women of the twentieth century* (pp. 93–116). San Francisco: Jossey-Bass.

Brown, D. R., & Pacini, R. (1993b). The Vassar classes of 1957 and 1958: The ideal student study. In K. D. Hulbert & D. T. Schuster (Eds.), *Women's lives through time: Educated American women of the twentieth century* (pp. 161–189). San Francisco: Jossey-Bass.

Brown, M. (1982). Career plans of college women: Patterns and influences. In P. Perun (Ed.), *The Undergraduate Woman.* Lexington, MA: D. C. Heath.

Burnett, J. R., Vaughan, M. J., & Moody, D. (1997). The importance of person-organization value congruence for female students joining college sororities. *Journal of College Student Development, 38,* 297–300.

Bushnell, J. H. (1962). Student culture at Vassar. In N. Sanford (Ed.), *The American college* (pp. 489–514). New York: John Wiley & Sons.

Callan, E. (1988). *Autonomy and schooling.* Kingston, ONT: McGill-Queen's University Press.

Carnegie Commission on Higher Education. (1990). *Campus life: In search of community.* Princeton, NJ: The Carnegie Foundation for the Advancement of Teaching.

Carroll, E. J. (1985). *Female difficulties: Sorority sisters, rodeo queens, frigid women, smut stars, and other modern girls.* Toronto: Bantam Books.

Cashin, J. R., Presley, C. A., & Meilman, P. W. (1998). Alcohol use in the Greek system: Follow the leader? *Journal of Studies on Alcohol, 59*(1), 63–70.

Chatman, J. (1991). Matching people and organizations: Selection and socialization in public accounting firms. *Administration Science Quarterly, 36,* 459–484.

Chickering, A. W., & Reisser, L. (1993). *Education and identity* (2nd ed.). San Francisco: Jossey-Bass.

Clark, B., & Trow, M. (1966). The organizational context. In T. M. Newcomb & E. K. Wilson (Eds.), *College peer groups: Problems and prospects for research* (pp. 17–70). Chicago: Aldine.

Cohen, J. (1988). *Statistical power analysis for the behavioral sciences* (2nd ed.). Hillsdale, NJ: Lawrence Erlbaum.

Connell, R. W. (1999). Making gendered people: Bodies, identities, sexualities. In M. M. Ferree, J. Lorber, & B. B. Hess (Eds.), *Revisioning gender* (pp. 449–471). Thousand Oaks, CA: Sage.

DeLucci, M. (1997). Liberal arts colleges and the myth of uniqueness. *Journal of Higher Education, 68,* 414–426.

Eddy, W. (1990). Greek and non-Greek affiliation: Relationship to levels of autonomy. *NASPA Journal, 28*(1), 54–59.

Edwards, R. H., Artman, J. M., & Fisher, G. M. (1928). *Undergraduates: A study of morale in twenty-three American colleges and universities*. Garden City, NY: Doubleday, Doran & Company.

Esterberg, K. G. (1997). *Lesbian & bisexual identities: Constructing communities, constructing selves*. Philadelphia: Temple University Press.

Farnham, C. A. (1994). *The education of the southern belle: Higher education and student socialization in the antebellum South*. New York: New York University Press.

Fass, P. S. (1977). *The damned and the beautiful: American youth in the 1920s*. New York: Oxford University Press.

Fass, P. S. (1997). The female paradox: Higher education for women, 1945–1963. In L. F. Goodchild & H. S. Wechsler (Eds.), *The history of higher education* (2nd ed., pp. 699–723). Needham Heights, MA: Simon & Schuster.

Feather, N. T. (1975). *Values in education and society*. New York: Free Press.

Fehr, B. (1996). *Friendship processes*. Thousand Oaks, CA: Sage.

Feldman, K. A., & Newcomb, T. M. (1994). *The impact of college on students*. New Brunswick, NJ: Transaction Publishers. (Originally published in 1969 by Jossey-Bass)

Figler, H. (1989). *Liberal education and career today*. Garrett Park, MD: Garrett Park Press.

Findlen, B. (Ed.). (1995). *Listen up: Voices from the next feminist generation*. Seattle, WA: Seal Press.

Fisher, V. D. (1991). Women and leadership: Do sororities help or hinder? *Campus Activities Programming, 24*(4), 64–68.

Fox, M., & Auerbach, D. (1983). Whatever it is, don't call me one: Women students' attitudes toward feminism. *International Journal of Women's Studies, 6*, 352–362.

Freedman, M. B. (1956). The passage through college. *Journal of Social Issues, 12*(4), 13–28.

Friedman, M. (1995). Feminism and modern friendship: Dislocating the community. In P. A. Weiss & M. Friedman (Eds.), *Feminism and community* (pp. 187–207). Philadelphia: Temple University Press.

Gilbert, D. (1998). *The American class structure: In an age of growing inequality* (5th ed.). Belmont, CA: Wadsworth.

Goldsmith, A. G., & Crawford, C. C. (1928). How college students spend their time. *School and Society, 27*, 399–402.

Gordon, L. D. (1990). *Gender and higher education in the progressive era*. New Haven, CT: Yale University Press.

Hall, R. M., & Sandler, B. R. (1982). *The classroom climate: A chilly one for women?* Washington, DC: Association of American Colleges.

Handler, L. (1995). In the fraternal sisterhood: Sororities as gender strategy. *Gender & Society, 9*, 236–255.

Harwarth, I., Maline, M., & DeBra, E. (1997). *Women's colleges in the United States: History, issues, and challenges*. Washington, DC: U.S. Department of Education.

Havemann, E., & West, P. S. (1952). *They went to college: The college graduate in America today.* New York: Harcourt, Brace.

Heath, D. H. (1968). *Growing up in college: Liberal health education and maturity.* San Francisco: Jossey-Bass.

Hesse-Biber, S. (1996). *Am I thin enough yet? The cult of thinness and the commercialization of identity.* New York: Oxford.

Hochschild, A. (with Machung, A.). (1989). *The second shift.* New York: Avon Books.

Hoekema, D. (1994). *Campus rules and moral community: In place of in loco parentis.* Lanham, MD: Rowman & Littlefield.

Holland, D. C., & Eisenhart, M. A. (1990). *Educated in romance: Women, achievement, and college culture.* Chicago: University of Chicago Press.

Horowitz, H. L. (1987). *Campus life: Undergraduate cultures from the end of the eighteenth century to the present.* Chicago: University of Chicago Press.

Horowitz, H. L. (1993). *Alma mater: Design and experience in the women's colleges from their nineteenth-century beginnings to the 1930s* (2nd ed.). Amherst: University of Massachusetts Press.

Hughes, M. J., & Winston, R. B., Jr. (1987). Effects of fraternity membership on interpersonal values. *Journal of College Student Personnel, 28,* 405–411.

Hutchins, R. M. (1936). *The higher learning in America.* New Haven, CT: Yale University Press.

Hutchinson, R. G., & Connard, M. H. (1926). What's a college week? *School and Society, 24,* 768–772.

Inness, S. A. (1993). "It is pluck but is it sense?": Athletic student culture in progressive era girls' college fiction. *Journal of Popular Culture, 27*(1), 99–123.

Kalof, L., & Cargill, T. (1991). Fraternity and sorority membership and gender dominance attitudes. *Sex Roles, 25,* 417–423.

Katchadourian, H. A., & Boli, J. (1985). *Careerism and intellectualism among college students.* San Francisco: Jossey-Bass.

Kessler, S. J. (2000). *Lessons from the intersexed.* New Brunswick, NJ: Rutgers University Press.

Komarovsky, M. (1953). *Women in the modern world: Their education and their dilemmas.* Boston: Little, Brown.

Komarovsky, M. (1985). *Women in college: Shaping new feminine identities.* New York: Basic Books.

Levine, A., & Cureton, J. S. (1998). *When hope and fear collide: A portrait of today's college student.* San Francisco: Jossey-Bass.

Lipset, S. M. (1960). *Political man: The social bases of politics.* Garden City, NY: Anchor Books.

Longino, C. F., Jr., & Kart, C. S. (1973). The college fraternity: An assessment of theory and research. *Journal of College Student Personnel, 14*(2), 118–125.

Lottes, I. L., & Kuriloff, P. J. (1994). The impact of college experience on political and social attitudes. *Sex Roles, 31,* 31–54.

Maisel, J. M. (1990). Social fraternities and sororities are not conducive to the educational process. *NASPA Journal, 28*(1), 8–12.

Malone, S. C. (1996). *Gender role attitudes and homogamy preferences of college Greeks.* Unpublished doctoral dissertation, University of Florida, Gainesville.

Mason, K. O. (1975). Sex-role attitude items and scales from U.S. sample surveys (Technical Report of the Population Studies Center at the University of Michigan). Rockville, MD: National Institutes for Mental Health.

McCosh, J. (1888). *Twenty years of Princeton College: Farewell address delivered June 20th, 1888.* New York: Charles Scribner's Sons.

McCoy, M., & DiGeorgio-Lutz, J. (Eds.). (1999). *The woman-centered university: Interdisciplinary perspectives.* Lanham, MD: University Press of America.

McGrath, E. (with Russell, C. H.). (1958). *Are liberal arts colleges becoming professional schools?* New York: Columbia University, Teachers College.

Miller, L. D. (1973). Distinctive characteristics of fraternity members. *Journal of College Student Personnel, 14,* 126–129.

Miller-Bernal, L. (2000). *Separate by degree: Women students' experiences in single-sex and coeducational colleges.* New York: Peter Lang.

Newcomb, T. M. (1943). *Personality and social change: Attitude formation in a student community.* New York: Holt, Rinehart and Winston.

Newcomb, T. M. (1958). Attitude development as a function of reference groups: The Bennington study. In E. E. Maccoby, T. M. Newcomb, & E. L. Hartley (Eds.), *Readings in social psychology* (3rd ed., pp. 265–275). New York: Holt, Rinehart and Winston.

Newcomer, M. (1959). *A century of higher education for American women.* New York: Harper & Brothers.

Nuwer, H. (1999). *Wrongs of passage: Fraternities, sororities, hazing, and binge drinking.* Bloomington: Indiana University Press.

Oates, M. J., & Williamson, S. (1978). Women's colleges and women achievers. *Signs, 3,* 795–806.

Pantages, T. J., & Creedon, C. F. (1978). Studies of college attrition: 1950–1975. *Review of Educational Research, 48,* 49–101.

Pascarella, E. T., & Terenzini, P. T. (1983). Predicting voluntary freshman year persistence/withdrawal behavior in a residential university: A path analytic validation of Tinto's Model. *Journal of Educational Psychology, 75,* 215–226.

Pascarella, E. T., & Terenzini, P. T. (1991). *How college affects students.* San Francisco: Jossey-Bass.

Peterson, H. L., Altbach, P. B., Skinner, E., & Trainer, K. (1976). Greek revival: Sorority pledges at a large university. *Journal of College Student Personnel, 17,* 109–114.

Pleck, J. H. (1987). American fathering in historical perspective. In M. S. Kimmel (Ed.), *Changing men: New directions in research on men and masculinity* (pp. 83–97). Newbury Park, CA: Sage.

Riesman, D. (1981). *On higher education.* San Francisco: Jossey-Bass.

Riordan, C. (1992). Single-and mixed-gender colleges for women: Educational, attitudinal, and occupational outcomes. *The Review of Higher Education, 15,* 327–346.

Riordan, C. (1994). The value of attending a women's college: Education, occupation, and income benefits. *Journal of Higher Education, 65,* 486–510.

Risman, B. J. (1982). College women and sororities: The social construction and reaffirmation of gender roles. *Urban Life, 11*(2), 231–252.

Rokeach, M. (1973). *The nature of human values*. New York: Free Press.

Rosenberg, M. (1979). *Conceiving the self*. New York: Basic Books.

Sadker, M., & Sadker, D. (1994). *Failing at fairness: How our schools cheat girls*. New York: Simon & Schuster Touchstone.

Sandler, B., Silverberg, L., & Hall, R. (1996). *The chilly classroom climate, A guide to improve the education of women*. Washington, DC: National Association for Women in Education.

Sanford, N. (1956). Introduction to personality development during the college years. *The Journal of Social Issues, 12*(4), 3–12.

Schleef, D. (2000). That's a good question! Exploring motivations for law and business school. *Sociology of Education, 73,* 155–174.

Schwager, S. (1988). Educating women in America. In E. Minnich, J. O'Barr, & R. Rosenfeld (Eds.), *Reconstructing the academy: Women's education and women's studies* (pp. 154–193). Chicago: University of Chicago.

Scott, B. A. (Ed.). (1991a). *The liberal arts in a time of crisis*. New York: Praeger.

Scott, B. A. (1991b). Promoting the "new practicality": Curricular policies for the 1990s. In B. A. Scott (Ed.), *The liberal arts in a time of crisis* (pp. 17–31). New York: Praeger.

Scott, J. F. (1971). Sororities and the husband game. In J. P. Spradley & D. W. McCurdy (Eds.), *Conformity and conflict: Readings in cultural anthropology* (pp. 145–154). Boston: Little, Brown.

Scott, W. A. (with Scott, R.). (1965). *Values and organizations: A study of fraternities and sororities*. Chicago: Rand McNally.

Sermersheim, K. L. (1996). Undergraduate Greek leadership experiences: A proven method for gaining career related and life-long skills. *Campus Activities Programming, 29*(3), 56–60.

Smith, D. G. (1990). Women's colleges and coed colleges: Is there a difference for women? *Journal of Higher Education, 61,* 181–195.

Smith, D. G., Wolf, L. E., & Morrison, D. F. (1995). Paths to success: Factors related to the impact of women's colleges. *Journal of Higher Education, 66,* 245–266.

Solomon, B. M. (1985). *In the company of educated women*. New Haven, CT: Yale University Press.

Spitzberg, I. J., Jr., & Thorndike, V. V. (1992). *Creating community on college campuses*. Albany: State University of New York Press.

Stoecker, J. L., & Pascarella, E. T. (1991). Women's colleges and women's career attainments revisited. *Journal of Higher Education, 62,* 394–406.

Strange, C. (1986). Greek affiliation and goals of the academy: A commentary. *Journal of College Student Personnel, 27,* 519–523.

Thomas, M. C. (1908). Present tendencies in women's college and university education. *Educational Review, 35,* 64–85.

Thornborrow, N. M., & Sheldon, M. B. (1995). Women in the labor force. In J. Freeman (Ed.), *Women: A feminist perspective* (5th ed., pp. 197–219). Mountain View, CA: Mayfield Publishing.

Tidball, M. E. (1980). Women's colleges and women achievers revisited. *Signs, 5,* 504–517.

Tidball, M. E. (1989). Women's colleges: Exceptional conditions, not exceptional talent, produce high achievers. In C. S. Pearson, D. L. Shavlik, & J. G. Touchton (Eds.), *Educating the majority: Women challenge tradition in higher education* (pp. 157–172). New York: Macmillan.

Tidball, M. E., & Kistiakowsky, V. (1976). Baccalaureate origins of American scientists and scholars. *Science, 193*, 646–652.

Tidball, M. E., Smith, D. G., Tidball, C. S., & Wolf-Wendel, L. E. (1999). *Taking women seriously: Lessons and legacies for educating the majority.* Phoenix, AZ: Oryx Press.

Tinto, V. (1975). Dropout from higher education: A theoretical synthesis of recent research. *Review of Educational Research, 45*, 9–125.

Tomaskovic-Devey, D. (1993). *Gender & racial inequality at work: The sources & consequences of job segregation.* Ithaca, NY: ILR Press.

Tyler, L., & Kyes, K. B. (1992, March). *Alcohol, sex, and contraceptive use among college seniors.* Paper presented at the 38th Annual Meeting of the Southeastern Psychological Association, Knoxville, TN.

Van Hise, C. R. (1908). Educational tendencies in state universities. *Publications of the Association of Collegiate Alumnae Magazine, Series III*(No. 17), 31–44.

Vannoy, D., & Dubeck, P. J. (Eds.). (1998). *Challenges for work and family in the twenty-first century.* New York: Aldine de Gruyter.

Veblen, T. (1918). *The higher learning in America: A memorandum on the conduct of universities by business men.* New York: B. W. Huebsch.

Walker, M., & Avioli, P. S. (1991). *College students' perceptions of their misuse of alcohol.* (ERIC Document Reproduction Service No. ED 343 480)

Waller, W. (1937). The rating and dating complex. *American Sociological Review, 2*, 727–734.

Wendell, B. (1904). Our national superstition. *North American Review, 179*, 388–404.

West, A. F. (1884). Must the classics go? *North American Review, 138*, 151–162.

Wilder, D. H., Hoyt, A. E., Doren, D. M., Hauck, W. E., & Zettle, R. D. (1978). The impact of fraternity or sorority membership on values and attitudes. *Journal of College Student Personnel, 19*, 445–449.

Wilder, D. H., Hoyt, A. E., Surbeck, B. S., Wilder, J. C., & Carney, P. I. (1986). Greek affiliation and attitude change in college students. *Journal of College Student Personnel, 27*, 510–519.

Wilkinson, L. (1990). *SYSTAT: The system for statistics.* Evanston, IL: Systat.

Winston, R. B., Jr., Nettles, W. R., III, & Opper, J. H. (Eds.). (1987). *Fraternities and sororities on the contemporary college campus.* San Francisco: Jossey-Bass.

Winston, R. B., Jr., & Saunders, S. A. (1987). The Greek experience: Friend or foe of student development? In R. B. Winston, Jr., W. R. Nettles, III, & J. H. Opper, Jr. (Eds.), *Fraternities and sororities on the contemporary college campus* (pp. 5–20). San Francisco: Jossey-Bass.

Wolf, N. (1991). *The beauty myth: How images of beauty are used against women.* New York: W. Morrow.

Wolff, R. W. (1992). *The ideal of the university.* New Brunswick, NJ: Transaction.

Woody, T. (1929). *A history of women's education in the United States* (Vol. II). New York: The Science Press.

Index

Academic Orientation scale, 68–72, 95–96
Academic Rigor scale, 74
Achievement, opportunities for, 147–151
Achievement Values scale, 18, 19, 20, 21, 22, 23, 24, 41–43
Adams, Elizabeth Kemper, 63–64, 65, 81
Adelphian Society, 31
Altbach, P. B., 44, 53
Alva, S. A., 53
American College Test (ACT), 8
American Universities and Colleges, 73
Appearance, concern for, 54–61
Arthur, L. B., 38, 40, 51–58
Artman, J. M., 88
Association of Collegiate Alumnae, 63–64
Astin, A. W., 6, 8, 25–26, 44, 67, 69, 93, 116, 126, 130, 155
Athletic community, 127–128
Atlas, G., 54
Attitudes Toward Feminism scale, 43–44
Auerbach, D., 28–29
Autonomy Values scale, 18, 19, 21, 24, 26–27, 40, 41, 43, 60–61
Avioli, P. S., 53

Baier, J. L., 41
Baker, L., 147
Bank, B. J., 131
Barnard College, 6, 8, 32, 87, 107, 112–113
Beard, Patricia, 8
Beauty Myth, The (Wolf), 54–55, 60
Beck, D. B., 28–29
Bellafante, G., 28–29
Bennington College, 15–16, 23, 44, 54
Boli, J., 66–68, 70
Bonvillian, G., 138
Boyer, E. L., 115, 133

Britten, F., 112
Bromley, D., 112
Brown, D. R., 87
Brown, M., 148
Bryn Mawr College, 6, 8, 65, 86
Burnett, J. R., 120
Bushnell, J. H., 87, 88

Callan, E., 26
Career Emphasis scale, 74
Careerism
  academic orientation and, 2–3, 10–11
  at Central Women's College, 10–11, 12, 68–84, 149
  college culture and, 3, 11, 72–79, 85–114
  entering students and, 68–72, 92–98
  gendered history of, 2–3, 62–68
  gender traditionalism and, 79–84
  grades and, 75–79
  majors and, 71, 75–79
Career Orientation scale, 68–72, 92, 95–96
Cargill, T., 38
Carnegie Commission, 115, 133
Carney, P. I., 41, 44
Carroll, E. J., 54, 55, 57–58
Cashin, J. R., 53
Central Women's College
  admission rate of, 6
  careerism and, 10–11, 12, 68–84, 149
  characteristics of, 4–7
  college culture of, 9, 16–20, 89–114
  community and, 11–12, 115–136
  enrollment in, 5
  feminism and, 28–30
  gender traditionalism and, 10, 11, 12, 27–28, 79–84

About the Author

Barbara J. Bank is professor of sociology and women studies at the University of Missouri in Columbia. She is the coeditor of *Gender, Equity, and Schooling: Policy and Practice* (Garland, 1997) and has authored or coauthored numerous papers, articles, and chapters in the areas of social psychology, gender studies, and the sociology of youth and education. She has twice been a Visiting Fellow at the Australian National University and has been the recipient of a Fulbright Senior Scholar Award and the William T. Kemper Fellowship for Excellence in Teaching.